INTO THE UNKNOWN

INTO THE UNKNOWN

The Inside Story of Rochdale AFC's First Season in the National League

CHRISTOPHER FITZGERALD

Foreword by Keith Hill

pitch

First published by Pitch Publishing, 2024

Pitch Publishing
9 Donnington Park,
85 Birdham Road,
Chichester,
West Sussex,
PO20 7AJ
www.pitchpublishing.co.uk
info@pitchpublishing.co.uk

A CIP catalogue record is available for this book from the British Library.

ISBN 978 1 80150 731 8

Typesetting and origination by Pitch Publishing

Printed and bound by TJ Books Limited

Contents

Contents

Dedicated to my wonderful family, who showed me both the patience and encouragement necessary to complete this piece of work.

Foreword

IN THE WORLD of football, every chapter has its twists and turns, and not all stories are bound by victories and glory. Sometimes, the narrative takes an unexpected path, one that challenges the very essence of a club's identity and resilience. This book documents one such chapter in the history of Rochdale AFC, a club close to my heart and one that I had the privilege of managing during some of its most storied times.

As I pen these words, I cannot help but reflect on the rollercoaster of emotions that Rochdale's relegation to the National League brought upon us all. Relegation is a bitter pill to swallow, and it tests the mettle of everyone associated with the club – players, staff and, most importantly, the fans – but relegation out of the Football League? Well, that's unprecedented here.

During my time as manager of Rochdale, I led the club to two promotions from the fourth tier of English football. The club has only ever experienced three promotions from that division in its entire history, so being responsible for two of them is an achievement I hold dear. I spent many years of my career as a player, youth coach and manager at the club, and, for the most part, I had the privilege of spending these special times with special people.

In football, success and failure often walk hand-in-hand. While fans celebrate triumphs and etch them into history, the pain of relegation lingers, leaving an indelible mark on the collective consciousness of a club and its supporters. However, true character is precisely revealed in these trying times, both on and off the pitch.

This book doesn't shy away from the raw emotions and the hard-hitting realities that come with facing the consequences of relegation. It delves into the heart of the matter, beginning by exploring the factors that led to this heartbreaking outcome. But, beyond the results, it also sheds light on the unwavering passion and dedication of the loyal fans who stood steadfast in their support.

Relegation is not the end; it is a new beginning, a chance to rebuild and rediscover the club's true essence. This is that story. New faces, new places and new challenges. As the saying goes, the measure of who we are is what we do with what we have. Rochdale's journey through the National League provided an opportunity to regroup, to learn from mistakes and to come back stronger than ever before.

While I am no longer at the helm of Rochdale, my heart remains with the club and its supporters. As you delve into the pages of this book, I invite you to join me in reflecting on the resilience of this historic club and the undying spirit of supporters, coaches and players alike.

No matter what the division, Rochdale will for ever remain a community, a family united by the love of the game. This story is a testament to that enduring spirit, and it is my hope that it serves as a source of inspiration for all those who have ever faced adversity on their own journeys.

The road less travelled can lead to the most remarkable destinations. This book, written by a diehard supporter of Rochdale AFC himself, illustrates this perfectly.

Keith Hill, Rochdale AFC manager
2006–2011 and 2013–2019

Introduction

AS I SIT down to write, I find myself in the midst of a storm of emotions that have been brewing for far too long. Rochdale Association Football Club, the team that has been an integral part of my life and the lives of countless others, has faced a chapter it has never encountered in its long history - relegation to the National League.

For a club that has proudly held its place in the Football League for generations, this is uncharted territory. Rochdale AFC – the Dale, as we affectionately call it – has always been synonymous with determination, resilience and a spirit that refused to waver in the face of adversity. But here, we find ourselves at the crossroads of history, where the battle for survival has taken a new and daunting form.

In our 116-year existence, we've endured heartbreaks and celebrated triumphs both major and minor, witnessed star players emerge and legends created, but never have we had to confront the reality of leaving the league we've called home via its trapdoor. Rochdale is a town in the shadow of footballing behemoths, but for those faithful to its one professional football club, the journey has always been a source of pride. Relegation to the National League feels like an unyielding low point that none of us could have foreseen.

But this is not a tale of despair; it's a story of hope, resilience and the indomitable spirit of a football club that refuses to be counted out. It's about the fans who rally behind their team in the darkest of times, the players who wear the blue and black stripes with pride and the community that stands united, ready to face the challenges that lie ahead – and, trust me, there are many.

More importantly, it is the story of a new journey and the colourful clubs and characters encountered along the way. Gone from the National League is the much-vaunted PR machine of Hollywood-owned Wrexham, but very much present is the chairman/manager model of Dorking Wanderers; the adventure-loving, flat-cap wearing local chairman of Oldham Athletic; the manager who is best mates with Gareth Southgate; the former West Ham United winger who has turned Maidenhead into a bear trap; the innovative young manager taking part-time Oxford City to new heights; the numerous chairmen looking to crack the EFL for the first time in their clubs' histories, and so many more.

For an entire season, I decided to drink in this new environment and fully embrace and document Rochdale's first experience as a fifth-tier club, striving to meet many of those who are already familiar with life at this level. So, grab your scarf, don your blue and black, and prepare to stand shoulder-to-shoulder with the loyal supporters as we relive this maiden voyage.

Prologue

ON 8 MAY 2023, Rochdale AFC's unbroken 102-year legacy in the EFL came to an undignified end. The sensation was akin to numbness; the sharper agony had been experienced two games earlier when relegation from the fourth tier was mathematically sealed. The media descended like grief tourists, capturing the prevalent anger and sorrow.

A fellow aficionado and friend voiced the prevailing sentiment at the time: Rochdale's uninterrupted membership in the Football League had been its badge of honour. Despite limited on-field triumphs, the club's steadfast adherence to financial prudence and living within its means, while remaining a Football League club, had been a source of solace. Now, that last refuge had been cruelly snatched away.

While it might be tempting to attribute the 2022/23 season in isolation as the cause of relegation, the catalyst and the path leading to this gloomy day could be traced back to 2017/18, and perhaps even further. This narrative is explored in detail in my earlier work, *The Rochdale Division*. The irony is, of course, palpable – Rochdale are no longer in the Rochdale Division.

For those unacquainted with Rochdale AFC or who have not yet delved into the pages of *The Rochdale Division*, this club, founded in 1907 and accepted into the Football

League in 1921, occupies an indistinct geographical niche between Greater Manchester and Lancashire. It thrives in the shadows of football juggernauts, offering a refreshing contrast to the extravagant norms. Remarkably, despite its diminutive stature, Rochdale has never courted financial overindulgence, staying true to its community-based identity.

Rochdale had inhabited the fourth tier of English football for so long that this division had unofficially come to be known as its home. Under the stewardship of manager Keith Hill, arguably the finest to occupy the role, this unglamorous, financially prudent club had been transformed since 2006. He made it known for a fluid style of play and a knack for exceeding expectations, the pinnacle of which came in 2015 when Rochdale secured its highest-ever league finish – eighth in the third tier. Subsequently, the club witnessed a steady decline, culminating in its return to the fourth tier.

We pick up the narrative at the end of a lacklustre second half to the 2021/22 season. Hill had long since departed, as had his successor, Brian Barry-Murphy, and many supporters had begun to question whether the then first-team manager, Robbie Stockdale, had exhausted his own tenure after guiding the club to an unremarkable 18th-place finish. Nevertheless, the board of directors chose to stand by him, affording Stockdale a busy summer of transfer activity.

His acquisitions included a desperately needed first-choice goalkeeper in Richard O'Donnell, a robust midfielder in Toumani Diagouraga, the seasoned presence of Ethan Ebanks-Landell in defence, and a physical striker in Devante Rodney. Yet Stockdale's penchant for bolstering options for his back three raised concerns, especially as midfield options appeared wanting.

At the start of the previous season, Stockdale had set the team's course to deliver the ball into the box swiftly. However, midway through that campaign, he inexplicably deviated from that approach, opting for a more ponderous strategy. This commitment to a laborious structure persisted into the new season, leaving supporters convinced that genuine change had eluded them.

Rochdale's 2022/23 campaign kicked off in disastrous fashion. The squad appeared out of sync both physically and tactically, losing all four of its opening League Two fixtures. To its credit, the board acted promptly, parting ways with Stockdale and his assistant, Jimmy Shan. Player-coach Jim McNulty briefly took the reins but was unable to spark a transformation.

A more pressing concern was that any new manager would now inherit a squad assembled on a budget that could not be considered modest, leaving little room for manoeuvre.

The quest for a new manager yielded several candidates, but the mantle was eventually bestowed upon Jim Bentley, the former gaffer of Morecambe and AFC Fylde. It initially appeared that the squad was quick to embrace the new manager's ideas, as evidenced by two thrilling 3-3 draws. However, a loss to the eventual league champions, Leyton Orient, signalled that the team, even under fresh leadership, might often fall short when the chips were down.

And so this promising start was short-lived. A series of narrow one-goal defeats exposed a recurring theme – the inability to synchronise two halves of football. The lowest ebb was a resounding 4-1 home defeat at the hands of Harrogate Town, a similarly positioned side. It became increasingly evident that, when pitted against rivals in the relegation battle, the team was found wanting.

A prolonged break due to inclement weather meant that Rochdale didn't take the field again until Boxing Day, three weeks later. The home clash with fellow strugglers Hartlepool United resulted in another disheartening defeat, further deepening the sense that relegation to the National League was all but inevitable.

The statistics painted a bleak picture. In the calendar year of 2022, Rochdale had triumphed in merely six home league games. The overall data was equally discouraging. The club had recorded more league losses in 2022 than any year since 1978, with a win rate of just 29.7 per cent, the lowest since 1986. The team had suffered 15 away defeats in 2022, second only to 1983.

The outlook appeared gloomy. A disappointing defensive performance at Doncaster only exacerbated the pessimism, though draws against Barrow and Newport offered a momentary respite.

A switch to a three-central-defender formation brought a ray of hope. The inclusion of Max Taylor on the right and Cameron John on the left bolstered the defence, allowing Ian Henderson to shine with two goals that secured three unexpected yet eagerly embraced points against Bradford City.

However, the team's performance began to unravel once more. A change that moved Taylor to the left to accommodate Sam Graham's return led to defensive frailties that Colchester United, another relegation rival, were quick to exploit.

The game also marked the debut of Sheffield United loanee Jake Eastwood in goal, who regrettably committed a costly error that gifted Colchester the win. From that point onward, the team's struggles intensified.

While further transfer window activity did little to improve results immediately, certain additions, such as free agent Danny Lloyd and Altrincham's Toby Mullarkey, showed promise.

The team persisted with the wing-back formation, and Ethan Brierley's return to the squad added creative flair to the midfield. Despite the youngster's contributions, Rochdale continued to grapple with inconsistency.

A loss at Grimsby Town and the recurring trend of drawing games that should have been won made the dire predicament evident, leaving Dale seven points adrift of safety when faced with a fateful game against Crawley Town. The result, a 2-0 defeat, marked the conclusion of Jim Bentley's managerial tenure. The timing of the board's decision would be a subject of debate for weeks after. *Should the decision have been made sooner?*

Jim McNulty was called upon to lead the team temporarily once again. This time, however, he secured two wins and a draw. Rochdale exhibited improvement in their opponents' half, with players such as Brierley, Lloyd and Abraham Odoh hitting their stride. Unfortunately, another loss soon followed, and the home crowd's patience again began to wear thin.

The mathematical confirmation of relegation to the National League came at the hands of local rivals Stockport County. It was a painful conclusion to a season riddled with struggles.

However, the team managed to ensure that their final home game in League Two ended on a positive note at least, with an attack-minded and high-energy performance against Sutton United.

On 8 May, a draw at Harrogate marked the end of an era and bid farewell to Rochdale's league football journey.

Behind the scenes, a different kind of drama had been unfolding. Since the summer of 2021, the club had found itself embroiled in both legal disputes and a disciplinary investigation initiated by the EFL pertaining to the private sale of shares by former board members and prominent shareholders to payroll company Morton House.

A determined group of investors had set their sights on acquiring control of the club, leading to a tumultuous period. Andrew Curran and Darrell Rose, representing Morton House, emerged as key figures in this takeover bid. Their approach involved persuading existing major shareholders, including recent chairman Andrew Kilpatrick and directors Graham Rawlinson and David Bottomley, to sell their stakes. Kilpatrick and the directors were willing to offload their shares privately, as were US-based shareholders Dan Altman and Emre Marcelli, after previous plans to create approximately 700,000 new shares to facilitate the takeover, and remove the pre-emption rights of existing shareholders, were thwarted by shareholders at an EGM.

Regarded as a hostile takeover, the move stirred apprehension among fans, who feared the influence of outsiders not aligned with the club's best interests. Simon Gauge, the fresh chairman, led his newly assembled board, the supporters' trust and like-minded fans in fighting Morton House, the representatives of which were deemed to have sidestepped protocols via their strategy to directly approach shareholders and bypass necessary club channels.

This clandestine approach disregarded established EFL ownership and directorial tests, raising concerns at the league's HQ about the integrity of the process.

This upheaval left the club in a precarious position, facing potential sanctions from the EFL due to these breaches of regulatory guidelines. Despite its claims of being unaware of David Bottomley's actions in his role as chief executive, and lodging complaints with the FA, the club was slapped with a suspended six-point deduction.

In the aftermath, Bottomley, Curran and Rose faced severe repercussions, receiving bans preventing them from involvement in football club operations for two years. On 26 August 2022, a high court claim between Morton House and the present board of directors and the supporters' trust was resolved. Gauge, reflecting on the financial toll of this saga on him and his fellow board members, estimated personal losses totalling around half a million pounds, including legal expenses – resources he said could have been better utilised for the benefit of the club.

In December 2022, the club issued a statement disclosing its ongoing financial challenges and the imperative to seek external investment. Although a recent share issue had generated funds from supporters, the board still remained open to the prospect of external investment, ensuring the club's long-term sustainability.

Former chairman Chris Dunphy had publicly expressed his willingness to assume control of the club and inject capital. However, he later withdrew his offer, admitting he had not fully acknowledged the complex financial implications involved.

As the club continued to engage with potential investors, 375,270 shares remained available for purchase at the end of the 2022/23 season. The key hurdle remained the necessity to sell at least 51 per cent of the shareholding to facilitate a takeover.

It seemed inevitable, therefore, that the club would navigate its path into the National League with the existing board in place, with the appointment of a new manager remaining the most critical and pressing of its concerns.

Dramatis personae

The key protagonists in Rochdale's debut on the National League stage:

Simon Gauge: Chairman of Rochdale AFC. Leading the search for investment while frequently having to dip into his own pockets to keep the club going.

Jamie Sarsfield: Working-class boy done good. As Rochdalian as a 'cruckled' ankle. Business owner and club director.

Murray Knight: The supporters' trust representative on the board of directors.

Jim McNulty: Head coach. Affable pragmatist involved with the club since 2015. Delivering on-field miracles while often working with two hands tied behind his back.

Louie Moulden: On-loan goalkeeper from Wolves. Great shot-stopper and great distributor. Son of former Dale striker Paul Moulden.

Tiernan Brooks: On-loan goalkeeper from Notts County. Capped by Republic of Ireland under-21s.

Ethan Ebanks-Landell: Team captain, solid centre-half who chips in with goals and assists.

George Nevett: Prodigious 17-year-old academy product. Ball-playing centre-half. Capped by Wales under-19s.

Cameron John: Much improved left-back or holding midfielder.

Jimmy Keohane: Dependable and versatile across the pitch. A football Swiss Army Knife.

Kyron Gordon: Useful centre-half/full-back hybrid. Product of Sheffield United's academy.

Harvey Gilmour: Tireless left-footed midfielder signed from FC Halifax Town. The engine in the centre of the park.

Ryan East: Impressive midfielder boasting a broad skill set. Signed from Bradford City.

Adam Clayton: Seasoned former Premier League midfielder. Signed from Bradford City.

Tyrese Sinclair: Dangerous and tricky wide forward player who can play on either flank.

Jesurun Uchegbulam: Talented young winger. Paid his own transfer fee so he could sign from Chesterfield. Once on the books at AC Milan.

Cian Hayes: Brilliant and skilful forward-thinking winger. Enjoyed two very productive loan spells from Fleetwood Town.

Kairo Mitchell: Grenada international forward. Signed from Notts County. Occupies defenders and scores goals.

Devante Rodney: Powerful and talented forward, struggling with fitness issues but still showed his worth.

Ian Henderson: Rochdale's record goalscorer. Still doing the business at 39 years old.

Kwaku Oduroh: Young right-back, on loan from Derby. Showed promise despite inexperience.

Finn Armstrong: Full-back or wide midfielder. On loan from Fleetwood Town. Product of the Burnley youth system.

Kyle Ferguson: Centre-half. Son of Rangers and Scotland legend Barry. Struggling with injuries.

Max Taylor: Centre-half. Manchester United academy product.

Michael Afuye: Young winger signed from Oldham-based club Avro. Used sparingly. Sent on loan to Guiseley.

D'Mani Mellor: Returned on loan from Wycombe Wanderers after featuring in Dale's relegation season. Wide forward. Product of Manchester United's academy.

Sam Mather: Talented Manchester United under-21 footballer who can play on either wing or through the middle. Joined Dale on loan for the latter stages of the season.

Dan Sassi: Centre-half on loan from Blackpool during the latter stages of the season.

Jacob Chapman: Australian goalkeeper, signed on loan from Huddersfield Town during the latter stages of the season.

Brad Kelly: Backup goalkeeper. Graduated from the Rochdale academy.

May/June 2023

OVER THE YEARS, Rochdale AFC had garnered a reputation as a club that sticks by its first-team managers. With a glittering trophy cabinet lacking, this ethos was most likely born as much out of necessity as it was empathy. However, having uncharacteristically gone through not one but two managers in the 2022/23 season, and still failed to avoid the drop into the uncharted waters of non-league football, the next permanent managerial appointment would arguably be the most important in the club's history.

It was felt by the majority of supporters that no rookies need apply, and that candidates should also have experience at National League level, either playing or managing. There was a tangible awareness that many a club similar to Rochdale had failed to apply the brakes once entering the fifth tier of English football and consequently ploughed further into the depths of its pyramid system.

To find the man who could prevent this happening, the board of directors had taken the unprecedented step of appointing a football consultancy, MRKT Insights, to conduct a thorough review of football operations at the club. It seemed an open admission that minds had been too focused on off-the-field issues previously and was an attempt to inject some 'football knowledge' into the club.

Still, it came as a great surprise to many when the directors subsequently announced they would, in fact, be sticking with the man who steered the club through the final eight games of the previous campaign. Jim McNulty was announced as 'head coach' on a two-year contract and, while he may not have boasted masses of prior management experience, nor possessed any experience at all at National League level, McNulty could at least profess to have experience at Rochdale itself, having represented the club for eight seasons as a player. He joined Dale in the summer of 2015 and went on to make 237 appearances before transitioning into a player-coach for the next two campaigns.

'The opportunity to lead our team and represent our club, which the fans cherish, has always been a dream of mine,' he said upon his appointment. 'To be given the opportunity at a club so close to mine and my family's heart is really special to me. Within a couple of years of being a Dale player, I knew that this would be the club where I hoped to fulfil that ambition.'

The board was also quick to highlight that McNulty's selection wasn't a decision made lightly, stating, 'Assisted by MRKT Insights, we have carried out a thorough recruitment process that included a long list, which was narrowed down to a five-man shortlist, culminating in his appointment. There was wide-ranging criteria that Jim came out on top of. In his time here as a player, he has seen what success looks like at this club. We are all looking forward to getting behind him as our rebuild and push towards regaining our place in the EFL gets under way.'

I felt I needed to meet with McNulty, to find out about the man who seemed so very ingrained in Rochdale's recent history and one charged with revitalising the club's on-field fortunes. Born in Runcorn, Cheshire, McNulty told me how he began his own journey.

'Runcorn is an overspill of Liverpool, so it basically is Liverpool,' he said. 'It's just a town consisting of a lot of families who moved out of Liverpool in the 1960s and '70s, my mum and dad being one of them.

'In Liverpool, football is an absolute religion. It was a huge part of my dad's life and was all he ever talked about. He played football mainly at amateur level, but eventually got to the dizzy heights of representing Wrexham's reserves. He was a goalkeeper, and a very humble sort of man.

'I spent my youth watching him playing amateur football for South Liverpool, which he did alongside working as a bricklayer. This was my indoctrination into football, I guess.

'The thing he would constantly say to me, and I'll never forget it, is, "Don't be a bighead." If he sensed there was ever any chance of that happening, that's what he said to me. That began to shape me. Subconsciously, I think it's probably why I'm very uncomfortable being complimented to this day. I don't necessarily think that's a great thing, because we have to be comfortable growing. It's certainly affected the way I treat my players. I want them to feel great, but I still want that balance of humility.'

McNulty's own football journey began when he was spotted by Everton playing for a local junior side at just seven years old. 'Everton put on a huge regional trial and about 400 kids were asked to turn up,' he said. 'They finally reduced this down to a final squad of 22, and I made that 22 along with quite a few guys who have gone on to become big names in football, Wayne Rooney being one of them. Therefore, I was in the football-education system very, very young, and I think that helped me. I think being coachable and being around coaches most of my life has allowed me to better understand what coaching is all about.'

While McNulty would go on to make his name as a centre-half and full-back, it was in the middle of the park where he first impressed. 'As I moved through the system, through the different age groups, I began to realise that all the midfielders were better than me, but I was a decent enough footballer to adapt to other positions,' he said. 'I was not quite big enough to be a centre-back at that point. I was a bit of a hybrid. I probably would have been more suited to this era actually, rather than my day. I'm not quite physical enough to be a big, dominant centre-back, but I had decent ball skills, so there was a place for me for a while.

'However, when I was about 15, it started to become obvious I wasn't going to make it at Everton, and so they let me talk to other clubs. At that time, Everton and Arsenal were probably seen as the marquee youth sides at my age group, mainly because we had Rooney, who just scored five goals against anyone we played, so I did get offers based on that reputation.

'Like my dad before me, I ended up signing for Wrexham, who were a League One club at the time. Denis Smith was the manager and he was a hard, hard man. My dad told me Denis had broken more bones than he'd had hot dinners. He certainly walked like a man who'd broken a lot of his bones.

'I was quickly put in the picture at Wrexham. I was a first-year pro and, having been at Everton, I thought I'd walk into the side. My dad's words about being a bighead came to the fore here, and rightly so. There were brilliant players at Wrexham, all of who could properly handle the ball and they could properly bollock you, too. They had Andy Morrell, who scored a lot of goals; Lee Trundle, who was outrageously talented; and Carlos Edwards, who played off one side. It was a joke and I could get nowhere near that side.

'The club then went into administration and I was offered a new contract on low money. You're more like a training body at that point. You're good enough to still be there, but you're not good enough to impact the first team, so they'll keep you around because you're a good sort. That's the stage I was at.

'At the same time, I was offered a part-time contract at Caernarfon Town in the League of Wales on way more money than what Wrexham offered full time. It wasn't head-turning money, but it was more money, so I took it. Despite it being more money, it was at this point I got a bit of a reality check. I had to get a part-time job doing night-shift work at B&Q combined with day work labouring with my dad.

'It was then I turned into a right moaning bastard. I'd been a pro and was one of the better players at Caernarfon, and I was making it known, you know? I'd exited a system that so many kids dream of being in and had not fully appreciated it when I was there, and now I was a part-time footballer.

'I remember we played Afan Lido and there was one guy I was giving mouth to. I was letting him know I'd been a pro and all that. I thought I was better than him, them, the entire level. This fella looks at me and calmly says, "After this game, I'm going to splat that big nose all over your face." And I was like, "Yeah, good one. Whatever. Blah, blah, blah," thinking it was just the usual bravado I'd heard a hundred times before.

'What I found out is, in the Welsh league, when someone says they're going to do you, they are actually waiting in the car park and they are actually going to do you. That was an eye-opener. I'm pulling out of the car park. He's blocking the exit. He's saying, "You're getting out of that car and we're going to dance, like we said."

'So here I am, in a Welsh league club car park, doing night shifts at B&Q, and getting my nose broken by some 32-year-old man who will die for the £60 he's being paid.

'It was then I knew I had to get back to full-time football, whatever the sacrifice.

'I wrote letters. Lots of letters. I had got into the League of Wales team of the season, so I was standing out. I wrote to TNS because they were the only full-time team in the Welsh league and had competed in the Champions League. My dad suggested I write to English Football League clubs, too. So, I did. I wrote to all of those who I could get to geographically, if I was to be offered a trial.

'My letter was pretty basic. It's the type of letter I see now, and the type I try to never ignore, as I know it's someone desperate for a chance. It said something like, "Hi, I'm Jimmy McNulty. I'm a six-foot-two-inch, left-footed, left centre-back, or left-back, looking for a chance."

'I got a response from Brian Horton at Macclesfield Town. He invited me for a trial. I played a few games. It was going all right, not brilliant, just all right. My trial was on a bit of a knife-edge. Then something happened that I still to this day believe was fate.

'Brian Horton was good friends with Sir Alex Ferguson. They lived close to each other in Alderley Edge. They'd go for Sunday dinner at the same place, that kind of thing, and became good friends. As a result, every year, Macclesfield used to play Manchester United in a pre-season friendly. Man United would send an XI that usually contained some household names.

'Prior to this particular fixture, on the Monday morning, Brian offered me a one-month contract worth £300 a week, plus £100 per appearance. I was earning about £600 at Caernarfon, including what I earned at B&Q and from my dad, but I knew I had to take the cut if I wanted to get back in. It was effectively Brian's way of saying, "I'm not convinced by you, but I'll give you this for now to impress me."

'While I mulled it over, I played against Man United on the Tuesday night. Rio Ferdinand was on for a bit, and so was Rooney. I marked a couple of wingers that night, one being Chris Eagles. I knew I'd had a good game.

'This is where fate intervened. The Macclesfield media team, as they do, asked Sir Alex how he felt our club's new signings had fared. He told them, "I thought the young left-back looked a good athlete." That's all he said. The next day, Brian offered me a one-year deal. I'm utterly convinced it was because of that one comment. And do you know what? My pro career took off from that moment.

'I always had a thirst for getting better, and that's something I try to instil into the players here at Rochdale. Every day is an opportunity.

'Once establishing myself at Macclesfield, I got bought by different clubs during quite a few Januarys in a row. First by Stockport, then by Brighton, then by Barnsley, before injuries levelled things out for me in the Championship. However, this is where I first properly met Keith Hill and David Flitcroft.'

Rochdale's legendary managerial duo were in charge of the Tykes, in the Championship, when they signed McNulty, but Jim said his association with Dale might have begun much earlier.

'I played against Hill's Rochdale team at Wembley in the League Two play-off final [in 2008] and Stockport won and went up. We then played Rochdale in a friendly that immediate summer. Jim Gannon, the Stockport manager, wasn't playing me because I hadn't yet signed a new contract. I was warming up, up and down the touchline, and Keith came out of his technical area at one point and said, "What the fuck are you doing on the sidelines?" He carried on trying to tap me up for quite a while until I decided to move to Brighton. He finally got me when he got the Barnsley job.

'Keith loved me and I loved him. He challenged me to do things I never thought I'd end up doing. I became so deep about things. He used to say to me, "You're capable of a lot more, but your destiny is in your own hands." "You're too nice," he would say. "Whatever happened to nice old Jim McNulty, anyone remember him?" He made me captain and asked me to challenge the players. Keith was an excellent motivator that way.

'Rather than immediately follow Keith when he went back to Rochdale, I actually went from Barnsley to Bury with Dave Flitcroft, even though I don't think me and Flickers were as compatible. We didn't see the game in quite the same way as me and Keith did. Before stats and everything came to the fore, me and Keith could reflect on a performance, as we used to know the same things about performance visually, before we'd even seen the stats, because the same things were important to us.

'We have slightly different styles now, but I'm managing in an almost different era to Keith, so why wouldn't I have? I'm glad I got to play for Keith at Barnsley and that he brought me here to Rochdale eventually, which is where I've felt at home ever since.'

* * *

TEN SENIOR ROCHDALE players from the relegation season remained under contract heading into the 2023/24 National League campaign, with three year-long extension options also triggered. However, the board sent a stark message to supporters regarding the budget Jim McNulty would be operating with.

'Several players who remain under contract have been placed on the transfer list with immediate effect,' a club statement said. 'Any player remaining in discussions and opting to stay with the club next season would be required to accept a significant reduction in salary.'

There was also the issue of McNulty's job title. Rochdale had traditionally eschewed modern football terminology, preferring the classic designation of 'football manager'. However, with input from the analysts at MRKT, it appeared that the individual overseeing the first team would now be referred to as the 'head coach'. This raised questions about who would be responsible for player recruitment.

According to McNulty, he would assume primary responsibility in this area.

'This is my team,' he told me. 'I interviewed for the job based on my vision for the team's style of play and the players I want to see in it. Before my appointment, MRKT presented a blueprint to the board outlining their vision for the club's future. They aimed to revitalise Rochdale as a selling club, a model the club once thrived on, where player transfers generate revenue.

'They wanted to create a brand that would help turn Rochdale back into the selling club it once was, where we move our guys on for money, but all the while playing attractive football and winning football.

'In terms of recruitment, on staff I have John [Shannon] for analysis and Kev [Gibbins] as my assistant. Kev is one of the most undervalued members of staff the club has probably ever had, which is why I was so keen to bring him straight back. He knows me so well. He will challenge me on everything that's important to be challenged on, which is perfect for me because I don't know everything, definitely not in this role, not yet.

'We each identify our own transfer targets – me and my team and MRKT, before going on to compare and contrast our lists respectively. I did sit down with MRKT initially and discuss a game model, which was an hour and a half of me going through the different shapes that I want to move the players into, what the players need to be doing in those shapes, and so on. They were taking notes and asking questions. They then went away and provided an initial scour of the market based on what I had told them.

'The initial lists MRKT produced were a mixture of players from a range of levels. Based on the nature of the budget available, a bulk of the players they came back with were from a level below where we play, so we had National League North and National League South players listed, some even lower. The players listed also came with data that, statistically, stated what they should be capable of.

'From that list, we then honed in on the most suitable targets. We've tried to refrain from naming individual players to MRKT in the initial stages, as I don't want to slant what they do. The odd time, there's been something I've already identified in a player that the data has reinforced, so it's nice when I see somebody flagged that I already like. Reinforcement is a very useful tool.

'Every signing that comes in is down to me, John and Kev, though. Some of them may have been brought in for us to look at, but, mainly, it is players we know of and like.

'Signing players will be a little bit different to what we have been used to in the Football League, however, as there is no transfer window to manage at this level, as such. Identifying the players is the easiest part. Other things then have to fall into place – we have to agree terms with the player, their club, if they're at one, their agent, if they have one. That's the difficult part, the part where everyone needs to be patient. Our budget is the humblest budget the club has had in my time here. The [board] is unhappy at how the budget has been spent in previous transfer windows and is keen that, what they perceive as past mistakes are not repeated this time. We need to do as much due diligence as we can on players. MRKT are very useful in this regard.

'Recruitment and shaping the squad ahead of next season has been the main focus this month, and the thing I've had to learn pretty fast, in terms of focusing my energies, is how to ignore a lot of the noise around being a manager. That's where being the head coach has been important, rather than a manager. There are situations I do have to manage, of course, but you can get distracted by so much else. There are so many other people around the football club, and around the game itself, who suddenly want to be in touch with you. Each one of those people want 15 or 20 minutes of your time and, before you know it, you've lost important hours or days in identifying players and helping the team get better.

'There are a number of managers who are my friends at this level, and they've told me that they were working towards transfer targets from February last season, so they were recruiting last season for this season, in effect, before the season was even finished. They were ready to go with their offers as soon as the last day of the season was done. I got this job ten days after the season finished and was then trying to build a staff. It hinders you a little bit in terms of trying to sign that first round of players, and, just as we began to move on them, they were gone. We got on the phone to certain players who said, "I've just signed for a club yesterday. [Rochdale] would have been perfect, too." This is the learning curve we are on.'

One player McNulty would need to do without for the coming campaign would be Ethan Brierley. The Rochdale-born midfielder was sold to Premier League side Brentford for an undisclosed six-figure sum before June was even out of first gear. Despite his young age, Brierley had been a standout in Rochdale's midfield the season prior, his passing ability putting to shame that of many of his more experienced contemporaries.

Having joined the Rochdale academy as a seven-year-old, Brierley made his first-team debut at 16 before going on to make 45 appearances for the club. His defining moment came the season just ended, however, when he sent over the perfect ball for Ian Henderson to net against Salford City, allowing him to break Reg Jenkins' long-standing record as Rochdale's all-time leading goalscorer. One bright spark in an otherwise dismal campaign.

Two of the very few remaining shining lights from the previous season were next to depart. Danny Lloyd chose not to accept a new deal, while Toby Mullarkey made the most of his relegation-release clause by opting not to return to the National League, from whence he came via Altrincham, instead deciding to remain in League Two by signing for Grimsby Town.

Perhaps less surprising was Liam Kelly deciding to reject a new offer and opt to join League Two Crawley Town. The diminutive midfielder had shown what he was capable of only in flashes during his time at Dale.

Next out of the door was goalkeeper Richard O'Donnell, signed by Blackpool, just relegated from the Championship. A considerable loss on the face of it, with only the relatively young and inexperienced Brad Kelly on the books posing a viable replacement at that point.

McNulty was quick to restore some of the trust deficit, however, by bringing in 24-year-old left-footed midfielder Harvey Gilmour from fellow National League side FC Halifax Town on a two-year deal.

'He can play a number of positions in midfield, and he's very comfortable with the ball at his feet,' McNulty said of the Sheffield-born player. 'He's proven himself at National League level and is someone who I think could play higher. He's just had a brilliant season with Halifax, playing a full campaign there, which culminated in him winning the FA Trophy Final against Gateshead.'

Gilmour's signature was quickly followed by those of free agent Kairo Mitchell, on a two-year deal, and Cody Johnson on a season-long loan from League Two neighbours Stockport County.

Mitchell, a 25-year-old forward, had played at National League level for Notts County the season prior, as well as a small portion of it on loan at Eastleigh. Interestingly, at the time of his signing, he was away on international duty with Grenada, for whom he already had 15 caps, as the nation attempted to qualify for that summer's CONCACAF Gold Cup.

'He is another player that I believe has Football League potential and has already gained good-calibre National League experience,' McNulty said. 'I'm really happy with his addition. I'm impressed with his relentless running for the team. He is a mobile target man in that sense, I guess. He will prove a handful for two centre-halves, never mind one. He can score goals for the team, but his presence on the pitch will also create goals for the team.'

Of 18-year-old midfielder Johnson, McNulty added, 'He's an exciting prospect that I know Stockport think a lot of. After watching him, we think he will be a brilliant addition to our squad.'

Next through the door was 6ft 5in centre-half Kyle Ferguson, son of Rangers legend and former Scotland international Barry. Ferguson, again brought in on a two-year deal, boasted both Football and National League experience, not to mention that which he had garnered on the continent and in the USA.

'He can handle all basic requirements of defending in the National League but is also very comfortable with the ball at his feet, so it's exciting to have him with us,' McNulty said of the signing.

Ferguson was followed by Swedish-born 19-year-old wide forward Moe Shubbar, who had been released by League Two side Crawley Town; another player with some non-league experience having originally played for Cheshunt and Edgware Town, and having been loaned to Worthing and Slough.

'He is a player that can be a very exciting prospect for the future, but is also ready to compete for a place in the team right now,' McNulty said.

The new faces were, of course, welcomed by the Dale supporters, but, as June drew to a close, the squad still seemed concerningly short on numbers, especially between the sticks.

July 2023

IT WAS EASY to picture Rochdale chairman Simon Gauge anxiously pacing the halls of Spotland Stadium, his mind filled with doubts and concerns. As a former airline pilot, he would be accustomed to pressure, but this situation had no doubt pushed him to his limits. Watching the club stumble out of the EFL under his stewardship would have been a keenly felt and devastating blow, and he would, no doubt, have questioned his own sanity for taking on the role of chairman two years prior.

The events leading up to this moment played like a gripping drama. In April 2021, the board of directors at the time proposed resolutions to release new shares in the club, teasing preferred investors with undisclosed identities. The supporters' trust, better known by its sobriquet of the Dale Trust, rose in protest, demanding an extraordinary general meeting (EGM) to remove two key board members. It was a battle of wills between the supporters and the establishment.

A historic night ensued, as the board withdrew its controversial proposals under intense scrutiny from shareholders and the determined Dale Trust. The motions to remove chief executive David Bottomley and director Graham Rawlinson from the board were then passed by a majority, marking a resounding victory for supporter power. From the ashes, a new board emerged, with Gauge at the helm, determined to reunite the club and its passionate fanbase.

Gauge, reflecting on his unexpected journey, admitted, 'This moment has chosen me rather than me it.' He had retired from his career as an airline pilot and had the time and energy to commit to the club. But it was the dissatisfaction with the club's recent struggles that fuelled his passion to make a difference. The opportunity to challenge the status quo and effect positive change was one he couldn't resist.

The decision to join the board was set in motion by a close friend of his late father-in-law, local businessman Peter Stock. Trevor Butterworth, a former club director, reached out to Gauge, seeking his involvement in addressing the club's turmoil. Graham Morris, a former club finance director, and other like-minded individuals, joined forces in sourcing additional individuals who were ready to step in after the failure of the old regime's proposals.

Gauge's connection to Rochdale ran deep. He had moved to the town more than two decades prior, his wife's family hailing from the borough. Watching Rochdale matches had become a regular ritual once he started bringing his youngest son along. The passion and authenticity of the game, free from the influence of money, captivated them. Standing by the tunnel, feeling the energy of the pitch and interacting with players, created a sense of belonging and community that couldn't be replicated elsewhere.

However, Gauge's newfound role as chairman came with unforeseen challenges. Morton House, a payroll company with no previous football industry experience, launched a takeover bid not two minutes after he took up the hotseat. The audacious attempt garnered national attention and triggered an investigation by the EFL. Despite initially claiming to withdraw its interest, Morton House persisted with legal action, alleging unfair prejudice caused by the Dale Trust and the board.

While these legal battles were eventually settled out of court, Gauge also faced the daunting task of keeping a financially struggling club afloat. He took decisive action to secure the future by leading on the redemption of the mortgage on Spotland Stadium, keeping control away from external entities. But the true test lay on the pitch, as the team fought against relegation.

Criticism from disillusioned supporters weighed heavily on Gauge's shoulders, and he withdrew into silence. Fans longed for meaningful engagement and found his statements of the board's desire to 're-engage with the fanbase' to be all too brief. A missed opportunity to connect with the very heart of the club left many feeling discouraged.

As the team prepared for its first season in the National League, Gauge faced the daunting challenge of managing a reduced income and the financial strain of many long-distance away games. Supporters wondered how the board would navigate these post-relegation hurdles.

When I spoke to the chairman, he pointed to the challenges of budget being nothing new to a club such as Rochdale.

'The club's financial position does not change, regardless of the league it is in, and hasn't really for the past ten years,' Gauge told me.

'The club has always lost money without cup success or player trading. If you look at the accounts for the years profit was made, either one of those two things happened. The club was effectively very good at this lottery for a period of time. This situation is no different to most clubs, the main difference being that, as a fan-owned club, when you turn to the club's owners to fund deficits, there is no one there!

'Relegation has fundamentally made no difference to this model. The playing budget has been cut to reflect the drop in income. The hardest thing is that there are players on EFL salaries in the National League, despite relegation clauses, which means the budget has not gone as far.'

While being fan-owned meant there was no one person with deep pockets at the head of the table, a positive development for the model had presented itself. The Dale Trust, Rochdale AFC's largest shareholder, secured its first place on the board of directors in the form of Murray Knight, elected to represent its interests at the highest level of the club's governance and decision-making. Knight's seat at the table was designed to reinforce the enduring pride in, and determination to live up to, the club's status as being fan-owned and fan-led.

Driven by a clear sense of purpose since its founding in 2004, the Dale Trust aimed to give fans a greater say in the club's affairs while building and safeguarding its shared ownership by supporters.

Having a Dale Trust representative on the board not only marked a significant milestone in the club's history, it offered the potential to promote a culture of opportunity, community and influence among fans.

'Collaboration with the board of Rochdale AFC involves regular meetings during which we discuss supporters' views, questions and suggestions,' said Knight. 'Our aim is to foster an excellent working relationship that brings supporters and the club closer together.'

One way the trust did this, Knight explained, was through regular fan forums, organised by the trust itself and attended by club management and directors. These provided an unfiltered and open platform for frank face-to-face discussion and, crucially, rather than restricting attendance to trust membership card carriers only, the doors were open to all supporters.

'Transparency and accountability are central to our operation,' added Knight. 'Major decisions are subject to member voting, and spending matters exceeding £3,000 are discussed with members.

'To ensure the trust represents the diverse fanbase and encompasses different perspectives, we actively seek the views and involvement of our members. Through regular pre-match gatherings and ongoing events, we encourage fans to step up and contribute, ensuring their voices are heard.'

This 'two-way street' fans enjoyed didn't come without a few speed bumps along the way – including the previously mentioned Morton House issue – however, what had emerged was an outstanding example of collaboration with stakeholders.

'Much of the work we do benefits facilities within the stadium, which naturally extends to the wider community,' said Knight. 'We also collaborate with local charities and have raised substantial funds for worthy causes.'

Furthermore, the trust was a key player in the development of a new five-a-side pitch at the back of the club's Pearl Street Stand, improving facilities for both the club and the community.

'The trust's collaborative efforts extend beyond Rochdale AFC,' Knight added. 'We actively engage with other supporters' trusts through our affiliation with the Football Supporters' Association, sharing experiences and knowledge for mutual benefit. Additionally, the trust provides support to various trusts that seek assistance.'

With growing numbers of fans signing up as shareholder members, providing vital income through voluntary monthly donations, the Dale Trust was making good on its commitment to help ensure the club's sustainability – with all eyes on the day when Rochdale AFC might make its return to the Football League.

* * *

BACK ON THE pitch, the revolving door continued to spin. The club bid farewell to Abraham Odoh, as he embarked on a new journey with Harrogate Town, and Tahvon Campbell, who set off on a season-long loan with Wealdstone. However, Jim McNulty welcomed a promising addition in the form of Kwaku Oduroh, a 20-year-old right-back, who arrived on a season-long loan from Derby County, and experienced midfielder Adam Clayton, on a one-year deal from Bradford City. This was an especially eyebrow-raising capture, given the 34-year-old had once played an entire campaign in the Premier League for Middlesbrough.

In a club media interview, McNulty expressed his unwavering commitment to building his squad, detailing how he was dedicating every spare moment to the task of recruitment. 'Whatever hours are left in the day after the training sessions have finished, I am spending on recruitment,' he said. 'There is still work to be done in and out.'

Another area of focus for McNulty was the club's youth academy, the players of which he revealed had been training with the first team at the rented Platt Lane facility in south Manchester.

Since 2007, when Keith Hill rose from the head of the youth academy to become permanent first-team manager, Rochdale had reaped the benefits of nurturing talented young footballers, both financially and in terms of its reputation. A remarkable list of names, including Will Buckley, Jamie Allen, Scott Hogan, Dan Adshead, Luke Matheson, Aaron Morley and, most recently, Ethan Brierley, had all come through the academy to secure contracts with esteemed teams in the upper echelons of English football.

Former chairman Chris Dunphy used to emphasise the necessity of player sales for a club like Rochdale to thrive in the modern football landscape. However, during his tenure, the club ensured that transfers were, more often than not, executed on its own terms rather than out of desperation. Dunphy, who is widely acknowledged for transforming Rochdale into a model of modern sustainability, upheld this reputation for around 15 years.

Since 2013, former Dale striker Tony Ellis had been in charge of maintaining this talent pipeline. However, he surprised everyone during the close-season by announcing his decision to step down from the role, upon which he was replaced by former Bolton Wanderers academy manager Mark Litherland, who himself did an about turn just weeks into the job, leaving for a post at Bradford City instead. The role was then filled by James Prieditis, who had been with the Rochdale academy for four years in varying positions.

McNulty seemed keen to bridge the gap during this period of transition. 'I've now got these young players learning how to be pros from the pros themselves,' he said in a club media interview. 'You can't become something unless you can see it for yourself. These players hadn't previously had the opportunity to see it. I've got the two teams training side by side. This, for me, is the way the football club needs to be and how it needs to remain.'

While the youth academy undoubtedly brought with it numerous rewards, it could also be a challenging environment for aspiring young players. At the end of the 2022/23 season, the entire under-18 squad was released due to the impressive talent within the under-16 and under-17 age groups. These younger cohorts had already showcased their potential by providing senior debuts to players such as Kevin Dos Santos, Oscar Kelly, Darren Ehimamiegho and George Nevett.

'I'll be using a lot of youth players in pre-season games,' McNulty said. 'Some of them will play on merit too, not just because we don't have other players to fill that position. It's a chance for all of them to impress.'

* * *

AFTER A CLOSELY guarded behind-closed-doors friendly against a Premier League club, the moment that Dale fans had been eagerly awaiting finally arrived. It was time for them to witness the unveiling of McNulty's freshly assembled troops as they clashed with Radcliffe Borough, a Northern Premier League side, at Stainton Park.

Prior to the game, McNulty referred to using these early friendlies as a way of practising strategy and ironing out inadequacies. 'We have to accept there will be compromises in these games that we wouldn't accept in competitive games,' he said.

That approach was certainly evident as he elected to field two very different teams in each half of the match, each with a complement of youth players. The second half also featured two trialist midfielders – former Fulham youth Jonathan Page and ex-Hamilton Academical man Lewis Spence – illustrating that McNulty still wasn't satisfied with the depth there.

Captained by former Dale midfielder Nicky Adams, Radcliffe certainly provided a decent workout for Rochdale, despite eventually losing 2-0 via goals from Ian Henderson and Tyrese Sinclair.

In the first half, Dale embraced a 4-4-2 formation, deploying young talent Darren Ehimamiegho and new signing Moe Shubbar on the flanks. What made this setup intriguing was the pair's freedom to tuck inside and bolster the midfield, while the full-backs received vocal encouragement to surge forward, leaving the central midfield duo of Cody Johnson and Harvey Gilmour to forge a tight partnership, sticking closer together.

Of this midfield two, the spotlight shone on Johnson as he showcased his remarkable long-range passing, drawing comparisons to esteemed former Dale man Aaron Morley.

Up front, Kairo Mitchell and Devante Rodney displayed a notable physical presence, with Mitchell's height proving to be a valuable asset, particularly for aerial duels.

In the second half, a similar approach was employed, with James Ball and Henderson leading the attack this time. Youth player Oscar Kelly played wider on the left and had a positive impact, contributing an assist for the second goal.

If there was to be one criticism, it was that Dale appeared somewhat open when in possession in their own third. The full-backs being high and wide left swathes of grass to exploit any time the opposition won the ball back. And, while the team did mix up distribution from goalkeeper Brad Kelly, especially in the second half, concerns remained any time unnecessary risks were taken there. Overall, however, supporters left with a feeling that players wearing the Dale shirt looked energised and displayed a togetherness that had been lacking in recent seasons, with senior players demonstrably guiding the younger. It was only one game – and the first game at that – but a positive tone had been set.

* * *

PRIOR TO THE next friendly, away at National League North side Chorley, Jim McNulty at last managed to add another goalkeeper to his roster in the guise of Louie Moulden, who arrived on a season-long loan from Premier League side Wolverhampton Wanderers. However, the deal for the 21-year-old, son of former Dale striker Paul Moulden and grandson of former Dale striker Tony Moulden, included a January release clause, should another club come in for him. As far as McNulty was concerned, it was a caveat worth conceding.

'He is a highly rated goalkeeper with experience at this level already, and he is well suited to the club's possession-dominant style, as we look to evolve our team from last season,' he said. 'He's a highly ambitious and driven individual who possesses an elite mentality – he trains and plays with great intensity.

'Richard O'Donnell was allowed to leave in the knowledge that we were recruiting Louie. He will be good for the environment, again reflecting the type of characters we want.'

Under the management of Andy Preece, a former player-manager at Bury, Chorley provided a more challenging level of competition for McNulty's players when compared to Radcliffe.

McNulty evidently aimed to gradually increase the difficulty of the tests his team faced before the start of the season, and a test this indeed was. Despite the addition of Moulden, Adam Clayton and new trialist Michael Afuye to the squad, Dale struggled throughout and failed to recover from Justin Johnston's clinical opening goal for the hosts after just 11 minutes. The 1-0 defeat served as a clear reminder that McNulty still had work to do in order to transform his team into a consistently cohesive unit that was capable of playing his desired brand of football. It was, however, still early days.

* * *

BEFORE A DOUBLE-game-week of friendlies, Jim McNulty took to the airwaves on BBC Radio Manchester's *Talking Balls* programme, captivating fans with what many considered to be the most exceptionally enlightening and candid interview from a Rochdale manager in quite some time.

During the conversation, McNulty expressed his ambition to initiate a shift in the team's mindset, embracing a more attacking style of football for the upcoming season. He spoke of early decisions made to reshape the team's culture, emphasising the importance of unity and selflessness. McNulty also delved into the challenges of adapting to different styles of play while grappling with budgetary limitations in player recruitment, stressing that the squad would not be complete by the first game of the season and would need to continue its evolution as the campaign progressed. Nevertheless, he expressed contentment with the players he had acquired so far, particularly praising the positive impact of Adam Clayton on the training ground.

When questioned about the impact of player departures on team morale, McNulty acknowledged their significance but underlined the resilience required in professional football. He believed that new players injected fresh energy and enthusiasm into the team, while negotiations and financial matters were best left to the club hierarchy.

Addressing concerns about his possession-based style of play, McNulty expressed confidence in the abilities of his defenders to select the correct pass, while acknowledging the need to increase the shot count. He defended his approach of seeking effective opportunities over sheer quantity, however, emphasising the importance of striking a balance between solid defence and attacking play.

This was immediately illustrated during a behind-closed-doors friendly at League Two Tranmere, with Dale impressively running out 2-0 victors thanks to a Tyrese Sinclair penalty and a second-half goal from Devante Rodney.

The team would then round off the week with a touch of poignancy. Originally slated to play Bradford Park Avenue on the Saturday, the game was cancelled in favour of a Friday night away trip to Walsall as a tribute to the late Wayne Evans, a former full-back for both sides who had died suddenly aged 51 while at home in the USA.

Evans, a well-known figure in football, had an impressive career in the 1990s, making 200 appearances for the Saddlers and subsequently playing almost 300 matches for Rochdale. Reflecting the profound respect and camaraderie shared among his friends and former team-mates, a memorial fund was established by a group led by Walsall legend Chris Marsh. Their aim was to assist Evans's family with the necessary expenses for repatriation, upon discovering that it would cost around £30,000 for Evans's wife to bring him back to the UK. As a heartfelt gesture, all the net proceeds from the match were dedicated to this cause.

Naturally, on such an occasion, the football was secondary. However, the addition of midfielder Michael Afuye, on a one-year deal following a successful trial period, brought a refreshing sense of excitement for Dale fans at least, and the team as a whole impressed once again in the eventual 1-1 draw. Rodney's second goal in as many games saw Dale lead for a good portion of the match against higher-league opposition.

* * *

IN THE MIDST of the club's so-far fruitless quest to find an investor, and with whispers circulating about the board's associations with individuals openly discussing such business in a local hostelry, supporters were taken aback by the sudden announcement of an EGM to take place on 9 August. The meeting aimed to seek shareholders' support for a resolution proposing that two directors provide a loan to Rochdale AFC, secured against Spotland Stadium.

Chairman Simon Gauge and director Richard Knight jointly released a statement to shed light on their intentions. Gauge expressed the pair's desire to alleviate immediate cashflow pressures, thus granting ample time to find the perfect investor for the club's future. The loan, he emphasised, presented an opportunity to find the most suitable match for Dale's long-term prospects. He offered reassurance to supporters that the loan was not for personal gain but, rather, to safeguard the club's interests. As both were already significant shareholders, Gauge said the pair were determined to protect their contributions in the event of any worst-case scenario, such as liquidation.

Knight echoed this sentiment, explaining that the pair had reached their limit in terms of purchasing available shares. Consequently, they made the decision to secure any additional investments into the club with the welfare of their own families in mind.

The pair's statement also referenced that the Dale Trust had applied for a Community Ownership Fund grant, as part of the government's levelling-up project, which would inject more money into the club.

The trust confirmed it was awaiting confirmation of the application's success. In its own statement, the trust explained that the fund aimed to provide community organisations such as theirs with access to funds that would have a long-term impact on the community. If successful in both the application and acquiring the necessary funds, the trust's plan was to use the money to purchase the playing surface at Spotland Stadium, which would be owned by the trust and then leased back to the club. This move would, the trust said, secure the future of the stadium, protecting it from potential 'ulterior motives', and safeguard the playing future of Dale and local rugby club Rochdale Hornets, with which the club shared the stadium.

* * *

THE FINAL TEST of Rochdale's pre-season programme was a home game against League Two's Bradford City.

Prior to the match, the club announced James Ball had left Spotland to join AFC Wimbledon on a free transfer and that George Nevett had signed his first professional contract, the 17-year-old academy defender agreeing a three-year deal having impressed in the friendly outings so far.

Dale once again performed well against higher-league opposition, running out 1-0 winners thanks to another thumping finish from Devante Rodney.

McNulty continued with the 4-4-2 supporters had seen previously, albeit this time with Henderson playing off the front, and usual right-back Oduroh stationed on the left of midfield.

Of note was how well the team defended as a unit. Cameron John, handed the number three shirt, looked to be first choice at left-back and upped his defensive work. The similarly maligned Ethan Ebanks-Landell of the season previous was particularly solid at centre-half during his 45-minute outing.

The endeavours of Rodney, looking every bit the ideal target man, were putting more pressure on opposing defenders, his strength leading to another fine goal.

However, the game did raise a question over the team's mobility against a more dominant midfield. Adam Clayton and Harvey Gilmour seemed at risk of being overwhelmed, prompting the consideration of a three-man midfield to test its viability. Moreover, there was room for improvement in terms of creating scoring opportunities, as attacks seemed characterised by fleeting moments rather than sustained pressure.

Sadly, any positivity from the football result itself was quashed by McNulty's post-match comments. He expressed the need for additional players to join the squad, but acknowledged his budget meant he would have to fish in rock pools as far as the transfer market was concerned.

'I still feel we need more,' he said. 'We've still got trialists and really young players coming off the bench, without any real injuries yet, which is concerning for me. There's a funny thing going on – we're the ex-Football League club, so we should have the ex-Football League budget, but our budget doesn't reflect that. We won't be able to sign tried-and-tested-type players for now.'

August 2023

WHILE IT IS a proud boast that Rochdale had remained members of the Football League since joining it in 1921, it isn't without fact that the club had flirted with demotion to the fifth tier of English football numerous times during that period.

Back then, however, there wasn't anything as perfunctory as promotion for non-league champions and relegation for the Football League's wooden spoon holders – that decision was instead left in the lap of the gods, or, more accurately, the vote of Football League club chairmen. Despite being at its mercy several times, Rochdale most notably benefitted from this controversial re-election system at the expense of fifth-tier champions Altrincham at the end of the 1979/80 season, a club which had comfortably won the division under its new guise as the Alliance Premier League.

In that fateful season, Dale, under the guidance of Bob Stokoe, battled not only on the pitch but also against the harsh winds of financial hardship. The side finished languishing eight points adrift at the bottom of the Fourth Division.

Meanwhile, Altrincham had forged a reputation as a progressive club with decent attendances. It seemed almost certain that Altrincham would secure the votes required for promotion, dashing Dale's threadbare hopes of survival. But fate had a different plan.

Legends abound of one single, pivotal moment. The chairman of Luton Town, Denis Mortimer, claimed to be entangled in the clutches of heavy traffic, while the chairman of Grimsby Town was said to have found himself standing in the wrong corner of the meeting venue, unknowingly withholding his crucial ballot.

Had those missing votes swayed against Rochdale, the entire tapestry of the club's Football League history would have been rewritten in an instant. Without a fleeting delay and an accidental misstep, the course of Rochdale's journey would have been for ever altered in an epoch-defining moment that would have arrived much sooner than eventually transpired.

Since a much fairer promotion and relegation system was introduced between the divisions in 1986/87, Dale had managed to steer clear of the demotion spots, cementing a reputation, for the most part, as fourth-tier survival specialists. Many a bigger club than Dale had fallen through the trapdoor in that time, often due to off-field problems overtaking matters on the pitch, but finally, in 2022/23, it was to be Dale's turn.

The National League, as the fifth tier is currently known, no longer carried quite the derisory reputation it once did, with 21 of the 24 teams competing in it boasting a full-time operation. Of course, the PR generated by Hollywood stars Ryan Reynolds' and Rob McElhenney's much-vaunted purchase of Wrexham, and the club's eventual promotion, had only boosted the league's reputation further.

There would be no such red carpet for Dale, however. In fact, with Notts County also achieving promotion from the division as play-off winners, having achieved 107 points during the season proper, the National League this time around looked very much wide open, with neither Dale nor Hartlepool United, the other side relegated from the fourth tier, among any pundit's outright favourites for an immediate return.

Financially, the two relegated clubs would receive normal EFL rations for one season only. After that, budgets would need to be supplemented by other means.

The fixture compilers did at least dish out a home match with which Rochdale could get their maiden campaign under way. Ebbsfleet United would be the visitors, a side that had achieved promotion to the fifth tier by clinching the National League South title with four matches to spare.

Under the ownership of Kuwaiti investors, Ebbsfleet were helmed by the magnetic Dennis Kutrieb, a well-regarded German coach who had seamlessly transitioned from a modest playing career to the realm of football management. Prior to joining Ebbsfleet, Kutrieb garnered acclaim for his coaching prowess at VSG Altglienicke, before going on to guide Tennis Borussia Berlin (TeBe) to the Berlin Cup Final and an impressive second-place finish in the league.

Even amid the disruptions caused by the Covid pandemic, Kutrieb's tenure at TeBe continued to flourish. His team dominated their league, ultimately claiming the championship and securing promotion. Such remarkable achievements earned Kutrieb the revered title of *Erfolgstrainer* (successful coach), bestowed on him by the German football publication *Kicker*.

This was enough to prompt Ebbsfleet to seek him out. Kutrieb took the reins of the Kent club during the tumultuous, pandemic-hit 2020/21 season in National

League South. He quickly became renowned for his attractive and attacking style of play, and steered the Fleet to an admirable third-place finish the following season, earning the club a coveted spot in the play-off final, which they ultimately lost. Not wanting to rely on such a lottery again, he masterfully guided the team to clinch the league title in the subsequent season, amassing more than 100 points.

By way of reward, the 43-year-old signed a contract extension, a move that clearly pleased club CEO Damian Irvine.

'Dennis has proven he is a great fit for this football club and has repaid the belief we had in him when he arrived in 2020 – a decision not without doubters and detractors at the time,' he said. 'Such success, with an exciting brand of football, of course, brings suitors to our door and it is no surprise Dennis has attracted interest from other quarters, including recent offers from the EFL. Like any ambitious club, we want to nurture and keep hold of our talents, particularly those we identified and recruited using our thorough processes and patience, such as those which delivered Dennis to Stonebridge Road.'

Despite football finance expert Kieran Maguire revealing that Ebbsfleet had lost £33,000 a week in season 2021/22, paying £314 in wages for every £100 of income, it was clear Kutrieb was more than just a well-backed manager. I caught up with the German ahead of the opening fixture to find out what he and his charges were all about.

'I spent my playing career mostly in the German fourth tier, with a brief spell in the third,' he told me. 'By the time I stopped playing, I was in the fifth tier, but was offered the chance to coach a team in the sixth tier, which I did for six months.

'Because I never really had a plan regarding what I wanted to do when I retired from football, this was a good situation for me. It gave me the time to assess if this was right. I knew I wanted to stay in football, as a coach, a manager, or even a player agent, but I just wasn't 100 per cent sure in what role. It turned out I really enjoyed the coaching.

'I began to get more involved and deeper into it. The club trusted me, and I got two promotions in three years – from the sixth tier to the fourth. I then made a move to another club where I got another promotion in two years and reached a cup final. It was then I realised I must have something to offer coaching, as you don't get three promotions and a cup final in six years with nothing.

'I got a message from the Ebbsfleet CEO, Damian Irvine, who said he was looking for a German manager and had been impressed by my stats. He asked if I could imagine doing the same in England. I said, "Yes, let's have a few chats and see where it goes."

'Damian explained to me that the club was looking for a German manager because he could swap an English manager with another English manager, but the basics would always stay more or less the same. He said the club had been inundated with CVs but nothing had really stood out to him as being different. He was looking for a completely fresh approach and he felt only an overseas manager could bring that.

'It was peak Covid time at this point, so meeting up proved quite difficult. However, we managed it, and I was able to have a look at the ground and meet the key people. It felt a good fit for me, so I said, "Let's do this."'

After arriving in Kent permanently, Kutrieb realised the enormity of the task ahead.

'Obviously, when you get promoted three times in six years in Berlin, you know the leagues inside out. You know every single player. I was pretty honest from the first day at Ebbsfleet because I said, "Look, I'm not shying away, I can definitely do this and be successful, but I will have two weaknesses: I don't know one player or one opposition team at this level." This is what I had to learn. One of my qualities is that I learn quickly, and I am very adaptable. Damian was great, essentially saying, "Don't worry, do your job and we will support you everywhere else."

'So, we slowly built up getting the recruitment right from window to window. I would say, maybe in the beginning, we got four or five signings wrong. In the second window, we had three wrong; in the third window, we had one wrong; and now we have none wrong, if that makes sense? With every game you play, you get better and better because you see all the other opponents – as individuals and as a collective. You assess their strengths and weaknesses on an ongoing basis and it lets you see who you might want for your own team and how to stop others playing well against you.'

Kutrieb also revealed that the secret to his success boiled down to one thing – hard graft.

'For me, instilling a higher work rate in the players was key,' he said. 'When I came in, the players were not used to training to my definition of what a full-time basis is. Yes, on paper the club was full time, but there was a big difference between our definitions. It wasn't magic, it was just that more work was needed to get the players to a level where they could play to my plan.

'That's the beauty of football. It isn't a German thing, a Spanish thing or a British thing, there are so many ways to play this game that are not tied to one nationality. It's down to the individual. Do you like to play on the floor? Do you like to go for the second ball? Do you like to sit deep? Do you like to play counterpressing or counterattack? There are so many options.

'The biggest difference I have made at Ebbsfleet in the three years I've been here is that we try to play on the floor as much as possible, because I think we have so many good players in England who are able to do that. I think the quality of the players, even at this level, is much better than to just kick the ball long and go for second balls.

'From this point of view, it was quite impressive for me how quickly everyone could adapt to what I wanted to see. It doesn't always go to plan, but that's normal in football because you have good days and bad days, but, in general, I was impressed with how much the players tried to adapt to the style of play.

'I think the most important thing is you need to make sure that your team is on one page and not all playing off the cuff. As long as you make sure that everyone knows what you want them to do, I don't mind a bit of in-game adaptability. I don't mind if they need to go long at one point, trying to win headers and flick headers and go from there. If that's what it takes to get an advantage, that's fine. I don't mind if a player has an off-day either, as long as they are trying. In football, you can carry an off-day player. It's not like tennis, where, if you have a bad day, you'll likely lose. In football, you have mates on the pitch who can cover for you. You can still keep the advantage and win the game.'

Having clearly succeeded in getting his Ebbsfleet charges to buy into his methods, Kutrieb remained ambitious for both the team and himself.

'My general aim is always to be successful and to get promoted again,' he said. 'I hate to lose games of football, and in any other sport for that matter. I'm just a bad loser. I think the challenge in football is that everyone feels they need to talk about their bigger aims. You don't need to talk too much about bigger aims, though, because those aims are just the result of winning football matches.

'I always said to our boys last season, "Don't focus on getting promoted. Focus on winning games, because if we win games, then we go up the table and, if we're up the table, we're getting promoted." That's what you can influence as a manager, and that's where you can make an impact.

'As for my personal aims, well, I didn't come over from Berlin to play non-league football for ever. I want to be in the Football League and, once there, I want to be as high as possible. I'm not rushed, though, and I think the consequence of hard work is being successful and this will always offer you possibilities to go to higher leagues.'

The chat had me convinced this would be no cakewalk for Dale. Ebbsfleet presented a formidable challenge, and the clash promised an exhilarating encounter that would set the tone for the battles to come. The game had also been selected by broadcaster TNT Sports (formerly BT Sport) for live television coverage, meaning an early evening kick-off and even more spice added to the contest.

Jim McNulty stuck with the 4-4-2 formation he had used in pre-season at a rain-lashed Spotland Stadium, deploying Tyrese Sinclair and Michael Afuye as wingers, who exchanged flanks after half-time. The inclusion of George Nevett, making his full professional debut, at left centre-back, brought equilibrium to the defence with his natural left-footed abilities and composure on the ball.

However, it was Ebbsfleet who ultimately emerged as 1-0 victors, courtesy of a fortuitous first-half goal from Luke O'Neill. The right-back intended to flick on Toby Edser's corner, but fate intervened, guiding the ball into the far corner of Dale's net. Perhaps better positioning to clear the ball ahead of the zonal marking could have averted the goal, but such wisdom is often clearer in hindsight.

Dale also had what appeared a clear penalty denied when goalkeeper Mark Cousins brought down Devante Rodney in an aerial duel. Compounding supporters' frustration, Kairo Mitchell's thunderous effort then crashed against the crossbar just before half-time. Alas, the home side proved otherwise unable to breach Ebbsfleet's deep defensive block, leaving them somewhat impotent in front of their own support.

Pleasingly, Dale displayed a varied approach rather than rigidly passing through opposition ranks. However, when Rodney and Mitchell exploited gaps in Ebbsfleet's expansive back three, they failed to capitalise, often recycling possession backwards.

Defensively, the team looked solid thanks to composed goalkeeper Louie Moulden's trustworthy presence. The Harvey Gilmour-Adam Clayton midfield pairing showed promise, with Clayton orchestrating play assuredly as the quarterback. Nonetheless, adapting to the formation sometimes hindered their coordination, straying too far apart and raising doubts about achieving the desired midfield balance between attack and defence. Furthermore, a lack of viable options on the bench proved a weakness, offering little chance to influence proceedings.

While there were positives to take from the game, there was also plenty for McNulty to ponder, too.

'We really needed the first goal today, because, if we'd got the first goal, I don't think we'd have looked back,' he said afterwards. 'Assessing it on its merits, I think we dominated the ball and dominated territory. We dominated chances. Ebbsfleet sat in a deep block and, if you gave me the chances we had today in another game, I don't think I'd trade them for anything else.'

Kutrieb revealed his own tactics for the game. 'We watched Rochdale in pre-season and saw they could use width to hurt teams on the counter, so that's why we sat deeper,' he said. 'We also saw they do zonal marking at set pieces, so we made sure we were first to the ball in these situations, which obviously led to our winning goal.'

* * *

PRIOR TO ROCHDALE AFC's EGM, the club held a well-attended fans' forum, where chairman Simon Gauge and his fellow board members were afforded an opportunity to lay out further detail pertaining to the loan both he and director Richard Knight were offering the club, secured against Spotland Stadium.

Gauge, in a pre-emptive statement, revealed that he and Knight, in an attempt to offer 'breathing space' in terms of cash flow, were prepared to lend Dale £350,000 for 'as long as the club needs it' at a commercial rate of interest.

He reiterated that the pair were not seeking to alter the resolution protecting the stadium in any way, but merely seeking shareholder approval under its existing framework.

Gauge also revealed the board had been working full time on finding an investor since January 2023 and had engaged with more than 200 parties.

He added that the club had been very close to a deal with one party of celebrity-fronted American investors, who wanted to invest in a fashion similar to that which took place at Wrexham, but, unfortunately, the consortium chose to purchase a Championship club instead. Coincidentally, a consortium fronted by former NFL quarterback Tom

Brady had announced that very morning its investment in Birmingham City.

There were said to be several other parties now being considered, but the issue for the board was not wanting to accept the wrong offer. The descriptions of potential purchasers ranged from 'tyre kickers' to 'brokers representing Middle Eastern sheikhs'.

At the EGM itself, the pair's motion was passed by shareholders on a show of hands. The resolution required a majority of 75 per cent, with Gauge and Knight just about receiving the requisite backing. The pair announced they would go on to discuss the terms of the loan with the rest of the board.

* * *

WHILE ROCHDALE WERE embarking on their first campaign in the National League at the lowest level they had competed at within the current English football pyramid, another club was also setting out on a debut campaign in the fifth tier – but at its highest.

Oxford City secured their place with a National League South play-off final victory over St Albans City, winning 4-0 in front of a record crowd of 3,100 at Court Place Farm.

The Hoops, going into the 2023/24 season, were managed by former Watford midfielder Ross Jenkins, who took charge in March 2022 having been caretaker since the January of that year. He guided the club to the play-off semi-finals, where they were beaten 3-0 by Dorking Wanderers, but he made no such mistake at the end of his second campaign.

'I look back at that first result now and I know we weren't ready,' Jenkins told me. 'We just didn't have enough to beat Dorking, who had been knocking on the play-off door for a couple seasons. We, on the other hand, were just enjoying the moment. Nobody expected us to get through and win the play-offs. But, I'll tell you something – it still hurt. I wanted to truly put my own stamp on things after that.'

Jenkins' Euro-trotting playing career saw him represent clubs in England, Romania, Bulgaria, Norway and Scotland. He certainly had plenty of experience to draw upon. It was at Watford, however, where he started out.

'I joined Watford when I was about nine years old,' he said. 'Back then, the academy was a really good setup. It's changed now, obviously, with the circumstances at the football club, and it being a club that is moving between the Premier League and Championship, it's harder for young kids to get through.

'When I was there, though, there was a big production line of kids coming through – loads of players from the academy making it to the first team, and I was lucky to be one of them.

'Funnily enough, I played with Will Buckley, who Watford signed from Rochdale. He was a very fast player. I remember a right-back getting subbed because they couldn't cope with him. I played under some really good managers as well, such as Brendan Rodgers, but we didn't quite get to the Premier League. I like to think we'd done the hard graft to contribute to where the club is now, and where it got to.'

Unfortunately, a series of injuries cut short Jenkins' stay at Watford and forced him to make some life-changing decisions.

'I sort of reassessed where I was in football and what I wanted to do,' he said. 'I didn't want to get to the end of my career and think, "Well, I wish I had done something different".

'I'd had a few offers when I was a kid to go to the top flight in Holland. I turned them down because I was playing in the English Championship. As an 18-year-old, I believed that was a really good achievement. I toyed with the idea a few times, but, ultimately, stayed put. Not many British players were doing it back then. However, when I was injured, it put a different spin on it. I was out for six or seven months. After that, I had a spell with Crawley to get myself fit and that made my next decision easy. I had plenty of offers from overseas but picked a country that not many people would pick – Romania.

'I had a good friend who was a scout out there. He said, "There's a club out here really wanting you, ACS Poli Timișoara." So, I did a bit of research. Big historic club, good stadium. I thought, "Yes, why not?" I turned up and I didn't speak a word of the language. I had to adapt to a new culture and get buy-in from the local players. They didn't like me at first. I had a fight on my first day in the changing room. But, after that, we shook hands and we got on really well. They saw I was wanting to fit in and learn. They respected me for that and it made my time there really enjoyable. I learned so much out there that you would take for granted here in the UK.

'When my time in Romania came to an end, I had a taste for the overseas lifestyle. Another scout I knew suggested Bulgaria to me. He knew the manager of OFC Pirin Blagoevgrad, who had previously played for CSK Sofia and spoke really good English, so I leapt into that one.

'Looking back, I learned so much tactically and technically from my spells in those two countries, and I firmly believe those leagues are underrated and overlooked. There are some players out there that I would take here at Oxford City in a heartbeat, but, obviously, due to Brexit, it's difficult to get those boys over as easily now. To a man, they're fit, they're strong, they're hungry, they don't take anything for granted. They work their socks off every session. They do double sessions every day. I learned a lot from the way they live, the way they communicate and the way they train.

'By now, I'm 25 and I know if I return to England at this point, I'd never go back abroad. I wanted one last stab at it. I get a phone call from Norway. It was Ian Burchnall, who a lot of people know in England now from his time at Notts County and Forest Green, but, at this point, he was manager of Viking FC. I signed for him and, I must say, it was the most enjoyable football I'd played to that point.

'Viking is a club with a lot of history. Roy Hodgson had managed them and players such as Brede Hangeland had represented them. It's a well-supported club in a decent stadium. We were in the Norwegian top flight but we got relegated in the end. We had a young squad and sold our better players, such as Julian Ryerson, who is at Borussia Dortmund now. Ultimately, it left us short of enough quality to keep us up.'

Next, Jenkins ended up in Scotland, signing for Hamilton Academical, which was where he picked up the injury that forced him to retire.

'When I was 19, I injured a disc in my back,' he said. 'Eight weeks' rehab, no problem. Then I'd done it again when I was in Scotland, aged 27, well, the disc just below it actually. So, I've now got two bad discs. When I saw the surgeon the first time, he says, "Yep, no problem. we'll fix it." I saw him the second time, the same surgeon, Damian Fahy at Chelsea, and he says, "Yep, no problem, I can fix you, but you might want to think about what you're doing after football."

'He was right. He did fix me, but I wasn't the same. I had severe pain down both my legs. I had a loss of sensation. It was scary stuff. I couldn't stand up at first. I had to lie on the floor. I was in some real big pain. I wanted to give it another go, you know, getting fit. But my calf muscles, my legs, they'd just lost the power. Not to the point I couldn't walk, obviously. I can walk and I can join in jogging. I can do bits. But to perform at the elite level of a professional footballer? No. It was gone.

'It was a sore one to swallow and it took me a while to get over it, if I'm being honest, because I knew I could still do it technically, but, for health reasons, I didn't want to be crippled when I was older. That was that – 27 years old and finished as a player.

'Luckily, I was thinking about the coaching side before I retired, so I'd done a little bit in Norway, studying, and, when I came back to the UK, I started on the various coaching courses you can do here. A lot of the old pros at Watford were giving me advice, too. It's the same advice I now give the young lads here at Oxford City. I say, "Don't just rely on football. Have another plan. I thought I was going to play to 37. I was super fit. I ended at 27."'

After getting over the disappointment of no longer being able to play, Jenkins found he had a knack for the other side of the game.

'When I was studying coaching, I actually got really into it,' he said. 'When you're an 18-year-old player, you just want to play. When you get older, you start to appreciate everything that goes into a football team. I wanted to progress and see if I could affect a team from the sides, and, luckily, I've been able to do it.'

Oxford City, in the shadow of their more illustrious neighbours Oxford United, are actually the older club historically. They also have the renown of having been managed by former England World Cup hero Bobby Moore and Harry Redknapp in the late 1970s. Yet the fifth tier, or step one on the non-league setup, is as high as they have ever competed. How did Jenkins end up being the man to achieve this?

'My girlfriend lives in Oxford,' he said with a wry smile. 'She came out to Norway with me. She lived with me out there. She then commuted to Scotland when I played there. So, I said, "When I retire, I'll move wherever you want to move to. Because you followed me, I'll follow you." I had no idea it would be that bloody year!

'I've actually another small connection to Oxford City. My brother was a player here many years ago, on loan from Stevenage. I used to come to watch him, unaware, obviously, I'd be managing the team in 18 years' time.

'When I moved down here, I knew Mark Jones, who was the manager at the time. I dropped him a message. I said I was retired and looking to get back into football. I asked if I could come along and just watch. So, I went along to watch. Mark then said, "Do you wanna do a session?" I said I was game for that, got my boots on, took a session, and then he said, "Do you wanna come on board?" I said, "Yep, absolutely." So, it happened quite quickly. I was first-team coach.

'As is the way in football, Mark then left the club and David Oldfield came in. An experienced player in his day, who had played at the top level, I learned a lot from David. I was still doing my badges while he was there, but then he left to join Weymouth and I was thrust into the hotseat on an interim basis. We managed to finish in the semi-final of the play-offs of the National League South, which was the highest achievement of the football club at that time. I was then offered the job permanently at the age of 31.

'The result of that game hurt, though, so I wanted to make sure we did as much prep over pre-season as possible. I was stubborn, real stubborn. I didn't just want players, I wanted the right players for us, and it took us a while to find them. We had a small squad, but we kept the cohort together and added players who definitely strengthened us. Players who people thought couldn't do the things that they are doing now. We've coached them well and that has brought success.'

With the Hoops being just a part-time outfit, Jenkins felt there was one key handicap his side faced when competing with the better-resourced full-time teams in non-league.

'It's purely time,' he said. 'It's not the lack of the players' ambition. It's not the lack of motivation. If I asked all the squad to come in Monday to Friday to train, they would. But circumstances dictate they can't. We pay part-time wages. We can't ask boys to leave their day jobs and sacrifice family life and food on the table for a part-time salary, just to make me feel better that we're full time.

'So, we've found a good way to combat that in terms of the physical aspect to the tactical aspect, to the knowledge, to how we drip-feed information. We don't overload them or drown them, but we give them the right information at the right time. It's easy saying it, but doing it over a long season is where it kicks in and it's hard.

'You are constrained to Tuesdays and Thursdays, maybe two hours each night. You're forced to find a different way to operate. Maybe a quick phone call on a player's lunch break, maybe a Friday night with a couple of them. You just need to find a way to bridge the gap to get information into them without flooding them on a Tuesday.

'But, you know, I'm lucky. I've got good staff around me. I've got players that are ambitious and hungry. I think the main importance of a good group is a good changing room. I think it's the oldest thing, and everyone says it, but it's bloody true.

'A dressing room requires everyone to pull in the same direction and, if you have Monday to Friday, you have more time to manage any nuances, but, with only Tuesday and Thursday available, you don't have that luxury, so you need everybody on board.

'We've achieved that and we've honestly got an excellent changing room. I've said to them, "If I was still a player, this is the changing room I'd like to be a part of."

'When I was interviewed to be manager here, I said, "I want the changing room to manage the changing room. I don't want to be sat in there with my finger pointing at people." I want people to jump on people and go, "Hey, that ain't good enough." That's what I have here now. A collective responsibility.'

Jenkins believed his side still had what it took to compete at National League level.

'The model of being part-time and non-league is that we might have to sell a few players,' he said. 'We only sell if the offer is too good, though. The long-term plan is to develop these players to either stay with us and progress with us, or move them on and let them progress elsewhere with the club benefitting financially.

'We take the underdog role, embrace it and try to show people what we can do. With that, we've got to juggle time, we've got to juggle distance, we've got to travel further, with overnight stays.

'We've got a budget for this, so we've got to make sure long term that we sustain our finances and we don't go under in terms of overpaying and rinsing the budget. We've got to be savvy with who we bring in, who we pay, what we pay. It's like any club really, but on a much smaller resource scale.

'But we know what we are. We have a nice compact stadium, a 3G pitch and we now don't clash with Oxford United in terms of fixtures, so, when they're away, we're at home, and we are seeing a few more faces. We want to entertain, we want to play in the right manner. We obviously also want to win games of football, but I believe we've got a squad on display that achieves both.

'We are a community club. We don't have any trouble. We try to make it a good experience for fans both home and away, and I hope we continue to do that in the National League.'

Rochdale supporters got to see this quaint hospitality early in the season as Oxford City was scheduled as the first away trip, a chance to regain optimism after the Ebbsfleet defeat. The Hoops' own fans were themselves smarting from a heavy opening-day defeat at Aldershot Town.

However, head coach Jim McNulty faced something of a setback before the match. Loanee Cody Johnson, who had exhibited an array of impressive passing during pre-season, was unexpectedly recalled by parent club Stockport County before he even had a chance to make a competitive appearance for Dale.

The absence of the midfielder, even from the bench, forced McNulty to take swift action to find a replacement. He moved promptly to secure the loan signing of 18-year-old Tommy McDermott from Port Vale, a deal that would remain in place until January. He then augmented this by capturing 22-year-old winger Jesurun Uchegbulam on a two-year deal from National League rivals Chesterfield, a signing he admitted he had been trying to get done for a while.

'He will add genuine competition for those wide players, adding to the good players that we've already got in that area,' McNulty said of the winger.

That did indeed appear to be the case, as it was Uchegbulam's introduction to the game from the substitutes' bench in the 67th minute that eventually added some impetus to Rochdale's efforts to break down a very defensive Oxford team, Ian Henderson finally breaking the deadlock on 71 minutes to hand the visitors a 1-0 victory and McNulty's side its first three points of the season.

McNulty stuck with his favoured 4-4-2 system, the only change from the Ebbsfleet game being Devante Rodney's mysterious absence from the squad. The match followed a similar pattern to the opener, but without Oxford's attack truly testing goalkeeper Louie Moulden.

It didn't take long for a smooth interchange near the box to lead to Henderson gaining possession inside it. He cleverly lofted the ball over the advancing keeper, only for the assistant referee to raise an offside flag against him.

Dale established a firm hold on possession as Oxford sat deep, evidently aiming to frustrate. Despite this resistance, McNulty's team persisted. Harvey Gilmour had an effort blocked in the Oxford area, and Henderson's sliding attempt was cleared off the line.

Early in the second half, McNulty adjusted his wide players slightly more centrally. Kairo Mitchell then forced Oxford goalkeeper Chris Haigh into action, deftly redirecting Jimmy Keohane's low cross goalward. Ten minutes later, Haigh parried Michael Afuye's cross into the path of Clayton, whose rapid shot was thwarted by the keeper's legs.

McNulty then granted McDermott and Uchegbulam debuts. Uchegbulam's initial involvement saw him sprint down the right and deliver a low cross that Mitchell narrowly missed.

The breakthrough finally arrived when Tyrese Sinclair found Keohane on the right side of the area. Keohane pulled the ball back for Henderson, who slotted home from the edge of the six-yard box with impeccable timing, becoming the first Dale player to score across three tiers of English football.

Dale maintained dominant possession until the final whistle, remaining relatively untroubled by the hosts.

'We dominated so much of the game today, we dominated so much of the ball,' McNulty said afterwards. 'We had to be really patient to wait for our chances and that's a new set of challenges for us as a team than what we've faced in the past few years.

'We've always been the team suffering in our own half, defending hard for large parts of the game and then hoping for something on the break. Today we were the other team. It's a new challenge, it's about moving the ball quickly, getting the ball into the most dangerous places as quickly as we can and moving a full set of ten outfield players, who were already set in their own half.'

* * *

WOKING FC IS a name most football aficionados have heard of but, with only a few notable achievements, including three FA Trophy wins in the 1990s, the club hadn't threatened to reach the Football League in more than two decades – until 2023.

Woking's full-time status was enabled the season previous by US investors Drew Volpe and John Katz, and, coupled with manager Darren Sarll's pragmatic approach, the team spent much of the season in third place, ultimately finishing fourth and having to settle for a National League play-off eliminator against Bromley, which they lost.

Sarll assumed the position of Woking manager in 2022, following a successful tenure at then National League outfit Yeovil Town. During his three years at Yeovil, he achieved remarkable milestones, including leading the team to the National League play-offs and making a notable appearance in the FA Cup's third round.

This season, he was gunning to take Woking a step further, and the trip to the Kingfield Stadium, a second successive away game for Rochdale, was to prove a tricky affair.

Despite there being only three days since Rochdale's previous match, Jim McNulty was still able to augment his squad further with the addition of midfielder Ryan East, who joined on loan from Bradford City until the end of the season, the 25-year-old going straight into the starting XI.

McNulty veered away from 4-4-2 for this one, electing to instead try a 4-3-3. This formational shift gave a first start for Jesurun Uchegbulam, who formed a forward triumvirate with Kairo Mitchell and Tyrese Sinclair. The midfield three consisted of East, Harvey Gilmour and Adam Clayton, with Jimmy Keohane, Kwaku Oduroh, Ethan Ebanks-Landell and Kyle Ferguson making up the back four.

Sarll himself seemed to be trialling something new with his own starting XI, but the experiment left his side lopsided and full of gaps, which Dale were quick to exploit. The midfield three were able to find the wide positions and, with a little more expediency, the visitors could have opened the scoring sooner than they actually did.

It finally fell to Sinclair to do the honours on 15 minutes when, following a direct ball from Louie Moulden, he skilfully found the net from an acute angle, seizing upon a hesitance by Woking goalkeeper Joe Day.

If anything, Dale should have gone on to aggressively press the Woking players' clear discomfort with their own system, but the half ended with the visitors only one goal to the good.

The inevitable half-time changes by the home side proved decisive ones, as Dale failed to adapt to the formational balance and shift in intensity now displayed by Woking. This was rammed home when Scott Cuthbert soared to deliver a precision header, which Moulden looked to have clawed to safety, only for referee Stephen Parkinson to adjudge that it had crossed the goal line. Woking then surged ahead in the 74th minute as Padraig Amond drew a handball in the area from Keohane, leading to substitute Reece Grego-Cox confidently converting the subsequent penalty.

Not content with just one, Grego-Cox secured his brace eight minutes later with a hooked finish, exploiting the fact that defender Ferguson was off the field following treatment for a head knock. Although Mitchell managed to provide Dale with a late glimmer of hope via an incisive finish following an even more incisive through ball from Clayton, it was too little too late.

Post-match, McNulty confirmed that Devante Rodney was suffering with illness, Ian Henderson, match-winner the previous Saturday, wasn't fit to start due to an ankle injury, and Tommy McDermott also missed out due to injury.

Still, he wasn't for making excuses.

'My overriding feeling was that, for most of the game, I didn't see our team's courage and personality with the ball,' he said. 'Credit to Woking for that, they put the pressure on, but it took us going 2-1 down for me to finally see some of the stuff that we've been implementing in training.

'Tonight was good evidence that, if we try to get into a fight with the opposition, the game can become anyone's. We need to try to make the game ours as much as possible. That's what I'll be looking for going forward.'

* * *

NESTLED IN THE vibrant town of Eastleigh, Hampshire, lies a football club whose resilience matches the spirit of its nickname – the Spitfires. The moniker pays homage to the iconic Supermarine Spitfire fighter aircraft of the second world war, signifying Eastleigh's strong historical ties to the aviation industry during that era.

In May 2023, Stewart Donald, former Sunderland chairman, returned to take over the reins of the National League club for a second stint. Donald's reduced stake at Sunderland allowed him to actively participate in another club's affairs. Notably, he had previously owned Eastleigh in 2010 but relinquished it in 2018 to lead the Madrox consortium's acquisition of Sunderland.

With Donald's return, the Spitfires aimed to soar to new heights, and they made the trip to Spotland undefeated in the new campaign. Manager Lee Bradbury also had former Scotland international Chris Maguire and former Dale loanees Scott Quigley and Paul McCallum among the players he could call upon.

However, as it emerged, Dale secured a comfortable victory thanks to first-half goals from Ian Henderson and Kairo Mitchell, a result that moved the side up to 11th in the National League table.

Jim McNulty made a tactical decision to reintroduce Cameron John and Henderson to the starting line-up, and it paid off handsomely. From the first whistle, Dale seized control of possession, with home debutant Ryan

East testing Eastleigh's keeper Joe McDonnell from long range. McDonnell parried the shot but it fell perfectly for Jimmy Keohane, who whipped in an inch-perfect cross for Henderson to tap in from close range.

At the heart of the action, the midfield trio of East, Adam Clayton and Harvey Gilmour orchestrated proceedings with poise, carving out chance after chance for Dale to extend their lead. However, it was Mitchell who stole the spotlight just before half-time. Receiving the ball with his back to goal from 30 yards out, he executed a sublime spin and unleashed an unstoppable missile into the top corner, leaving McDonnell helpless.

The second half saw Dale's dominance continue, with Tyrese Sinclair's shot deflected wide by a sprawling McDonnell. Moments later, the keeper denied Mitchell again, using his legs to thwart the striker's attempt after Gilmour's incisive through ball.

McNulty's flexible 4-3-3 formation allowed for fluid positional interchanges and provided a solid defensive foundation. Gilmour's intelligent movements on the left created dynamic triangles with Clayton and East, while Keohane's forward forays from right-back added an extra dimension to Dale's attacking threat. The team's adaptability shone through, with Henderson dropping deep to influence play, and the ever-available East excelling in midfield while displaying a crucial forward-thinking mentality.

Defensively, Dale looked resolute, though it must be acknowledged that Eastleigh's misfiring forward line struggled to pose a genuine threat. Mitchell's well-timed runs into channels at the other end of the pitch added another dimension to Dale's attack, keeping the opposition back line on their toes.

While some argued post-match that Dale could have capitalised further on their superiority by scoring more goals, it was nonetheless a resounding victory that highlighted the team's potential when firing on all cylinders.

'Today we were very professionally ruthless,' McNulty said afterwards. 'I thought we were dominant, and it could have been way more [than 2-0].

'I've seen so many aspects of a selfless performance today, too. The team is everything. Trying to instil that into the group is the most important thing for me. I think it will serve us well in the long term.

'We should have a constant belief in a certain way of playing, and we should stick to it. The noise game to game is very different. It's difficult not to be distracted by the noise but it's my job to protect the players from the noise and keep them focused on what we collectively believe.

'When it comes to fruition, such as in games like today, I think it's amazing. One of the most amazing things for me today was in the last minute of the game – and it probably went unnoticed by so many people – but Eastleigh were on a counterattack and the sprint recoveries from our players, flying past every single one of their players, showed the desire and willpower to get back for the team.

'When there are seven or eight players back, it's easy to think, "Let someone else deal with it," but all ten of ours got back and forced Eastleigh out of play. Moments like that are the epitome of the team for me.'

McNulty also revealed that Jesurun Uchegbulam, who had performed brilliantly at Woking, would sadly be out of action for the next month after tearing a hamstring in that match.

* * *

ROCHDALE FANS DIDN'T need to cast their minds back too far to remember the club's last tussle with Bromley. An FA Cup first-round encounter at Spotland in 2017 saw Keith Hill's charges, then at League One standard, dispatch their National League opposition without breaking a sweat, winning 4-0 with Ian Henderson grabbing two of the goals that day.

Ahead of Bromley's first league clash with Rochdale, the club's current manager, Andy Woodman, a former goalkeeper, revealed to me that he was hoping for a different outcome this time as he considered Dale's home as something of a good-luck charm.

'Ironically, while on my journey around the lower leagues as a player, I made a debut for two different clubs at Rochdale and kept a clean sheet both times – Northampton and Brentford,' he smiled. 'So Spotland is a ground I've done quite well at. I hope that continues.'

The positive clean-sheet trend didn't continue for Woodman, unfortunately for him, but his side did hold Dale to a 2-2 draw as both teams finished the game with ten men.

Chinweke Okoli's header gave the visitors the lead, before two from Tyrese Sinclair turned the game on its head. However, Bromley equalised just after the hour mark and, although Dale dominated, they had to settle for just a point.

Jim McNulty named an unchanged starting XI from the Eastleigh win, with new loan signing Max Conway, a 19-year-old left-back from Bolton Wanderers, replacing the ill Devante Rodney on the bench for this Friday night contest.

Dale maintained the same 4-3-3 formation, with Sinclair on the left and Harvey Gilmour on the right. The players were visibly growing more comfortable with

McNulty's tactics, resulting in increased creativity and forward-thinking play.

However, Bromley had set up to absorb pressure and counterattack, with Corey Whitely the first to exploit this, firing an effort off the post. Louie Moulden then denied Ben Krauhaus, but could do nothing to prevent Okoli's headed opener from the ensuing corner.

Sinclair's performance stood out as he posed a constant threat down the left. The game then pivoted in the 38th minute when Joshua Passley was sent off for bringing down Cameron John in the area, allowing Sinclair to convert the resulting penalty straight down the middle.

Ryan East impressed again with his composure and influence in midfield, firing inches wide from outside the area before Kairo Mitchell had a goal ruled out for offside.

Six minutes into the second half, Dale took the lead through a moment of brilliance from Sinclair. He cut inside and curled an exquisite effort into the far top corner from the edge of the area for his third goal of the season.

However, complacency seemed to set in thereafter, affecting both attack and defence. Greater vigilance was needed to prevent counterattacks, while Dale's attacking play lacked precision in crossing and capitalising on shooting opportunities.

These lapses were duly punished as Bromley equalised just after the hour mark through Michael Cheek's neat finish following another swift counter. The lesson still hadn't been learned, and Dale were further chastened following yet another counter when Adam Clayton had to bring down the goal-bound Whitely, earning a debatable straight red card from referee Aaron Jackson.

Now Dale's goal and numerical advantages had been squandered.

Cheek fired the resulting free kick narrowly over, before Sinclair struck the upright in pursuit of a hat-trick, but the home side were left frustrated despite showing more promise.

'The fans were great tonight,' McNulty said afterwards. 'They were baying for the opposition's blood because they could smell it. The players could too. We, as coaches, need to continually work on how to extract that blood from the opposition. We're putting destructive phases of play together right up until the last third of the pitch. We're scoring less goals than our [expected goals] suggests we should be scoring, so we just need to handle those certain moments a bit better so that we can really start to kill games off.'

McNulty also shed light on Rodney's continued absence through illness. 'Dev has been for a number of chest scans, the final of which discovered some complications with his viral infection,' he said.

'We'll lose Dev for much longer than we thought, which is a genuine shame. With the way we're playing, Dev, in and around the opposition box, could be devastating. He's picked up this virus, which has taken a bit of a nasty turn, and we're told now that it's going to take quite a bit of time before we see Dev again, unfortunately.

'It's testament to his character that he sat on the bench for us last week – when he didn't really know what was wrong with him, but he knew something wasn't good. He was willing to sit on the bench with the team low on numbers, because [Ian Henderson] is carrying an injury as well.'

* * *

FOLLOWING THE FAILURE of an attempt to acquire Yeovil Town in May 2023, Julie-Anne Uggla and her son

Matt, through their 394 Sports Ltd group, successfully completed a 51 per cent takeover of York City from Glen Henderson the following month.

Henderson himself had only taken charge of York the previous summer, in a deal that involved the club's supporters' trust acquiring the remaining 49 per cent.

The Uggla family's substantial wealth and extensive network stemmed from Canadian-born entrepreneur Lance Uggla who, according to the *Financial Times*, had amassed a fortune of £650m by 2020, largely through the success of IHS Markit, the financial data company he founded and subsequently sold for a substantial sum.

Julie-Anne and Matt, Lance's former wife and son, respectively, assumed directorship of 394 Sports Ltd, the company that had acquired the controlling stake in York. Together, they co-chaired the club. Julie-Anne, an entrepreneur born in Zimbabwe and raised in Canada, had established the city-guide technology business Cities Talking, while also raising significant funds for charitable causes.

With Matt seemingly taking on the football side of the business, I sought him out ahead of Rochdale's visit to the old Yorkshire capital to find out about the new journey the Minstermen were embarking on, and just what had inspired him to buy a football club.

'I was born in Canada but moved to London with my parents when I was about two years old,' Uggla told me. 'I then grew up there.

'My parents have both done really, really well in life, yes, but I started my own property company when I was about 19 years old. It just kept growing and growing to the point it now runs itself. It got to the point where I wasn't actually having to do much because it was throwing off enough rent that I could buy four or five more properties the following year. It was very much a rinse-and-repeat business.

'I ended up hiring my best mate to run the whole thing once I had my daughter, but, as she got older, I started to get bored on the work front again. A friend of mine mentioned Yeovil Town was up for sale. I found this interesting because I grew up a massive football fan, supporting Arsenal, and the thought of club ownership had never seriously crossed my mind. The more I thought about it, the more it interested me.

'So, without realising what I was signing myself up for, I approached Yeovil to see what was what. Let's just say that interest ended for both parties in a not very nice way. I felt scapegoated a little bit, which wasn't nice, because people don't ever fully know what goes on behind the scenes.

'The experience hadn't dampened my enthusiasm for football club ownership, though. I felt I had unfinished business. Through the holding company set up by myself and my mum, we looked at about 50 different clubs that were open to investment – Rochdale was one of them, actually. There were bigger clubs, too, but they presented too much of a beast to take on right away.

'Anyway, of all the clubs, York City presented the easiest and simplest transaction opportunity, allied to the fact it was based in a beautiful city with massive growth potential. So, we approached York, and I think it took just a couple of weeks to get it over the line.

'We also liked the fact York was in the National League. It's proper football. The Wild West of football. A real place to grow from. I get asked how far I think we can take York. I think we have the potential to make the Premier League, if people really, really wanted to make that happen. It would take a lot, but, if you look at the size of York as a city and then you look at Bournemouth, Luton, those types of places, I don't see them being bigger places, or the people there being any more passionate about football.

'And that was another factor for us choosing York City. You get clubs who think they've found their level and have no ambition, or there are those where you could pump a lot of money into them, and bring in good players, but they're soulless places. That's not what it's about for us. It's about going on a journey with the fans.

'The two most important things to me are my relationship with the players, and my relationship with the fans, because, at the end of the day, there is no football club without the fans. This is their club and it's the most important relationship that I'm going to have, because everyone else will come and go over the time I'm here, but the fans are here for life.

'To me, as a football fan growing up, it always felt that the owners and chairmen were so far removed from the supporters. They felt like these mythical creatures that you couldn't have anything to do with. Well, I want to engage with people and let them know as much as I possibly can. We're going on this journey together, so I want them to all feel welcome.

'My mum is less involved on the footballing side, and more looks after the commercial aspects of the club. We obviously have a board of directors, but with me and my mum having such a majority stake, the decisions are ours to make. I take advice from a lot of people. I have Darren Kelly, who's our general manager here, and David Stockdale, who's still playing, but is also our head of recruitment.

'In terms of growing the club, I think there are two markets. You've got the people inside the city and then those in the surrounding areas. We are running the traditional programmes, such as going into schools and giving out tickets, but I think also having a successful team on the pitch helps with all the stuff off the pitch, because people then want to be associated with it.

'The new generation now lives on social media. This is what Dorking Wanderers do really well with their documentary on YouTube. They let people know what's going on. It makes the fans feel like they're part of the team. They turn up for a game and recognise all of the players. I think humanising the players in this way is vital.

'You want to create that inclusive club culture where there are no scandals, no crazy stuff, just a classy place that people want to be associated with. So, if you're going out to big businesses, they're looking at you and see that you pay your players, the players are all happy and decent people, and the fans are happy, meaning the club is a major part of the community. That's what a business wants to invest in and that is what will make a football club grow.

'I've moved to York from London as I believe it's vital to be part of this community. You can't really take your finger off the pulse. I have to be here to make sure that all the stuff we're trying to get going is actually moving and, if it's not, then it's about understanding why and being around to sort it.'

Despite having a decent history against Rochdale, York had been absent from the Football League since relegation in 2016, in which time the club had fallen as low as the sixth tier. In their first season following promotion from National League North, the Minstermen finished 19th in the National League in 2022/23. However, with the Ugglas' backing, York were expected to achieve much more in the 2023/24 campaign.

As it transpired, York's quest for success was thwarted during the bank holiday clash, with Dale running out 3-1 winners at the Community Stadium, a result that cost manager Michael Morton his job.

Jim McNulty brought Kwaku Oduroh back into the starting XI at right-back for this one, which pushed Jimmy Keohane into an advanced midfield role, allowing Harvey Gilmour to drop back to cover for the suspended Adam Clayton.

And Dale went for the jugular from the first whistle, Tyrese Sinclair, Ryan East and Kyle Ferguson all having chances within the first quarter of an hour, before Cameron John had a goal ruled out for offside.

Dale earned a penalty after Ethan Ebanks-Landell was brought down while attacking a corner. Sinclair confidently stepped forward, delivering a powerful spot-kick into the top corner, securing his fourth goal of the season.

Unfortunately, the match took a contentious turn when Oduroh was shown a harsh yellow card for a foul on Maz Kouhyar. Louie Moulden then showcased his athleticism, brilliantly tipping Dipo Akinyemi's resultant free kick over the crossbar. Nevertheless, from the subsequent corner, Adam Crookes found himself unmarked and nodded the ball into the far corner in the 11th minute of added time, despite only six minutes originally being signalled by the fourth official.

Shortly after the half-time break, Dale were once again awarded a penalty. Kairo Mitchell orchestrated a delightful through ball to Keohane, who was hauled down by Crookes, resulting in a red card for the York man as the last defender. Sinclair, displaying power and precision, stepped up to net again, despite the goalkeeper's valiant effort to stop the ball.

Despite now having a numerical advantage, the Dale players found it challenging to assert themselves in the manner they had in the first half, enduring a period of pressure from the hosts. Moulden was called upon to make several outstanding saves to preserve his team's lead.

In the dying moments of the game, Dale sealed the victory, however. A long ball from Moulden was controlled by Mitchell, rebounded off York substitute Paddy McLaughlin and fell perfectly into the path of Ian Henderson. With composure, Henderson lofted the ball over the advancing goalkeeper, notching his 139th Dale goal.

This win put Dale into fifth place in the National League standings to round off August, marking a good first month's competitive work for McNulty.

'I was pleased with the first-half performance,' he said after the match. 'When it was 11 v 11, we cut York open. I couldn't believe we went in at half-time level. I'm really pleased we've got the win, and the momentum we've generated, but I have an overriding feeling that we were let down by the officials today. You want a good portion of accuracy and consistency from them, but it became a mess. We played 14 minutes' added time in the first half when they signalled six. I don't understand it. That led to the ref awarding a foul that wasn't a foul, and a booking, and we ultimately conceded from that. Defending that corner is on us, yes, and we need to handle that better, but we shouldn't have still been playing at that point.

'In the second half, we lost control a bit. There is no way it should have caused as much stress as it did. I didn't recognise some of our decision-making. The third goal brought relief, but it shouldn't have come to that. We were good for the win, of course, but we need to get better at making some of those decisions second half.

'The fans have been amazing this season. There is an understanding from them as to how we are trying to play and there is an appreciation of that. I'm glad we are giving them something to cheer again. I'm proud to be Rochdale manager.'

* * *

AS AUGUST DREW to a close, I was invited by Jim McNulty to what had become Rochdale's training base in south Manchester, to see first-hand how he implemented his ideas and, as he put it, to 'get a feel' for what he was trying to achieve.

Located in Fallowfield, Manchester Metropolitan University's Platt Lane Sports Complex offered a variety of top-quality pitches, a fully equipped gym and a host of meeting rooms, all of which McNulty said suited his needs.

'We've got everything we need to allow us to train in all weathers,' he said. 'There is nothing like this available to us in the Rochdale area at the moment, so we're here for the next year at least, certainly.'

As the players filed out of the complex at the end of a tough session, McNulty led me to the meeting rooms.

'The perception is that we're doing really good at the moment,' he said, pensively, as we found a seat. 'But the situation on the pitch can change at any moment. I'm highly aware that our squad is wafer thin. I think we'll have been the only team in the National League for the past few weekends that didn't have a striker on the bench, for example.

'Ian Henderson is 39 years old. I see moments in his energy and performance levels where I think he shouldn't be out there all the time, you know? He deserves to be moved in and out of this team now. We shouldn't have full reliance on Hendo. It's wrong. Kairo Mitchell I brought to the club for reasons that I think are hugely important to this team, but I didn't bring him in to have the weight of the world on his shoulders in regards to scoring all the goals. The narrative needs to be controlled with these two forwards.

'Our marquee marksman is Devante Rodney and he is struggling with a really bad viral infection. We're going to be without him for months. I'm having to use Harvey Gilmour up front and he rolled his ankle in training today, so we might have to play another full-back on the wing. The players are able to rotate some positions, but it comes with real limitations. I've got Kairo playing with two broken ribs at the minute, too. I can't tell the fans or media this, because then every opposition player will target him and batter the fuck out of him. He's tough and he's playing for the team because he knows we've got no one else.

'We need help in these areas to be serious about doing anything this season. It's a big, big task to keep a very small squad fit all season without some help. I've been so happy with George Nevett, and deservedly gave him a pro deal, but the rest of the young guys are not ready yet. They train with us here every single day because I'm trying to accelerate their learning, but they are not ready for full exposure to this environment. So, our current league position is masking what is going on behind the scenes and it could take just one thing for us to end up in that toxic place of last season again, and that's what I want to avoid.

'Tyrese Sinclair is getting brandished as the standout winger in the league at the moment. The team model constructs so many moments for him and the other wingers to be effective. That's why he's got standout stats. I'm on at Tyrese every single day, though, because I think he hasn't actually started yet. He hasn't shown what he can truly do. He hasn't got enough assists. The amount of moments he's been in the final part of the pitch, in the hard space, inside the opponents' box, he can be getting more assists.

'I'm having to approach this season by getting the players to believe in my model.

'The games are a challenge because these other teams in the National League are better at some things than we are. I say to the guys all the time, there's two different sports going on in this league, ours and everyone else's. The second we don't play ours, we're in danger. We don't have the budget to play attritional football and be at the top. We can't afford the biggest, the strongest, the fastest. We need to play in a unique Rochdale way, like we once did.

'We're trying to get this club back to how it used to be. I had never contemplated my future being away from this club as much as I did last season. I was in conversation, actively thinking about taking up different roles at Premier League clubs that would allow me to utilise my potential intellect and experience of the game. With the direction the club was travelling in, and the choices it was making being less clear to me, my future felt like it was probably going to be away from Rochdale, which is something I could not have foreseen years earlier.

'So, this season, having got the job, I knew we had to play football that represented me. I don't think it's right or wrong, I just think it's me. It's got to be authentic. We have to be so brave playing this type of football, knowing that it could go wrong at any moment.

'I believe in our players. I believe in who we've recruited and we're going to continue to try to do it this way because I believe in attributing meaning to performance, just like the New Zealand All Blacks' approach. The players sometimes laugh when I monologue like this, but they get it. They get the importance I place on everything having meaning.

'I break it down to a simple question – what are we trying to do? Win? Yes, but how? You're in a position that helps someone else in the team initially and that action ultimately rewards you as part of the team. We've introduced notepads into team meetings. I love American sports, NFL, basketball and so on. You watch the players there, the first thing they get out is a notepad. Footballers don't do it. There's an embarrassment about being professional in football. There's, like, a coolness in not trying. I've broken that here.

'I'm trying to introduce a language to the players, to help them see better how what we do in training relates to game situations. Language is a big thing for me. Instead of other types of words that are loose and don't attach real meaning to events, we keep using specific words or phrases in training, so that, in those moments on the pitch, a simple phrase called out can trigger an action.

'For example, we have something called a box-defence structure. Ethan Ebanks-Landell is by far the best in the group for this. I hear him out there, he'll say, "Box defence, box defence." The other players know what that means in that moment. If they defend that moment properly because of our box-defence structure, it's like a dopamine. Sometimes it might look naive, but in other moments it looks fucking tremendous, and it rewards the players so much that they know they can do it again and be successful.

'Then I see other teams who don't have a language, with players all on different pages. They're all trying their best, but they're chasing shadows. They all believe they should be doing something different. They're all talking and cutting each other off. They have no unified belief and language, and, as a result, it makes them appear disorganised.

'But, even in saying all that, I still don't know if I'm getting it right. Results are the biggest marker, yes, but I feel better now having a rock-solid belief system to judge performances by. I've been part of football clubs where, if we won, the manager was happy, and if we lost, they weren't. But there was nothing to judge a performance by. There was nothing to say why we won, or why we lost. There was no template. An approach based on results only can be very dangerous. Victories can conceal flaws and defeats can mislead. Winning or losing, we should still be able to judge performances correctly.

'When I took over on an interim basis at the end of last season, I'd say to the players, after games that didn't go our way, despite a good performance, "You've got so little to believe in. I admire so much what you're doing because you've got so little to reinforce your belief that what you're doing is OK, and you've got so little support for what you're doing."

'They've got that this season, so you can now see them moving the ball out from the back and going through teams with belief. They have to keep the belief that this is the right approach, though, as I said. We cannot abandon this belief and try to play like other teams. Against Woking, for example, we shit ourselves and had no bravery. I said, "That's what hurt me the most, that you lost all belief that everything we've done for eight weeks out there will actually work."

'Part of the issue is that there's a goal behind them. Take that away and no one will get the ball off them. They'll pass it about all day and try anything. Not even a pack of tigers would get the ball off them. Put that goal back, though, and there's a fear. That goal challenges your belief system. That's what we need to overcome. Forget the goal is there and just play. I think we're getting this now.

'For me, and it goes back to what I said at the start, it's the final third where we need to be more clinical, but the team needs more help there. It's almost the hardest part to coach. It's the one part of the pitch where you just sometimes have to buy, you know what I mean?

'None of the players are letting me down. Every one of them is trying their best, but we need help in this area. I think there needs to be a bit more transparency about the budget I am working with. Basically, anyone I bring in now has to be free. I looked to bring in Chris Conn-Clarke on loan from Fleetwood. I'm a big fan of his. We were looking at a small contribution to his wages. Then Altrincham came along and paid a fee for him. Yes, they bought him – and there's no way he will be on less money, either. That's what we are having to compete with.'

National League table as at 31 August 2023

	P	W	D	L	F	A	Pts
Solihull Moors	6	4	2	0	11	4	14
Barnet	6	4	1	1	13	8	13
Chesterfield	6	4	1	1	11	4	13
Hartlepool United	6	4	0	2	15	11	12
Rochdale	**6**	**3**	**1**	**2**	**10**	**7**	**10**
Altrincham	6	2	4	0	12	10	10
Woking	6	3	1	2	10	8	10
Ebbsfleet United	6	3	0	3	10	9	9
FC Halifax Town	6	2	3	1	6	5	9
Maidenhead United	6	2	3	1	6	5	9
Gateshead	6	2	2	2	12	10	8
Wealdstone	6	2	2	2	7	9	8
Dagenham & Redbridge	6	2	1	3	6	8	7
Aldershot Town	6	2	1	3	10	14	7
Eastleigh	6	1	3	2	7	8	6
Boreham Wood	6	1	3	2	6	9	6
Bromley	6	1	3	2	5	8	6
Kidderminster Harriers	6	1	3	2	2	5	6
Oxford City	6	1	2	3	8	9	5
Oldham Athletic	6	1	2	3	7	10	5
AFC Fylde	6	1	2	3	12	16	5
Dorking Wanderers	6	1	1	4	7	14	4
York City	6	0	3	3	7	11	3
Southend United*	6	3	0	3	12	7	-1

* Southend deducted ten points for failing to pay an existing tax bill.

September 2023

THERE ARE SUPPORTERS old enough, like me, to have attended many of Rochdale's clashes with Halifax Town AFC in the Football League.

The scintillating game at The Shay in 2002, where Rochdale cult heroes Lee McEvilly and Paddy McCourt kept the club's play-off hopes alive, or the acrobatic overhead kick goal by Jason Peake in 2000, shaped two of the more recent memorable encounters.

Dale's relegation to the National League would renew this cross-Pennine rivalry with our friends in Calderdale for the first time in 22 years, but it would not be the same Halifax we would face.

In 2002, Halifax Town was placed in administration after relegation to the fifth tier, but was saved by local businessmen and backing from the club's supporters' trust.

Despite manager Chris Wilder's remarkable effort the very next season, including overcoming a ten-point deduction to secure league safety, the club went on to ultimately fold in 2008, three years shy of its centenary.

Despite efforts to reach an agreement with creditors, a 'miscalculation of the debt' and an insistence on a 100 per cent repayment by HM Revenue and Customs proved terminal. Regardless of hopes for a reprieve, the club's appeal to the Football Association was rejected, leading to its closure.

The club's supporters and a consortium of businessmen, including current chairman David Bosomworth, Stuart Peacock and Bobby Ham, then played a crucial role in creating a new club, which applied for a place in the Northern Premier League.

FC Halifax Town was accepted into the Northern Premier League First Division North, the eighth tier of the football pyramid, on 30 June, just seven weeks before the season's start. The early days of the new club were marked by challenges, including building trust with suppliers and sponsors, addressing concerns from players about previous payment issues, and gaining the support of cautious fans who were still recovering from the loss of the old club. Despite these hurdles, the new directors, including Bosomworth, aimed to rebuild FC Halifax Town and eventually return it to the Football League.

It was from this humble beginning that the club began its arduous climb back to prominence, eventually reaching the hallowed grounds of the National League once again, steadily, from 2017. Remarkably, Halifax also achieved a moment of triumph when they clinched the FA Trophy in the 2022/23 season.

I caught up with FC Halifax Town Supporters' Club chairman Kit Walton, who explained how fans had backed the club through its reformation and the years that followed.

'The supporters' club, of which I have been chairman for 25 years now, has contributed to the growth and development of FC Halifax Town mainly via financial assistance,' he explained. 'We have contributed at least £10,000 every year, which has been used for the general running of the club. During lockdown, the club led its own financial appeal, with our support, and around £55,000 was donated, which obviously helped a great deal. In reality, the chairman is believed to contribute around £100,000 annually, so our contribution is welcomed, but will never be enough. We have, I believe, one of the lowest budgets in the National League.

'We have contributed £17,000 so far this year, of which £10,000 paid for a player's operation to be done privately. The club can't afford injury insurance, and obviously they can't wait for the NHS. The rest of the money went towards the funding of a feasibility study on laying a new pitch; which was required to allow the club to apply for large grants. The club shop only operates online, but the FC Halifax Supporters' Club runs a physical shop, which is definitely needed. We also have our own monthly lottery, as the club has no one to run one.

'With all that said, we are short of manpower, so haven't been able to assist in helping the club foster community engagement, but the club has employees whose job it is to do this anyway, as have most clubs at, or above, our level.

'Our relationship with the club's management and ownership is very much an "arm's length" situation, in that the club has only a CEO, marketing director and part-time secretary. Admin is minimised to allow a larger playing budget, but this means we find it incredibly difficult to progress any proposed initiatives. The chairman is always available to talk, but he prefers to leave the running of the club to the aforementioned two-and-a-half people. The chairman does meet us and attends "Open to Question" meetings when asked, but, as we have now had the same owners for 15 years, many fans feel we have stagnated.

'With that said, the very survival of FC Halifax Town is a hell of a success story in itself. It's been a perennial struggle, which I don't see changing anytime soon. I do know that the chairman is desperate to get us promoted to the EFL, and sees this as the land of milk and honey. If he is correct, and we get there, I believe we would have a much bigger voice, and the potential to drive our initiatives forward.

'We *do* represent the fans, and take up issues with the club when we think it's needed. We make suggestions and recommendations to the chairman, but, I must say, these are rarely acted upon – you'll recognise the phrase "leave it with me", I guess? As already mentioned, the club is so stretched employee wise that anything we want takes a ridiculous length of time to progress. As a group, we suffer in the same way as the club, in that we have only six committee members and a few reliable volunteers, but we have nowhere near enough resource to help with anything except bucket collections and the aforementioned merchandise shop.

'We currently have an initiative prepared to provide pitch covers, for example, but, by the time we are allowed to publicise this (the club and local council are negotiating), it will likely be too late for this season. One committee member has recently started an away travel club with the assistance of other fans, and this seems to be going really well so far. You won't be surprised to hear the club has no one to arrange away travel, of course.

'Membership of our supporters' club is free, and forms are available online and from committee members. We regularly appeal for additional helpers and committee members, but most people prefer to sound off online rather than give up their time to do anything meaningful.

'We try to introduce new initiatives, such as the pop-up shop, but tend to follow the interests of committee members rather than work to a grand plan. However, we have evolved via the addition of committee members who have dragged the supporters' club into the 21st century by harnessing the power of the internet. Ten years ago, we had no Facebook page, Twitter offering, merchandise offering or lottery, so we are moving in the right direction.

'However, there are many obstacles - mainly manpower and communication - which we have failed to overcome. I think the truth is we have learned how to live with them, and operate as well as we can within the obvious restrictions. At the end of the day, we want FC Halifax Town to progress, and, to a certain extent, this is probably best achieved by offering our support to the club, rather than rocking the boat.'

On the forthcoming renewed derby match, Walton said, 'I'm a real-ale drinker, so am very much looking forward to the Rochdale game, as the town is a relative paradise to me and my friends.'

Unfortunately for Rochdale's players there was no such paradise, as they decided to wait for the reacquaintance of this cross-county rivalry to put in their poorest performance of the season so far, suffering a 1-0 defeat at a Spotland that was sunny in weather if not in disposition.

Ian Henderson marked his 400th appearance for the club, and the return of Adam Clayton, following his suspension, meant Harvey Gilmour, having overcome his rolled ankle, reverted to the right and Jimmy Keohane returned to full-back. This familiarity was reassuring but proved Dale's ultimate downfall in a paradox that meant Halifax were able to plan accordingly.

Rob Harker's goal in the 22nd minute proved to be the deciding factor, bringing to an end Dale's streak of three unbeaten matches. The striker was left with an easy tap-in following a cross from Angelo Cappello, who had won possession high up the pitch after a mistake by Keohane.

Dale pushed hard but couldn't quite find a way to score, as Halifax were a yard quicker in every department.

Halifax's plan seemed obvious – to send Dale through the centre of the pitch, something which was easier for the Shaymen to achieve given Dale's two wider players did this naturally to utilise their preferred foot. Switching this about seemed a certain move for Jim McNulty, and it was hard to understand why he didn't at least try it for 15 minutes. Forcing the opposition full-back to defend against a player going down the line certainly would have opened up the play.

Similarly, with Cameron John landing a booking, introducing Max Conway at, or just after, the break would have provided the visitors with another threat to deal with. Conway's appearance in the 84th minute was far too late to make an impact.

'I feel like the worst we should be taking from a game like today is a 0-0 draw,' McNulty said post-match. 'I think we, as a group, got things wrong in the first half. We addressed this at half-time and then found more space second half. Teams do unexpected things when they come here to play us. Halifax were very organised today and proved very tough to break down, but I don't think we exploited what little they did offer us.

'I also thought today you could see the shallowness of the squad. Hendo and Kairo need a bit of help, but we had no forward on the bench to bring on. That is really going to show in some games and today was one of those.'

* * *

KIDDERMINSTER HARRIERS IS a club with which Rochdale had become well accustomed to battling in the Football League in days gone by. However, the team that was once enriched with Scandinavian talent and led by Jan

Mølby 25 years ago had by 2023 vanished. In its place stood a team that had had to fight its way back to the fifth tier through the National League North play-offs.

Currently under the management of a former playing stalwart, the Worcestershire club was determined not to be mere participants in the current campaign. Russell Penn, who had made more than 200 appearances for the Aggborough side during his playing days and had also earned eight caps for the England C team, now led Kidderminster with renewed ambition and determination.

I caught up with him ahead of Dale's trip to Worcestershire to hear more of his backstory and to find out how the Harriers had evolved since previous heydays.

'I got released by Scunthorpe as a young scholar aged 19 and then I signed for Kidderminster, which is a local team for me,' Penn told me. 'I'm from Dudley originally, so I'm only down the road.

'I had four fantastic years playing for the club in the fifth tier, which was known as the Blue Square Premier back then, racking up nearly 200 games and 45 goals.

'I then got my money move into the Football League when I was 24 and spent the next ten years continually improving. From Burton Albion, to Cheltenham, to York City, to Carlisle, to Wrexham – just improving each time, making play-offs and enjoying FA Cup runs.

'I'm one of the lucky ones. I probably played around 600 games in my career and I put that down to extreme hard work and a bit of luck.

'When I was about 30, I was playing for York City for the second time. You have so much time on your hands as a professional footballer, and I was coming to the end of my playing career, so I decided to do my coaching badges. By the time I was 33, I had completed them all the way up to UEFA A. Leadership is something that has always appealed to me. I was captain at all my clubs, so coaching and management was always something I was going to do. I was back at Kidderminster by now, and I hit a bit of luck in that the manager was leaving and I was one of the older pros, who tend to get given the role on an interim basis in those scenarios. We won three out of the next four games and the chairman said, "Go on, have a crack at this full time."

'I took the job on but, 22 games later, Covid comes along. It acted as a bit of a blessing in some ways. Football shut down, so, for six months, I was just doing my homework on management. Every day, I'd have three or four hours on the laptop or on my phone, just researching, getting my staff ready for whenever football might start up again. It was a bit different to trying to get everything done during the usual hostile two months of summer. We had a good nine months of build-up in total. We'd had a really poor previous season, hence why I got the job in the first place, so I had released 90 per cent of the players. We were literally starting from scratch. From a selfish point of view, it was great, as I was able to build my own team at the football club.'

Kidderminster had remained a full-time operation since dropping out of the Football League in 2005. Penn thinks this had been a distinct advantage.

'There's a reason why all these full-time teams get promoted from the National League North and South,' he said. 'They're fitter than everyone else and more tactical. We also worked really hard to build the supporter element back up because, when we got relegated to the North, the crowds slumped to about 1,200. They were still there, in the town, so we had to give them something to get them back through the turnstiles.

'We've had an average gate of between 2,000 and 2,500 over the past two years, delivering supporters a fantastic FA Cup run, which drew us against West Ham United in the fourth round two years ago; two play-offs and then a promotion.

'Our job now is to consolidate in the National League but to also keep the fans entertained. We recruited well over the summer. I believe it will be enough to be competitive, but we also lost two of our major players, the captain and vice-captain. We believe we'll still have enough over the next 36 games to stay above the line, but we're not just looking to finish 20th. We want to finish as high as possible.

'We're now coming up against teams like ourselves, and better, every single week, so we have to be on it. The biggest thing in this league is budget. You never see a top-budget team get relegated from the National League and, if you do, it's only once every 25 or 30 years. Budget goes a long way here.

'You're also coming up against players and managers who have been around the block more frequently. They've been there and done it all before. You just have to work that little bit harder and that little bit wiser.'

The late summer continued at Aggborough as Rochdale rolled into town, with the sun blazing down a touch under 30°C on to a crowd of 2,507. Jim McNulty, with the Halifax disappointment still clearly ensconced, opted to shuffle his pack. Max Conway, Kwaku Oduroh and George Nevett all came into the starting line-up in place of Ian Henderson, Kyle Ferguson and Jimmy Keohane. Pleasingly, Jesurun Uchegbulam returned to the bench, having recovered from the hamstring injury he picked up at Woking.

McNulty adopted a 4-5-1 formation to start the match, with Harvey Gilmour positioned as the most advanced midfielder just behind Kairo Mitchell in the attack. Tyrese Sinclair returned to the right side of midfield after a period of absence there, allowing Adam Clayton's attacking prowess to be utilised on the left flank.

The Harriers had been struggling with a five-game winless streak ahead of this fixture, but took the lead in the 18th minute when Joe Leesley expertly dispatched a Jack Lambert ball into the top corner after the latter had been allowed to waltz into the box unimpeded.

Gilmour came close to levelling the score with a well-aimed drive that narrowly missed its mark. However, Dale did eventually find the elusive equaliser with just 15 minutes remaining, captain Ethan Ebanks-Landell meeting a corner with a fine looping header.

In stoppage time it appeared as though Dale might even have stolen a victory, but Henderson's goal from inside the penalty area following a free kick was disallowed due to a late offside call.

If Henderson's goal had been counted, it would have marked a victory that the team couldn't wholly have claimed as deserved. The performance in the first half was lacklustre, characterised by a limited range of attacking strategies. The players appeared fixated on a singular approach, settling into a predictable passing rhythm. They failed to seize crucial opportunities, neglecting moments where a change in tempo, a well-executed through ball, or a decisive cross from wide positions could have unlocked the opposition's defence.

It was McNulty's substitutions that finally made a notable impact on the game, as did a tactical adjustment made at half-time, which resulted in more crosses being delivered into the opposition's penalty area. This simple yet effective approach compelled the Kidderminster players to actively defend rather than maintain their positions.

Oduroh, while a decent full-back, appeared less comfortable when venturing into advanced positions. Keohane's introduction in the second half added a new dimension to Dale's play in this regard, with him assuming a role akin to that of a midfielder, exploiting available space.

Uchegbulam's cameo appearance on the wing held promise, too. His ability to take on the opposition's left-back demonstrated a vulnerability that might well have been exploited sooner.

After the match, McNulty mentioned that the hot weather had significantly affected the pace of the game and had led to frequent stoppages. The Dale head coach said he believed the Kidderminster players had also deliberately slowed down the game when the ball was out of play, which had disrupted his own players' rhythm.

'I think that's something the opponent does well, actually,' he said. 'I identified pre-game that, when the ball is out of play, they take their time to allow themselves chance to reset. I think the officials have to play their part by being mindful of that.

'That said, we don't help ourselves by going one goal down. We've done this in a few too many games now, which just makes it harder for us. Teams sit in and, when the ball is out of play, they try to keep it out of play for a long time and, if it's not going to be officiated well, then it's something that they can and will do.'

These difficulties aside, McNulty said he was satisfied with what he believed was a valuable away point.

'I thought the team reacted really well in the second half – showed character, showed bravery, showed belief, and I'm glad that we can go away from this game with a point on what was a tough day.'

* * *

BARNET HAD BECOME something of a yo-yo club between the fifth and fourth tiers of the English football pyramid since their first introduction to the latter in 1991, but they had not escaped National League level again since 2018.

Two games of many readily came to this writer's mind ahead of Rochdale's home fixture with the Bees, the first being that Barnet's former home, Underhill, was the venue for Dale's first victory in London, a 4-0 win for Mick Docherty's side in 1995. The other memory was not so fond: a 6-2 defeat at the same venue a year earlier, with Scottish striker Dougie Freedman bagging four of Barnet's goals.

Dale's more recent home record against the Bees had fortunately been much better than on the road, the past five meetings at Spotland all ending in victory, and it was a trend that would continue on a windy September Saturday afternoon.

Barnet's playing operation was helmed by Dean Brennan, a seasoned non-league campaigner who had inspired his charges to a magnificent start to the season, guiding them to the table's summit. However, it was to be Dale who knocked the Bees off their perch with the players turning in their best attacking performance so far to secure a 4-2 win.

Jim McNulty reverted to a 4-3-3 with Harvey Gilmour the most advanced of the midfield three. Jesurun Uchegbulam and Tyrese Sinclair were the wide players, very wide in fact, and this caused Barnet issues all day.

In the 23rd minute, Sinclair received a pass over the top from goalkeeper Louie Moulden and skilfully chipped the ball over Laurie Walker in the Barnet goal to open the scoring. However, Barnet quickly responded as the troublesome Nicke Kabamba headed the ball into the net from a cross delivered by Dale Gorman from the right.

Sinclair continued to shine, however, and was on hand at the back post to turn in his seventh goal of the season in the 42nd minute, courtesy of a precise pass from Uchegbulam out on the right.

Uchegbulam then played a pivotal role in Rochdale's third goal as well. He set up Adam Clayton, who delivered an accurate ball into the box, allowing Gilmour to tap in from close range early in the second half.

It was then that Dale contrived to hand the momentum to the guests. Clayton nonchalantly played a free kick short and turned over possession, which allowed Kabamba to bring Barnet within reach again with a powerful strike in the 67th minute, converting Harry Pritchard's well-placed assist.

Young George Nevett was enjoying another fine game in the heart of the Dale defence, but it seemed Barnet's tactic was for Kabamba to pull on to him to win headers. When substitute Kyle Ferguson was introduced, this seemed a natural antidote, but the 6ft 5in defender was deployed at right-back, and so didn't actually solve the problem. The Bees then began to pile on the pressure and an equaliser was looking inevitable until, in the closing stages, Rochdale sealed the victory with a clinical counterattack, Sinclair racing down the left before providing a pass to be expertly finished by substitute Ian Henderson.

Despite the frantic final quarter, Dale deserved the win, with the approach of constantly switching between playing out and going long causing real concern and doubt for the opponents.

After the match, McNulty expressed his satisfaction with the players' performance.

'It was an 11-man performance, and we were total value for the win against what has been a very good, top-of-the-league team so far in this division this year,' he said. 'I think a lot of Barnet. I've watched a number of their games, and I was very aware of their threat.

'I think that we gave them a little bit of a gift for their second goal, to make it 3-2, and potentially brought some nerves to the occasion.

'But we're always getting challenged from the outside. Even though we're so well supported from the outside as well, there are still people challenging our belief.

'When we do score training-ground goals like today, particularly three of them, it's just so nice to watch the players celebrating what they've just done, knowing that they've practised it. I thought that we could have got even more. I thought that we looked very dangerous in all aspects of the game.'

* * *

ELSTREE STUDIOS, THE renowned film and television production complex, can be found in Borehamwood. Established in 1925, it is one of the oldest and most prestigious studios in England. Over the years it has been the backdrop for iconic film franchises such as *Star Wars*, *Superman* and *Indiana Jones*, as well as popular TV shows such as *EastEnders* and *The Crown*.

But there is another treasure to be found in this Herefordshire town, a professional football club with its history entirely rooted in non-league football. Established in 1948, Boreham Wood FC has since embarked on an extraordinary journey, rising through the ranks from local leagues to the London Spartan League in 1973. The determination of those attached to the club propelled it forward further still, to the Isthmian League and the Conference South.

But the pinnacle of its achievements came in the 2014/15 season when the club reached the fifth tier for the first time. Under the management of Luke Garrard, in his ninth season at the helm – an impressive tenure given the relatively high turnover rate of managers in lower-league football – Wood were aiming to repeat the feat of reaching the play-offs, as they had the previous season.

Having got off to something of a slow start this time around – Wood met Dale while in 16th position – Garrard was taking nothing for granted when I spoke to him ahead of the midweek fixture, confirming he would be relying on all of his experience both on the pitch and in the dugout in order to carve out a result.

'We're very lucky we're operating a full-time model now,' he said. 'In my first year, we went from training in the evenings in the first 10 to 12 games, to a hybrid model of two mornings, then to full-time. You look at Wealdstone probably being the only side in this division that still do evenings now. Maybe Oxford City? Then there's the hybrid clubs in Dorking and Maidenhead, who are a mix of evenings and mornings. And the rest of them? They are very much full-time.

'I remember playing in this league about 10, 12 years ago and there was a hell of a lot more part-time sides. The National League now? It's an extension of League Two, most definitely. There are probably only six or seven clubs that haven't ever played in the division above. So yeah, it is tough, it is relentless, it is unforgiving. Every manager works tirelessly to ensure that they're prepped and ready for their Saturdays and Tuesdays, and I respect hugely the work that people do within the division, because it is a full-time job in a full-time division, even for part-time teams.'

Garrard started his playing career as a trainee at Tottenham Hotspur, before turning professional at Swindon Town. He then moved to Bishop's Stortford and AFC Wimbledon, before beginning his love affair with Boreham Wood, where he ultimately combined both playing and coaching.

'I started out as a sessional coach with Boreham Wood, then moved to become under-18s manager, then academy manager, and then I became the assistant manager for three seasons before I got the job as manager, the role in which I am now enjoying my ninth season.

'Good relationships are the reason I've lasted so long. I think the relationships I have at this club are very strong; my relationship with the hierarchy, most importantly of all. I was very fortunate to get the job initially, I know that, but, once you get put in the hot seat, you have to deliver to ensure that you don't get brought right back out of it.'

Garrard was given the job at the age of just 30, with Boreham Wood perilously close to the National League drop zone.

'I was very appreciative that the job was my first job in first-team management and could quite easily have been my last,' he said. 'If we weren't successful in that first year, in staying up, I would've been the guy that took Boreham Wood straight back down. That would have been my legacy. So, yeah, relationships are massive. It's something that I have cultivated over the 18 or 19 years that I've been here.

'It's all well and good having these relationships, but, year on year, we have had success on the pitch, too. Whether that's fighting relegation, to finishing mid-table, going to Wembley in my third year, or having a season where we had our boys cherry-picked because we had such a successful season, and then finishing 18th the following year. These are all successes. From that year on, we've had good runs in the FA Cup and we've had two play-off semi-finals.'

Garrard revealed coaching was something that had always been in his blood.

'I always wanted to be a coach,' he said. 'I always felt that I could become a manager. I was a bit of a student of the game when I was playing. I liked to see what the sessions were about and why they were done the way they were. I'd ask questions. I worked at Boreham Wood academy and, in working with the under-18s and under-19s, I'd probably have taken 800 games. Therefore, it wasn't like I was coming into management wet behind the ears. Did I think I was going to do it at the age of 30? Most definitely not. When the chairman asked me, and I remember it very clearly, he asked, "Are you ready?" And I said, quite flash, "Yeah, I'm ready. I'm good to go". I was not even close to being ready. Managers at that level had forgotten more than I knew at the time.

'Year on year, we've had infrastructure improvements with regard to media rooms for our analysts, new breakfast rooms for the players and so on. I've seen the club not wanting to stay still. They want to strive on and try to get into the EFL. That aligns with my thinking and where I want to be as a manager.

'Do I want to manage as high up as possible? Yeah, I'd be lying if I said I didn't, of course, but it's got to be the right club. I live six miles up the road from Boreham Wood. It's more than just a manager/chairman relationship for me. In an ideal world, I get this club into the EFL because then I'll probably ride off on my horse and retire happy. I genuinely feel that it's coming, it's close. We need to keep continually building and progressing like we do year on year. I'm not going to give it a time frame. I could easily stipulate that we do it in two, three years, but the chairman might see something in someone else and get them in to finish the job sooner. I can't ever be complacent.'

Garrard certainly wasn't complacent against Rochdale, his side earning a point from a game neither side truly deserved to win.

Jim McNulty named an unchanged XI from that which beat Barnet and, once again, the slick passing through the lines and retention of possession were on display throughout the first 45 minutes. However, this time, it was more akin to the performance at Kidderminster and came without an end product, with Tyrese Sinclair in particular struggling to find his range.

The first half ended goalless but, just two minutes after the restart, Dale took the lead. Cameron John's right-footed shot ricocheted off Boreham Wood goalkeeper Nathan Ashmore and hit the crossbar before falling to Kairo Mitchell, who calmly slotted home.

However, the lead was short-lived as Tyrone Marsh scored with a header from a left-sided cross, just a minute later. Equally disappointing is that the goal was very similar to that which Barnet scored first at the weekend, and this seemed to take the fizz out of Dale's endeavour, leading to a sustained bombardment from the hosts. Mercifully, it was withstood to the final whistle.

It was another game where the Dale players really needed to prioritise stopping crosses into the box, especially immediately after scoring themselves, and, where that wasn't possible, at least getting closer to their opposition in the area. The natural solution would have been seeking to play in the opponents' half for a good five or ten minutes after taking the lead, thus negating any immediate counter-threat from the restart. In terms of Dale's own threat, the swapping of wings may have yielded fruit. Jesurun Uchegbulam was getting no change out of the opposition left-back on this occasion, so switching sides with Sinclair could have been an option to make the most of the first-half dominance.

'I'm pleased with the point overall at what is a tough place to come,' McNulty said after the match. 'Boreham Wood made the play-offs last year and pushed Notts County all the way [in the semi-final]. Based on tonight, I can see why. They totally know what they are doing.

'I thought we were very good in the first half, but I'm disappointed we conceded so quickly after going ahead in the second half. We, in effect, helped them get back into the game. We recovered from that against Barnet, but didn't really tonight. We sustained a large spell of pressure, but the courage we showed in dealing with that was excellent. Once I've calmed down and zoomed out, I'll look back on this as a good point.'

* * *

WHILE THE NATIONAL League does contain several old faces fallen from Football League grace, or well-established non-league household names, it is perhaps Dorking Wanderers who best encapsulate what the fifth tier is all about.

Established in 1999 by a close-knit group of friends, the club had experienced a breathtaking transformation. From its humble beginnings as a parks team with just a handful of loyal supporters, it had emerged as a formidable presence in the National League. Nowadays, Dorking's matches at Meadowbank Stadium could draw the attention of up to several thousand passionate spectators.

At the heart of this remarkable journey stands the indomitable figure of Marc White, a true one-man show. As manager, owner and chairman of the club, White had orchestrated an astonishing 12 promotions within a span of 24 years.

Even with the weight of these responsibilities, White navigated the demanding landscape of football alongside a full-time job at his marketing company. Having once been a youth player at Fulham, he honed his skills in London before venturing into the realm of entrepreneurship. While he may not boast formal coaching qualifications, White said his passion and unwavering commitment to Dorking had bestowed upon him a wealth of knowledge and experience throughout the club's ascension through the ranks.

I met up with White prior to Dale's scheduled fixture in the town, to hear his story first hand. A colourful character, decked in a puffer jacket and high-profile cap, at 49 years old, he had the infectious charisma of a man more than half his age. It was easy to see how he related to the players he managed.

He started by explaining the Dorking journey.

'I was a Wimbledon fan,' he said. 'Me and my friend used to go up there regular. We ended up getting bored with it, though, and we just thought we'd start our own team on a Saturday for a bit of fun. We started a team in division five of the park league, which was the lowest physical level of the English football pyramid. We'd all pay £5 each to play, rent the pitch for £50, got a local pub to sponsor the kit, and we were off. That, in a nutshell, is how Dorking Wanderers started.

'Initially, it was just very much a social thing. You know, play a game and then go to the pub. But then we started winning a few titles. I was player-manager and the appetite for success crept up on us. We just aimed to keep doing what we were doing, but, all the while, moving forwards. We'd maybe done four or five promotions before we had to act. First, it's having to put a rope around the pitch, and then it became a path, and then it became some terraces, and then it became a tea hut, and then a bar, and then changing rooms of a certain size, then floodlights. We did it all ourselves, too. There's no big benefactor. We put a lot of time, effort and money into it. It became a local project for us and now we have more than 1,000 members, from mini kickers at four years old, to walking football.

'When you tell all this to someone who doesn't know our full story, it does sound a little bit like, "Where's the catch?" but there isn't one. It's a true fairytale story. Obviously, there's a huge amount of people involved now behind the scenes, non-exec board members and volunteers, and I'm still steering the ship – one careful owner-type thing – but we're still very true to our roots, still very true to what we set out to do, which is to keep football real and for the people.'

White now finds the club's ascent an all-consuming task.

'It takes over my whole world,' he said. 'I work relentlessly. I'm always trying to structure the business accordingly, so that we can go forward, but in a way that's manageable for me. The biggest thing about progression is keeping up with it off the field. You have to keep building your ground in your wake.

'Even last year, when we got promoted to the National League for the first time, the work we had to do off the field was almost more than what we had put in on the field. We needed to find about £700,000. We needed a TV gantry. We needed a whole away end, a new toilet block. You name it, we needed it. It's not like Chesterfield, Oldham or

Rochdale, who come to this level with everything in place, we've got to implement it.

'For example, if we made the play-offs this season, we'd be stuffed as it stands, we really would. The league won't let you compete in the play-offs unless you're physically able to be promoted to the Football League. We're in the middle of buying our ground from the local authority, and there is a lot of wrangling there. It's always been that way, though. The ground we're in now is four years old. But between us being here now and the time we were in the park league, we spent about nine years at a place called Westhumble. We built it from scratch. Even back then, we had to go to parish council meetings to get approval for floodlights and so on. It's always been an uphill battle.

'We have about 60 or 70 local sponsors now, and we've got a full-time commercial member of staff, but any shortfall will still come to me. At the start of this season, we offered a third of the club to fans via share purchases, too. We work relentlessly to raise money by raising the profile of the club. We're very aware that we have to put ourselves out there. We've got a YouTube documentary, for example. We're always the underdog, really. We have to be, with where we've come from.'

As well as keeping the club operational, White also had to oversee on-field matters.

'Basically, I'm a football nut, just like everybody else,' he said. 'I know football managers at the highest level who don't watch football games unless they're paid to. On the flipside, there are people who go out to watch five games a week for fun, and I'm that guy. So, growing up, I was a football nut. I watched countless games. I was a good player as a kid, but also worked in the City of London, and leadership was a key element of the business I was involved in. I ended up blending the two qualities together and the rest has come from experience on the job.

'I've actually found management easier the higher we've gone, if I'm honest. We've left behind the days where we had to beg, borrow and steal to try to recruit the best people. Also, the higher you go, you're talking to more people who understand football. It's a lot easier than working with a bloke who is still hungover because he met some woman the night before at a nightclub. I'm always learning, though, obviously, and I had lots of good chats last season with the more experienced managers in the league, such as Parky [Wrexham manager, Phil Parkinson] and [Chesterfield manager] Paul Cook.

'They spoke heavily about the need to be really good at recruitment. I know, it sounds obvious, but I've always been big on recruitment and our success has been based on retaining 70 per cent of our squad at all times. We don't turnover players, we only add people in. It was reassuring to hear that that approach is accepted the leagues all over. That said, if we ever do get to the EFL, I'm fucked. You need to have an FA coaching badge to be a manager and I ain't got one.'

Despite having lofty ambitions for Dorking, White did still have to manage the fact that his side was a part-time outfit.

'We're doing either two mornings a week or two evenings,' he said. 'To bridge the gap with full-time clubs, we try to silo our skillset. What do I mean by that? Well, we've got three technical coaches working on marginal gains, such as dead-ball situations, for example. We can't replicate things like recovery and fitness, that the full-time clubs can achieve by training all week, but we *can* have the best free kicks in the league, or the best corners. It's those areas where we can make a difference and those things that *could* prove the difference in a match situation.

'One thing in the National League you will notice is that it's a bit of a haven for clubs rebooting. So initially, Football League clubs are like, "Fuck me, what a disaster, we're in the National League," but local businessmen come out of the woodwork and, before you know it, the club has rebooted. It creates a really interesting league because there are only two promotion spots and you've got all these full-time and part-time teams vying for them. It's a real eye-opener.'

White had garnered a reputation as a man of the people, too. The previous season he regularly put considerable amounts of his own money behind the club's bar for visiting supporters to enjoy. Dale fans would be hoping for a similar gesture after making the 241-mile trip to Surrey.

'We say, if the visiting team sells out their ticket allocation, then we drop £500 behind the bar for their fans,' he said. 'There are enough rivalries in this game and we don't need more. Coming up through the leagues, and I know it sounds stupid, but the people I've met who I love the most are those who make the sandwiches and make the tea. And, when you visit these clubs, it's like you are going into their living room. That gets lost the higher up the leagues you go, but it's the ethos I want here. We've always tried to look after people at our club like that. You know, "Come into our living room."

'Football clubs are ultimately the hub of the community and they should be protected as such. They are there before and after bad owners, and before and after good owners, too. I'm a big advocate for that. We work closely with all the local schools. We host business partner networking events. During Covid, we were handing out the food parcels. It's a reciprocal relationship.'

This writer certainly found the Dorking hospitality a welcome tonic upon arrival. Having taken the sleeper train from Glasgow to London due to work commitments the previous evening, which was not so much an Agatha Christie experience as *Children of Men*, a libation was very much needed.

The Rochdale players did their bit, too – eventually. The visitors secured a stunning comeback victory against their ten-man hosts with a stoppage-time goal by Ian Henderson after captain Ethan Ebanks-Landell had equalised in the 89th minute.

Jim McNulty opted to place Jesurun Uchegbulam back on the bench for this one, with Harvey Gilmour moving to the right so that Henderson could return to the starting XI in a more central role.

Dale certainly looked the slicker passing team in the first half, with Dorking pressing well enough to force the visitors into finding a pivot rather than a forward pass. When Dale did get through their hosts' lines, play more often than not broke down in the final third, with either a bad decision or a Dorking recovery tackle winning out.

After the break, the Dorking players kept at their task and took advantage of some paper-thin defending to take the lead. Jimmy Keohane allowed Dorking's recent signing, Tom Blair, to cut across him on the left and place a shot from the edge of the box towards the near post, which beat Louie Moulden.

Dale then toiled for most of the rest of the second half and seemed bereft of ideas in the final third. This was despite Kairo Mitchell doing his best to hold the ball up as a direct option, rather than have his team-mates play the ball about in front of the Dorking players, which they seemed to prefer. It was as if the Dale players were afraid to have a shot from open play, even though a direct free kick from Adam Clayton, which produced a fine save from Harrison Male, showed they could test their hosts from range. In plain terms, the full-time outfit was being outmanoeuvred on the chessboard by a part-time operator. The Dorking players were also using their artificial home pitch to a distinct advantage, well used to playing on a surface that saw black rubber spraying everywhere. To the uninitiated onlooker, it was ridiculous.

McNulty finally introduced Uchegbulam for Ryan East, which allowed Gilmour to move back infield, where he was at his best. This, combined with Max Conway's introduction at left-back in place of Cameron John, helped boost impetus, as Conway was able to push forward more quickly, allowing Tyrese Sinclair to cut inside more often.

By sticking to their task, despite the growing unease from the visiting fans, the Dale players grabbed two late, decisive goals.

A free kick found its way into the Dorking penalty area, and Ebanks-Landell calmly volleyed the ball into the net with his left foot from 12 yards. Dan Pybus then received a second yellow card and was sent off for a foul on Sinclair before, in the 96th minute, Henderson's opportunistic finish from Keohane's initial shot, after Uchegbulam had turned Ryan Seager inside out, secured a fifth win of the season.

The best thing about football is that sometimes it transcends all analysis and can exist solely in the emotive. The jubilant celebrations at the full-time whistle are all that will ultimately be remembered of 'Dorking Away' and, in retrospect, all that will subsequently matter.

'This team doesn't give up,' said McNulty afterwards. 'That's why I'm really proud of them. Honestly, if we'd lost that game 1-0, I would have stood here and said the team fought all the way.

'Truthfully, once we did get that first goal, we felt like a serious outfit that was on the hunt for the second, and I think we were good value for it in the end. We really stressed Dorking. They did everything to hold on. By the end there was a lot of last-ditch tackles, guys getting sent off, and we were always putting them under it.

'The challenge for us was, could we be that team that can reverse a fixture late on and, fortunately, we were. I was very happy with that, and I think our fans were too.'

McNulty also highlighted that, despite being a part-time outfit, Dorking had crafted a solid reputation as a home team that was difficult to thwart.

'That was probably our most difficult game this season, and we've won it. I was speaking to their manager at the end of the game, and he said that they were in the top five last season on home form. I know they beat some notable teams here. I know they beat Notts County here.'

McNulty, despite not wanting to blame the pitch, felt compelled to acknowledge its impact on the game.

'It's a difficult place to come, the surface makes it very difficult. Every time we were playing our way, and we were nearly away from them, somebody would get back and make a tackle. The pitch would slow you down slightly. Our players would have to take an extra touch all the time. It was a really difficult factor.

'You don't want to talk about the pitch, you don't want to blame the pitch, but whether we had won 2-1 today or lost 1-0, I couldn't not mention the pitch because it was a massive factor in the game.'

* * *

CHESTERFIELD WERE ALMOST every pundit's tip for the National League title before the 2023/24 season got under way, primarily fuelled by the fact the Derbyshire club was the remaining powerhouse of the previous season's triumvirate following the promotion of both Wrexham and Notts County.

Rochdale supporters certainly needed no introduction to the club, given the pair had clashed 113 times in league and cup since their first encounter in 1922.

Chesterfield's relegation from the EFL in 2018 was a bitter blow for a club that had left behind its historic home, Saltergate, in 2010 for a modern 10,000-seat stadium. With a rich history as a founding member of the Third Division (North) in 1921, and a constant presence in the Football League for 97 years, the club had overcome significant financial turmoil prior to the bold stadium move thanks to its supporters' trust and local benefactors.

However, budget overruns on the new stadium project and increasing financial demands left Dave Allen, the Sheffield casino owner who held majority ownership, disillusioned despite his substantial investments. The club had tasted some success during recent years, achieving promotion to League One in 2014 under the shrewd management of Paul Cook, even going on to the play-off semi-final for a shot at Championship glory. Nevertheless, Cook's departure to manage Portsmouth, followed by the sale of key players, allied with escalating financial disagreements and a mass boardroom walkout, saw the club embark on a downward spiral.

Amazingly, Cook was now back in the Chesterfield hotseat, looking to guide the Spireites back to the EFL with the backing of new chairman Mike Goodwin. At this juncture, he had his team sitting top of the table, chasing a seventh straight victory and looking very formidable.

The producers at TNT Sports clearly saw Rochdale's first National League clash with Chesterfield as an enticing prospect, as the Tuesday night encounter at Spotland was selected for live broadcast.

The Chesterfield squad contained an embarrassment of riches, so much so that former Northern Ireland international Will Grigg wasn't even among the starting line-up. It was little wonder Cook admitted to the broadcaster pre-match that he still didn't know what his best XI was.

Jim McNulty's squad, much more humble by comparison, still offered a small degree of flexibility and he chose to bring Jesurun Uchegbulam and Kwaku Oduroh back into the starting line-up. It wasn't enough, however, to stave off a home defeat in front of 3,044 supporters. Two goals conceded from crosses, either side of Kairo Mitchell's controlled finish from a sumptuous George Nevett through ball, settled the contest and handed the home side a first loss in five matches.

Quite simply, Chesterfield had the players to exploit Dale's zonal marking approach to set plays. Armando Dobra, perhaps the shortest player on the pitch, rose highest to head home Michael Jacobs' cross from the right after only six minutes, the ball bouncing off the inside of both posts before crossing the line. Not one home player picked up his run, and those in the box were left looking perplexed at the lack of communication.

Dale were level seven minutes later as Nevett marauded forward from the back and sent forth a beautifully weighted defence-splitting pass which allowed Mitchell to produce a composed first-time finish under goalkeeper Harry Tyrer.

The hard work was undone, however, when another header put the Spireites back in front in the 25th minute. Liam Mandeville received a short corner on the left, wasn't closed down, and crossed for Tom Naylor to nod in. Again, two defenders either side of him failed to attack the ball, although Naylor did give himself a slight advantage by pushing off Harvey Gilmour.

In the second half, the Chesterfield players eased into game-management mode and were content to let their Dale counterparts play in their own half. The wings were not providing their usual fruit for Tyrese Sinclair and Uchegbulam, even when they swapped flanks. Likewise, the one weakness at the heart of Chesterfield's defence, that being the ball played in behind, yielded little more when exploited.

Still, against the league leaders, who were able to bring talent such as Ollie Banks and Grigg off the bench, it was a creditable performance.

'I've never been as proud in defeat as I am tonight,' said McNulty after the match. 'The bravery of the players, under the lights and in front of the TV cameras, I thought, was amazing.

'Truthfully, I thought we pushed them all the way. I thought we were the better team, in my opinion, and it's a shame that, for such a courageous performance from the players, we take nothing. But I don't feel disappointed, I really don't.

'Chesterfield are the big boys in the division, and you can see why. They can score in a number of ways, they have serious power and serious squad depth, which is what that budget gets you. It gives you access to those players and, if three of their star players aren't doing it, they can bring on another three.

'It indicates where we're at versus where they're at, when we're signing their fourth-choice winger [Uchegbulam].

'We've got a serious run of games right now, with a real threadbare squad, but I'm taking momentum and positivity from tonight's game, and the players should too.'

* * *

ROCHDALE AND SOUTHEND United were no strangers in the Football League, with the teams facing each other almost 60 times since their initial encounter in 1958. One particularly significant match took place in May 1969 at Spotland, where Rochdale's 3-0 victory in front of a bumper crowd secured a first promotion from the fourth tier.

In more recent times, the two teams had last met in the third tier of English football some four years prior, since when Southend, similar to Chesterfield, had experienced a significant decline, eventually dropping out of the EFL altogether. The club, owned by Essex property developer Ron Martin for the past 25 years, faced severe financial troubles that had escalated to the point where there were genuine concerns about Southend's ability to start the 2023/24 season.

The club was given a 42-day deadline to settle a tax bill of £275,000, and the financial situation had become so dire that Martin had expressed a willingness to sell up for a nominal amount of £1. The situation worsened as players refused to participate in pre-season training due to alleged non-payment, and there was even an instance where the water supply was cut off at the Shrimpers' Roots Hall stadium. Consequently, the National League hierarchy rapidly lost patience with the club and set some very definite terms so that Southend could start the season.

I caught up with fellow journalist Chris Phillips, of the *Southend Echo*, to find out just what had befallen the club.

'In short, this has been the result of long-term mismanagement right at the top,' he said. 'Short-term solutions have been applied to long-term problems and the bottom line is, basically, there hasn't been enough money to keep it going properly. The club is in a mess and it's sad to see.

'The coaching team kept going throughout all of pre-season and Kevin Maher has been incredible as the head coach. The players stopped training together for a week as they waited for their wages, and staff went three months without getting their salaries.

'Everyone is now fully up to date with their wages at the club and that enabled Southend to start the season. Nobody envisaged we would then beat one of the favourites for the title, Oldham, 4-0.

'While the club might be up for sale for £1, with everything else attributed to it, you're probably looking at having to pay about £10m by my estimations. It's not simple to explain, but the club doesn't own the ground, the training ground or the site for the proposed new stadium. The new stadium has been put on the back burner now to make it a simpler transaction to sell the club, but it's still far from straightforward.'

And with no buyer found and debt still outstanding, the National League was faced with no alternative but to dock the Shrimpers ten points at the end of August, an appeal against which fell on deaf ears. Martin once again appeared in court on 23 August and pleaded for more time to settle the club's debts, claiming, '[The debt] will be discharged by the process of the [club's] purchase.'

However, this tested the patience of Judge Sebastian Prentis, who was reported to say, 'If this was not a football club, with the attachment of its fans, I would be winding you up today.' He gave Martin until 4 October to settle the outstanding debt. 'You will be wound up on the next date if it's not sorted,' Prentis added.

The adjournment prevented Southend adding to their squad, leaving the team with just 16 registered players as the club prepared to take on Dale. Maher was undertaking his 100th game in charge and the hosts should have made sure it was a game to forget, but instead contrived to squander a two-goal lead allowing the Shrimpers back to Essex with a point.

Dale adopted a 4-3-3 formation to start the match, with two wide players, thus positioning Harvey Gilmour further forward in the central area. The approach inspired Dale's strongest start to a game so far, as they consistently troubled Southend across the field, with Jesurun Uchegbulam exploiting the vulnerabilities in an opposing defence that lacked physicality.

In the tenth minute, Rochdale broke the deadlock when Uchegbulam skilfully evaded Jack Bridge before testing Shrimpers goalkeeper David Martin with a low shot. Capitalising on the rebound, Jimmy Keohane instinctively slotted the ball into the net.

Adam Clayton's composed presence in midfield played a pivotal role in Dale's positive play, and, with pace ahead of him, the entire side looked dangerous. Once again, Uchegbulam was instrumental, controlling the ball on the touchline without facing a significant challenge before delivering a cross that Kairo Mitchell headed home from close range. Mitchell's consistently improving ability to position himself effectively for scoring opportunities paid dividends, and five goals in 13 games was a fair return for someone who wasn't initially signed to top the scoring charts.

However, Dale's inability to defend crosses had become a concerning recurring issue, as these balls were too often catching the defenders off guard, and Southend quickly pulled a goal back within two minutes. A right-wing cross from Harry Taylor found the unmarked Harry Cardwell, who expertly nodded in his eighth of the season.

In the second half, the Shrimpers switched to a four-man defence in an attempt to thwart Dale's threat down the right-hand side. They did better than that, however, and managed to level in the 64th minute when Jack Wood delivered a precise right-wing cross that Cardwell clinically headed home at the far post for his second goal of the game.

A change was then made with Tyrese Sinclair coming off for Ian Henderson, altering the shape to a more traditional 4-4-2. Gilmour shifted to the right, and the tiring Uchegbulam moved to the left wing. However, this adjustment had little impact on proceedings as Dale failed to vary the style of play, resulting in a rather uneventful conclusion to a contest that should have been won convincingly.

The point left Dale seventh in the table to end September, which was cause to celebrate, but there really should have been two further points on the board.

'I think we should have had the game won by half-time,' agreed Jim McNulty afterwards. 'We were very good in the first half, but guilty, in my opinion, of some complacency.

'Not being 4-0 up at half-time, we then allowed the element of doubt to creep in by conceding a goal.

'There's always that potential with being at this stage as a team – we're not a top, top team yet and it's early for us – so, we let that doubt in, and we haven't got enough confidence to take total control to kill the game like we should have.

'Southend changed shape to try to stop us when they got it back to 2-2, which is credit to them. They showed good character to come back and they're happy with their point today. We're unhappy with the point, which is probably a decent sign of where we are.'

National League table as at 30 September 2023

	P	*W*	*D*	*L*	*F*	*A*	*Pts*
Chesterfield	13	10	2	1	32	21	32
Barnet	13	9	2	2	27	16	29
Solihull Moors	13	7	6	0	23	12	27
Bromley	13	7	4	2	20	12	25
Gateshead	13	6	4	3	32	16	22
Altrincham	13	5	6	2	24	19	21
Rochdale	**13**	**5**	**4**	**4**	**21**	**17**	**19**
Woking	13	5	4	4	17	13	19
Hartlepool United	13	6	1	6	22	25	19
Aldershot Town	13	5	3	5	23	25	18
Dorking Wanderers	13	5	3	5	15	17	18
Oldham Athletic	13	4	5	4	18	17	17
Eastleigh	13	4	5	4	16	21	17
Ebbsfleet United	13	5	1	7	20	22	16
Wealdstone	13	4	4	5	15	19	16
FC Halifax Town	13	3	6	4	12	13	15
Dagenham & Redbridge	13	3	3	7	12	17	12
Boreham Wood	13	2	6	5	14	20	12
Oxford City	13	2	5	6	19	26	11
York City	13	2	5	6	19	26	11
Maidenhead United	13	2	5	6	8	17	11
AFC Fylde	13	2	3	8	19	30	9
Southend United*	13	5	3	5	21	17	8
Kidderminster Harriers	13	1	4	8	7	18	7

* Southend deducted ten points for failing to pay an existing tax bill.

October 2023

SOLIHULL MOORS FC, situated at the charmingly named Damson Park, was established in 2007 through the merger of Moor Green and Solihull Borough. After gaining promotion from National League North during the 2015/16 season, Moors had successfully solidified their position in the fifth tier. In 2017/18 they came close to achieving promotion to League Two for the first time, securing second place under the guidance of former England goalkeeper Tim Flowers. Unfortunately, the team narrowly missed out on promotion after losing in the play-offs. After another tilt at promotion, this time losing in the play-off final to Grimsby Town, Moors had to endure mid-table obscurity the season previous to 2023/24.

Chairman Darryl Eales, hailing from nearby Birmingham, boasted a successful entrepreneurial and investment career. Notably, in 2014 he took charge of Oxford United, helping propel the club to League One as well as to two Wembley finals.

Fondly reminiscing about his days watching Solihull's founding club Moor Green with his father, he shared his excitement about how his family and friends became shareholders at Solihull, highlighting the club's familial and community-oriented essence.

'I lived in Birmingham during my childhood,' he said. 'We lived around the corner from Moor Green when they used to play in Hall Green. That was probably when I was between the ages of about seven and 15. I remember going quite often with my dad and enjoying the community aspect of it. Principally, though, I watched Birmingham City. They were my main team.

'About ten years ago, I'd got to the end of my primary career, which was running a private equity business, and I bizarrely decided to buy a football club. I looked at buying Birmingham, but realised, very quickly, I couldn't afford it. Most of my mates said it would have been foolhardy to own the club I support anyway, because it would take quite a lot of the pleasure out of it. They pointed out that, if we lost six games in a row and I went to a local pub, I'd just get grief.

'So, I ended up buying Oxford United, and I had four successful years there. If you think you understand football, you want to try owning a football club. You realise quickly that you know nothing. It was fascinating to learn about football from the inside – managers, players, cultures, all the rest of it. I learned as much during that short period of my life as I have about any other industry over a much greater period of time.

'I got lucky because I had a very good manager in Michael Appleton but, after four years, I realised it had gone from being a scary, exciting adventure to something I was thinking about far too much. So, in 2018, I sold it, thinking I'd probably just go back to watching local football and a bit of Birmingham City. By this time Moor Green and Solihull Borough had merged, and a friend of mine said the newly formed Solihull Moors was under a degree of financial pressure. They were victims of their own success because they had got promoted from the National League

North to the National League and they just weren't ready, being a club with no real history and no real fan base.

'This is where I got gloriously naive, because sentiment took over and I thought it was going to be a lot easier at this level than it's ultimately proven to be. The team was struggling in a relegation fight when I got involved, and barely survived. When I bought the club and took over the chairmanship the next season, I said to Tim [Flowers, the first-team manager], "I don't want another relegation scrap, that's my only condition." We ended up finishing second and made the play-offs.

'At Oxford, I was on my own and that was one of the major stress factors while I was there. When I took on Moors, I tried to get about 20–25 other people involved, including my family. They're investing on a lower level than myself, but the financial burden is at least shared.

'My view is that, generally, for most football clubs at this level, your playing budget is your loss. You can run the club everywhere else by using commercial revenue and gate revenue. The playing budget tends to be how much the owner or owners have to dip into their pockets.

'The caveat to all of that is teams such as Chesterfield or Oldham, which get big home gates, can, if sensible, probably break even. In the real world, clubs will always spend just that little bit more on the playing budget because, once you get into contractual arrangements with players, it's hard not to. It's a fine balance between not selling yourself short with a player and putting them on too long a contract that it ends up being a drain on the club. It's fraught with risk and, if it was easy, everyone would be doing it, wouldn't they?

'At Oxford we used a player-trading model which, let me tell you, is not an easy thing to get right. Peterborough has done this magnificently for years now but, at Oxford, we were lucky and made about £7m, without which I'd have been absolutely crippled. I say we were lucky, but I had a very good recruitment team working at the club, led by the manager, so we made our luck, I guess.

'The problem with the National League is that you don't sell players with the same amount of value, so it's very difficult to implement a player-trading model at this level. The reality is, you need top-end League One or Championship clubs to be buying your players and they aren't really. Bottom of League One and League Two clubs is invariably where we do business, and they aren't paying the money you need to make the model work long-term.

'Therefore, promotion has to be our ultimate aim and that is our recruitment model. Players aren't coming to us for the money. They certainly aren't coming for the prestige. Nobody wakes up in the morning having dreamed they'd signed for Solihull Moors. We want players who want to help us become successful and, by default, they too will become successful, better known and more likely to progress.'

Having almost steered the club to the EFL in 2021/22, Eales was faced with making tough decisions when that form wasn't replicated in 2022/23.

'Supporters view their club through a very small window,' he said. 'They have a view on team selection and players based on this window. The first-team manager has a much bigger window, as he sees the players at training and spends a lot of time with them. It is based on this bigger window that the first-team manager picks his team.

'This broader canvas applies to club ownership too. I am making decisions for the best interests of the club based on more than just a five-minute window. I had to do this last season by letting first-team manager Neal Ardley go. The season before, he got us to the play-off final against

Grimsby. He was convinced we were going to win the game. He felt the best two teams in the division were Stockport County, who had won the title, and Wrexham, who had already lost in their play-off eliminator. He was adamant we were going to win and achieve promotion. We didn't win and, as a result, there was an almighty hangover the following season. Even I felt this hangover. I would give myself a mark of five out of ten for my own performance during the first part of last season. There was part of me casting jealous glances at Grimsby's fixtures, thinking, "That should be us." A lot of that was in the manager's head as well and, consequently, the players' heads too. We didn't address that quickly enough in the first 15 or 20 games of last season. We kept on trying to find excuses as to why we weren't performing as well as should have been.

'In a funny sort of way, it probably didn't matter. Last season, on the basis that Notts County and Wrexham were so much better than everyone else, it meant if you were ever going to have a bad season, that was the season to have it.

'We got to Christmas time and I asked myself, realistically, what was going to change. We had the same players, but, instead of performing at eight or nine out of ten each week, they'd dropped to maybe a six. That's all it takes in football, such fine margins. I knew we weren't going to get promoted that season anyway, so I took the long-term view and changed things.

'You'll recall I took a bit of stick for letting our star striker, Andrew Dallas, join league rivals Chesterfield on loan. From my point of view, Andrew's contract was going to end when the season did, and he had already stated his intention to play league football the next season. Chesterfield were offering a very attractive package to just take him on loan, so it made complete sense to me. The same applies to Ryan Barnett, who went to Wrexham.

'I don't criticise the players. They want to play at the highest level they can and, usually, it's a win-win relationship for them and our club. Added to that, 99 per cent of the Moors fans that I know, which is the majority of those who go to the games, completely understood. It's the keyboard warriors, who view the game through that small window, who spout the negativity. They probably don't even go to games. I just think anything on social media is a bit like me and you down the pub having five pints and talking bollocks about football. It's not meaningful analysis. It's just people venting. I need to rise above that to keep what is best for Solihull Moors at the forefront of everything I do.

'And that goes for the first-team manager, too. I loved my relationship with Neal Ardley, but no one person is bigger than the club. I'm not spending ages trying to make a bad decision. Like when I was in business, I would say, "I might be the CEO, but I need everyone contributing to making better decisions in the best long-term interests of the business."

'So, I brought in Andy Whing who, honestly, has been a breath of fresh air because he's like a kid in a sweet shop. He thinks he's got the perfect job for him. He's local and he never thought he'd get this chance this early in his managerial career. I had the benefit of knowing him as a player when I was at Oxford. He puts his heart and soul into everything he does. We've started the season well and I'm hopeful this year we can go one step further.

'I think that the critical relationship at a football club is between the chairman/owner and the manager. If that is a good relationship, generally the club does well. Of course, you can't get too close to a manager due to the short-term nature of results and pressure. You have to be able to hold them to account. You tend to find that's how a football manager thinks anyway; they want everything now as they know they might not be here tomorrow.

'Expectations have gone up due to our play-off finishes, but our supporters know that reaching the English Football League is an aspiration rather than a divine right. In the National League, there are clubs who have been there previously who believe they should be there now. I tend to find the history of clubs like that acts as a shackle. It's a dead weight that pulls them down rather than allows them to look up. History counts for nothing in the National League, only the here and now.

'I suppose the problem with being an owner is you're always walking that line between trying to run the club commercially and seeking the glory of success. In many regards, that means the owner has to be a fan of the club – not necessarily a lifelong supporter, but certainly a person invested in the success of the club. If you're not, I don't know why you would want to get involved, to be quite honest. I'm a bit one-eyed on this. I'd still prefer owners to be, at least in part, local people or people who have some obvious connection to the club.

'I mean, look at Birmingham City now. They've got very wealthy American owners fronted by Tom Brady. That's brilliant, yes, but why? What's in it for them long term? That's what you should always be asking. I think this is where governance needs to change. It's not about Financial Fair Play. I'm not against a billionaire owner putting millions of pounds into a football club as long as it's sustainable. If they leave the club in a better place than they found it, then that's fine. If they leave an infrastructure that is sustainable, then great. It's those who come in and then pull the plug when the novelty wears off, or worse. That's not what football clubs need. One of the rules in football needs to be that you can't separate the ground from the ownership of the club. The ground needs to be the vehicle that the shareholders own. You've seen owners of a club in the past move the ground into a separate propco [property company] and, for me, that makes their intentions very clear. It shouldn't be allowed. I mean, without the ground, what is a football club?

'Most fans just want their clubs to be well run and to be proud of the way their team plays. They don't expect to win every game, and they know some seasons will be good and others not so good, but they just want their club to be part of the community and reflect their values. And that's what I'm doing at Moors, because how else do you get people to come to watch you? Birmingham is just around the corner and there are two big teams there. Being part of the community and being integrated into the community is how we make people feel like they are part of this club. Too many clubs now play lip service to the community and almost use the community to fund the club rather than the other way around.'

However, Eales believed that for clubs at National League level to truly prosper, there would need to be some radical reforms to structure.

'It's a belief of mine that the cut-off between the divisions in the current EFL pyramid should be between the National League and the National League North and South, not between League Two and the National League. The National League, to all intents and purposes, is League Three. The only thing we don't get is the £1.2m of central funding, which probably means, ironically, that our clubs are better run because they're dependent either on their owners or commercial revenue, and so can't run ahead of themselves.

'The biggest frustration with the National League for me is that there's not a three-up, three-down system with League Two. I believe what should actually happen is the National League and League Two should merge and form a League Two North and a League Two South, with the top two of each going into League One, and one relegation/promotion spot to each of the National League North and South.

'I think this form of regionalisation is important for the finances of clubs at our level. There would be less distance to travel for a start, which is more sustainable, and it would mean bigger crowds more regularly, which would drive revenue.

'Kidderminster, for example, are our nearby rivals but they face a Christmas double-header with Boreham Wood, who are bloody miles away. Where is the sense in that for the staff and the fans? As it stands, at the beginning of each season, National League clubs are asked by the fixture compilers to suggest ideal dates to play certain opponents. We say we don't want a five-hour coach journey on a Tuesday night, for example. I would say, 90 per cent of the time, we don't get anything resembling what we've asked for. If the league was regionalised, this wouldn't be an issue.

'Another of my big bugbears at this level is the artificial pitches. There shouldn't be any. They should be banned. The argument from those clubs who have them will be that they are needed for revenue during the week, where they are rented out to the public. If we became part of a regionalised league structure, we wouldn't need them as the central funding would cover that shortfall.

'I'm a bit of a traditionalist, I think football should be played on grass. The best players don't like playing on artificial surfaces, and they tend to think it gives the home side a disproportionate advantage. Take Dorking, for example. They play a game where they hoof the ball like a nine iron into the corners of the pitch and our players are thinking the ball's going to bounce out, so stop running. It doesn't though, it sort of spins backwards, almost at the first bounce, and the Dorking player is anticipating this. It takes you a while to adjust to that, even within a game.'

The contest between Solihull and Rochdale at Damson Park was very much played on grass, and, with Andy Whing having guided Moors to third in the table by this stage, they looked every bit a side with EFL ambition, running out 2-0 winners on the night. Dale had been the losing side now in the first game of each of the three months of the season so far.

With games coming thick and fast, Jim McNulty's thin squad was starting to feel the exposure. Circumstance rather than choice seemed to dictate that both Tyrese Sinclair and George Nevett began on the bench for this Tuesday night encounter, with Max Taylor and Ian Henderson replacing them in the starting XI.

Henderson took up a familiar central role just behind forward Kairo Mitchell, with Harvey Gilmour providing width on the left and Jesurun Uchegbulam likewise on the right. Taylor partnered captain Ethan Ebanks-Landell in the heart of defence.

Despite the eventual outcome, the visitors actually started the game the brighter, with the by-now trademark interchanging of the ball from the defence through the midfield the dominant feature. Unfortunately, this failed to translate into anything meaningful in the final third and so the home side grew into the game the longer Dale remained toothless. Taylor, too, looked off the pace and picked up a careless booking. A similar foul not long afterwards prompted referee Jamie O'Connor to give the defender a final warning, putting him on the thinnest of ice.

The second half saw the visitors begin to look a little laboured. This was best personified when Uchegbulam failed to track back after a run up the wing, allowing Joe Newton to march down the line and feed Jack Stevens for a finish that was all too easy – 1-0 to the Moors.

When Dale did manage to create in the final third, they were let down by more wayward finishing. Mitchell could and should have fired home using his left foot, but the delay while he sought to get the ball on his right saw him tackled and the chance was gone. Likewise, the usually deadly Henderson wafted at a ball he would typically have thundered home, and goalkeeper Tommy Simkin gathered easily. From this came the sucker punch. Simkin sent his subsequent kick long, parting the Dale centre-backs. Moors' Josh Kelly was on to it in a flash and neatly lofted the ball over the advancing Louie Moulden in the Rochdale goal. A tactic that had worked so well for Moulden himself in previous games had been used against him here to devastating effect.

Dale pushed on for something, anything, but ultimately drew a blank. The lack of a replacement centre-forward in the absence of Devante Rodney was truly brought to bear.

'I don't know how we've lost that tonight,' McNulty said after the match. 'We've created more than enough chances to win the game and they barely tested Louie beyond the goals they actually scored. I think it comes down to the fact that they took their chances and we didn't. That's football. I'm not going to over analyse this tonight.

'The fight was there throughout. There were honest mistakes, but they tried and pushed. We tried to invade their box and tried to get the ball in the back of the net, it just didn't go in. We will look to bounce back on Saturday.'

McNulty also confirmed that he would be missing left-back Cameron John for as long as eight weeks with a hamstring injury.

'He's been in good form and in a good place mentally,' he said. 'It's a shame to lose him.'

* * *

ESTABLISHED IN 1870, Maidenhead United had woven a decent enough football history on behalf of the town. From early FA Cup ventures to mergers and non-league battles, the club's journey had been one of both grit and achievement.

However, it was the notable exploits of one man in particular that immediately drew interest. Former West Ham United winger Alan Devonshire had overseen two lengthy and successful managerial reigns at the Berkshire club – the first in the 1990s and the second, his current stint, which began in 2015.

Taking the part-time club to the National League in 2018 – and keeping it there for five seasons – had been nothing short of miraculous. Devonshire had also developed a reputation for turning Maidenhead's York Road ground into something of a bear trap for former EFL clubs, with home supporters gleefully chanting 'you've been Devonshired' to opposing fans on the receiving end of a chastening.

I caught up with the 67-year-old to find out first hand just what created the bond between this small part-time outfit and a former top-flight footballer.

Devonshire began his professional career with West Ham United in 1976. He spent more than a decade at the club, becoming a highly regarded winger. His skilful dribbling, accurate passing and versatility on the field made him a key player for the Hammers during the 1980s.

'I was at Crystal Palace under-18s first, and was promised pro terms when I got to my 18th birthday,' he told me. 'However, it didn't materialise because Bert Head was the manager at the time and, in the March of 1973, he got sacked. So, Malcolm Allison came in as the new manager and he got rid of six of us, and I was one of them – he didn't even see us play.

'I played in non-league after that, out wide on either side, or playing in the hole, as they say these days, before West Ham picked me up in 1976.

'At the Hammers, I was mainly played on the right at first, but then someone got injured and I was put on the left. I found it a lot easier there and that's when things really took off for me.

'In non-league, it's a lot more physical and the referees aren't as good, so you don't get protection. I remember when someone came up to me at West Ham and said, "Well, how do you find the physical side of it?" And I laughed. I just said, "It's a piece of piss," because, at the end of the day, I was getting a little bit more protection from better referees and so my legs weren't kicked to pieces.'

Devonshire played a significant role in West Ham's success, including the FA Cup triumph in 1980 and a Second Division title win in 1981/82. Devonshire was also capped at international level, representing England eight times in the early 1980s. However, his international career was limited due to him sustaining a brutal injury in 1984.

'After I won the cup with West Ham in the May, I got picked for England to play Northern Ireland at Wembley about three weeks later,' he said. 'I was in and out of the England side after that until Bobby Robson got the job. Bobby really liked me. He actually tried to sign me when he was Ipswich manager, so I knew I had his backing. I played four games on the bounce for England and then I get that bad, bad injury.

'I remember it vividly. It was 7 January 1984. We played Wigan in the FA Cup third round and, after seven minutes, I get hit on one side and tackled on the other. I snapped my medial ligament, my ACL [anterior cruciate ligament] and my PCL [posterior cruciate ligament]. The doctors had to move my hamstring and put it in the middle of my knee to stabilise it, so the injury was quite a bad one. I've never known anyone else in football to do that injury.'

Devonshire somehow managed to recover and went on to play again for West Ham for a further six years, and then Watford for another two, before retiring in 1992.

'I think I had 12 surgeons all say I wouldn't play again, but I love to prove people wrong,' he said. 'I did play again but I was never the same player. A lot of people say to me, "You got eight caps for England but, without that injury, you'd have got 58." It's all talk, of course. Speculation. That injury is my one regret in football. Because of it, I will never truly know what I could have achieved as a player. Still, it was out of my control and I had to get on with it. It's not as if I self-destructed. I still played until I was 35.

'When I hung up my boots, I literally did nothing for three or four years. I just switched off and took a break from it all. The thing is, though, I just love football and I wanted to be involved in some way. It wasn't just the games I missed, it was all of it. The training and general involvement of being around a club.

'A friend called and asked if I would help out with a bit of coaching here and there at a local team. I did, and I loved it. Then Martyn Busby, who was manager of Maidenhead at the time, phoned me up and asked if I'd like to be co-manager with him, so I did and I loved that too. Then, after about three weeks, he said he had to leave. I don't even know what the reason was really, but he just said he had to go.

'The way things happened, I kind of just took over on my own and it snowballed from there. It's a lovely club and I got on really well with the chairman and his wife at that time. For the size of the club, we had a reasonable amount of success. After eight or nine years, the chairman and his wife left the club and I decided to leave with them. To this day, I'm lucky that every job I have ever moved on from has always been on my terms.

'I had a good few good years in the fifth tier as manager of Braintree after a few spells at other clubs, but the budget was small and there was a time when we had a few player injuries to deal with, so I had five youth-team boys on the bench. In the National League, that isn't sustainable, but the club didn't have the money to do anything different.

'Peter Griffin, the current chairman of Maidenhead, then gave me a call, asking if I would go back. I'd actually signed up most of the Braintree team for the following year, but the chance of going back to the club I never really wanted to leave anyway, was too good to turn down.'

Devonshire's managerial career has been marked by his ability to achieve positive results with limited resources and his dedication to nurturing talent in the lower tiers of English football.

'It's been a tough time since coming back to Maidenhead, but an enjoyable one,' he said. 'As a part-time team in what is mainly a full-time division, it's hard work. I've had a lot of players leave us for the Football League over the years now, and I like to think I've helped with that. That's my kind of buzz out of all this. I'm not in it for myself. It's not a financial thing for me.

'It's just about helping younger boys, who've had the same disappointment I had when I was 18. I know a lot of kids now are at pro clubs from six years old, and then they're suddenly released at 18 with no real explanation. I can relate to that, so I want to get them in here and help them develop.

'My son Lee does all the scouting for me. He's been brought up with football and he's very talented at seeing a player in someone. He'll recommend them to me, I'll take a look, and then we'll make a decision.

'We now train Monday, Tuesday mornings, and then Thursday nights. We decided to get the players in on Monday mornings just to recover. We don't do anything heavy, but, because we don't see them on a Sunday, it just gives us chance to ensure they recover properly so that we can train properly on a Tuesday and Thursday night.

'We just try our best. That's all we can do. We try to set the boys up in a certain way to be hard to beat, but also to be talented and to attack. We're not a defensive team at all. I've got a system that works for the players rather than a system that works for me. That's the way we have achieved the success we have.'

Thankfully, the Rochdale players weren't completely 'Devonshired' on their visit to an unseasonably warm York Road, but they came mighty close, squandering a first-half lead and having to come back again to seal a 2-2 draw.

Jim McNulty was able to add Cian Hayes to his matchday squad, having signed the 20-year-old winger on a one-month loan from League One side Fleetwood Town earlier in the week, as well as forward Devante Rodney, who had been sidelined with illness for much of the season to date. However, while one hand did giveth, the other did taketh away. Full-back Max Conway had been recalled by his parent club Bolton Wanderers, having made only seven appearances for Dale, leaving the squad painfully short in the full-back department when considering Cameron John's injury.

McNulty brought George Nevett and Tyrese Sinclair back into the starting line-up after their midweek rest, such as it was, meaning Max Taylor and Ian Henderson reverted to a seat on the bench.

The visitors started the match well enough too, attempting to build up the play rather than force it, with Sinclair the liveliest threat out on the left, albeit without a tangible end product. The Maidenhead players showed flashes of their own potential when managing to get through Dale lines, and so both sides exchanged a few testing jabs before a meaningful thrust got through.

Kairo Mitchell made it 1-0 to Dale when he expertly controlled a loose ball, after his marker had tried to intercept a long-range pass from captain Ethan Ebanks-Landell, and sent a fine left-footed finish past Craig Ross from the edge of the box in the 27th minute to mark his fourth goal in six games.

After the half-time break, Dale seemed to lose focus. Perhaps it was the unseasonable heat, perhaps it was fatigue from the relentless procession of Saturday-Tuesday games with little scope for rotation, perhaps it was even a combination of both, but the goal through which

Maidenhead equalised was disappointing held against any mitigating factor.

After a substitution and a system switch, Maidenhead's Reece Smith pushed the ball all too easily past Nevett on the left, before jinking the other way, and remained composed enough to roll the ball beyond Louie Moulden.

McNulty chose to throw Hayes and Rodney into the mix as both sides looked for a winner, but the Dale players were looking stretched, losing possession more easily now than in the first 45 minutes. This was punished when Chanka Zimba capitalised on Bradley Keetch's precise ball over the top, finding himself in acres of space on the right. With a burst of speed that left Nevett trailing, and exploiting Moulden's momentary hesitation, Zimba maintained composure to calmly slot the ball inside the far post to secure a 2-1 lead.

Mercifully, Dale managed to hit the hosts on the counter just as all looked lost. Rodney received the ball out wide on the right from Ebanks-Landell in the 86th minute and, under pressure, did well to whip the ball across the face of goal with his second touch, which Sinclair hammered home at the back post unmarked.

Dale ended the match in the ascendency thereafter, but the Magpies of Maidenhead stood resolute.

'I think the team – and that means all of us – are disappointed with a point and with the goals that we conceded,' McNulty said after the game. 'Fifteen games in, and a third of the season gone, is a good time to reflect. We're enjoying this new chapter in the National League. I'm enjoying trying to make a success of it, trying to win games, with all the challenges that we're under, but there are consistent things that have hurt us in those 15 games – we acknowledge them, we can't ignore them.

'I said in a post-match interview after a home game a few weeks ago that it's really clear to me what we need to get better at. We've conceded in trends so far. There's a trend of conceding from crosses, from mishandling balls into wide spaces behind us, and how we deal with it from there.

'At the top of the pitch, there are moments of quality in certain areas, but also moments where we should be scoring more.

'But how we get better at it can't come from the marketplace, it has to come from within. We've got what we've got, we are where we are. We're still adjusting financially as a football club which has dropped to this level.

'This is a perfect period of reflection now, to look in the mirror, me included, to recognise what's been costing us, what we can be better at, and how we go about doing it.

'Everyone knows that if we leave a game disappointed, it's usually because we should have won. I think it would be a travesty if we lost that game. What I can't deny, is that the players have got this fight and spirit, and it warms me. I feel fortunate, lucky and thankful to have that from them.

'The fight got us a point today, because it's tough when you come to these places, and you get reversed from being 1-0 up. Your ego and confidence go through the floor, but I knew it would be tough.'

* * *

ONE OF THE most notable ignominies of a club losing its place in the EFL is the need to qualify for the right to participate in the FA Cup, and so it was for Rochdale, having been drawn away against Hereford FC in the fourth and final qualifying round.

England's premier cup competition had held some fond memories for Dale under the recent reign of Keith Hill, a fifth-round clash with top-flight outfit Tottenham Hotspur, which was forced to a replay, chief among them.

Since the club's formation in 1907, Dale had needed to qualify for the FA Cup from the 1908/09 season until 1924/25. The club had entered at the first-round stage ever since, playing a total of 256 ties (including replays) of which 94 were won, 59 drawn and 103 lost.

Hereford FC, a phoenix club of the now-defunct Hereford United, who Rochdale had met 46 times previously in the Football League, operated at National League North level, just one below Dale, and were managed by former Celtic and Scotland right-back Paul Caddis.

Caddis enjoyed a diverse career in club and international football. The Scot, hailing from the Ayrshire coastal town of Irvine, began his journey at Celtic, progressing from the youth ranks to make his first-team debut in 2008. During his time in the East End of Glasgow, he received call-ups to the Scottish national side and also featured in the UEFA Champions League against the likes of Barcelona.

After falling down the pecking order at Parkhead, he made the move to Swindon Town in 2010, before joining Birmingham City, with later stints at Bury, Blackburn Rovers and Bradford City, where he continued to ply his trade in various tiers of English football. Upon retiring from playing, Caddis transitioned into coaching and took up a role in Fleetwood Town's academy in 2021 before moving to the Hereford hotseat in May 2023.

Caddis had managed to guide the Bulls to 16th in National League North by the time of Dale's visit to Edgar Street and boasted the likes of former Aberdeen striker Adam Rooney among his squad members.

Jim McNulty, meanwhile, was forced to make changes to his starting line-up ahead of this tie. Kairo Mitchell and

George Nevett were away on international duty with Grenada and Wales under-19s, respectively, so Ian Henderson and Kyle Ferguson stepped into their roles. Mercifully, the parent clubs of loanees Louie Moulden, Ryan East and Cian Hayes all allowed them to play, or McNulty's selection dilemma would have been much more of a headache.

Unfortunately the stronger line-up failed to make a difference in the West Midlands, and it seemed that McNulty's now established preferred system of building up play through patient possession had been mastered by the lower-league opposition, who simply grew in confidence the longer Dale's approach failed to hurt them.

It proved terminal in the 78th minute. When Dale attempted one such passage of play out from the back, Hereford pressed. Alex Babos dispossessed Adam Clayton in midfield as he attempted to pirouette on the ball, and fed Ethan Freemantle on the left edge of the box, who cut in to finish easily past Moulden. It was just this incisiveness that the Dale players were themselves missing all afternoon. The 1-0 defeat was keenly felt by both the supporters who had travelled to the match and those who stayed at home.

McNulty cut a dejected figure afterwards, the fact this would be the first time Rochdale would not compete in the FA Cup proper for almost 100 years weighing heavily on his shoulders.

'I'm hurting, the players are hurting and the fans are hurting,' he said. 'I feel I can't talk too much about the game – who should have won, who should have scored – because I'm in pain.

'My best moments in this job are seeing the players happy and seeing the fans happy. I feel devastated when they're not. We missed a lot of chances. The ball didn't go in. That always gives the opposition a chance. Always. It's a similar assessment to a lot of our games. My prime objective is to produce a style of football, moments and outcomes that make everyone happy. That didn't happen today. It's important we now pick ourselves up for a massive league game next weekend.'

* * *

THE ROMANTICISM OF the 'local-businessman-done-good' running a town's professional team is all but a nostalgic fantasy in the upper echelons of club football these days, where overseas corporations or Middle Eastern royalty now hold the purse strings for the majority.

Lower down the pyramid, such cases can still be found, however. Rochdale has had its own idealisation in this regard, of course, with Fred Ratcliffe, David Kilpatrick, Graham Morris, Andrew Kelly and Chris Dunphy, among others, notable in the town for their trade and favoured by the supporters for dipping into their own pockets, when necessary, to help with the club's running over decades gone by.

While this may now be viewed as an old-fashioned and outmoded business model, Oldham Athletic, a club of Premier League founding member fame, probably remains one of the last bastions of this wistful archetype thanks to owner Frank Rothwell.

The local businessman completed a £12m takeover of Oldham following the controversial and unpopular regime of Abdallah Lemsagam, under which the Latics dropped out of the Football League altogether.

Rothwell, who made his fortune from his own Manchester-based cabins company, took Oldham on in July 2022, when the club was just days from being liquidated.

He is now regarded with something approaching messianic reverie by the Oldham supporters.

Having endured Premier League relegation in 1994, Oldham suffered a further blow when they slipped from the second tier in 1997. For the next 21 years, Oldham battled in League One until Moroccan-born and Dubai-based Lemsagam assumed control in 2018. However, his tenure only accelerated the club's decline, marked by a distressing four-year period encompassing 12 different managers, two relegations and the ominous threat of oblivion. It was at this critical juncture that Rothwell stepped in as saviour.

The man who saved Oldham Athletic is no ordinary figure, however. Having left school at the tender age of 14, Rothwell has been a resident of the town for nearly half a century. With his unmistakable northern charm and a penchant for tinkering with tractors, he could easily be a character in a Harry Enfield sketch, embodying the stereotypical image of a flat cap-wearing northerner. He stands in stark contrast to the polished, impeccably suited businessmen who dominate the modern corporate world of football. It is precisely this down-to-earth nature that makes him all the more captivating and endearing to the supporters of the club he has saved.

Oldham and Rochdale supporters were looking forward to re-establishing their derby rivalry at Spotland on the 21st of the month. Ahead of the fixture, I wanted to chat to Rothwell, to gain an idea of how he handled the Latics' first campaign in the National League the previous season, and, as just six miles separate the two clubs, to draw parallels with Rochdale, if any presented themselves.

'I wasn't a season ticket holder, or anything like that,' he told me when asked how he first got involved with Oldham. 'I would go to Boundary Park on a Tuesday night to watch the team, if I had the time to spare. You know, as a local bloke who fancied going to a football match. I'd probably seen 100 games that way over the past 30 years. It was one such game in March 2022 that planted the seed in terms of owning the club. We were playing Leyton Orient. I'd not been for a couple of years, but the drums were banging, supporters were chanting and kids were having a great time. This was all despite the club struggling.

'I said to my son, "We could do something here with Latics," and he basically said, "On your bike, the last thing we need is to buy a bloody football club."

'Towards the end of that season, there were men of my age invading the pitch to sit on the centre circle. You've got stewards saying, "Come on, Jack, I've known you all my life, let's move," and Jack would be like, "No, we need to protest against this lot." So that was the passion for the club, you see? It was all ages. I didn't want to see that disappear.

'I had been given the Freedom of the Borough of Oldham by the council in 2021 and I was also made the town's business ambassador, so I had plenty of contacts. Darren Royle, son of legendary Oldham manager Joe, approached me about putting a consortium together, as he could see the club going to the wind. Truth be known, I'd had that conversation with many business people throughout the town previously, and all of them said no, no and no again.

'Darren showed me a business plan of how Oldham could become self-sustainable with the right ownership. I looked at it and put it to my family again. We decided we could maybe get involved without a consortium. Darren told us the chap who owned the stadium, Simon Blitz, was due to be in Oldham the next week, so we set up a meeting. Simon was interested in selling, and named a price, but said he wouldn't sell us the stadium unless we first bought and owned the football club. He said, "I don't want to be the person responsible for the demise of Oldham Athletic." I thought, "Wow, this guy isn't even from Oldham, and he cares this much."

'Quietly, we decided to speak to Abdallah to see what he wanted for the club. My son, Luke, led the negotiations there. We did the deal, bought the club, did the due diligence on the stadium, and here we are now.'

Rothwell set up his Manchester Cabins business in 1979, aged 28, from his home in Royton, on the Oldham/Rochdale border. He retired in 2021, leaving the family business to be managed by his son, and his daughter Su. The company currently employs more than 50 people in its Oldham factory and depot, and turns over almost £20m a year.

'I got married at 19 to my darling wife Judith,' he said. 'We have both now outlived our parents. Are we on borrowed time? Maybe. We need to make sure this wealth we've created goes to our children. We're putting things in place now. We don't want the kids having to sell half of all the businesses to pay a tax bill, should we suddenly depart this earth. Therefore, I don't actually own Oldham Athletic, my kids do. It's mine and Judith's graft that has paid for it, and I'll be involved as long as I'm able to be, as Mr Chairman, but I've protected both the club and my children by giving it to them now.'

In the present, Rothwell was indeed Mr Chairman and was fully ensconced in helping Oldham achieve what he believed was its full potential.

'The size of Oldham Athletic Football Club dictates that it is not a National League club,' he said. 'Therefore, promotion has to be our one and only aim this season. We sold 4,000 season tickets at the early bird price alone. If you are younger than 35, you can't remember Oldham Athletic winning anything. For a club of this size, with this support, that's not good enough. Thirty-five years since we've had an open-top bus parade? This town needs that again. Deserves it, even.

'Financially, the club needs it too. I've been in business now for 50 years. My philosophy has always been to only take a wage out of it. If the business doesn't make a profit, I don't get a wage. Simple. However, football doesn't play by these rules and so, every month, we have to put money into the club. Far more than we thought we'd have to. That's why we need to get promoted. We need to get to our natural position at the top of League One/bottom of the Championship and build from there. This town can support that and make the club sustainable.'

Rothwell said he found his introduction to the National League an eye-opener and something of a humbling experience.

'Last season, our first in the National League, I remember we were away at Bromley,' he said. 'They had a plastic pitch and all that business, and I thought, "Oh yeah, this is proper non-league." We got hammered. I couldn't believe it. I didn't expect that.

'The chief exec came up to me after the game, introduced himself, and said, "I understand you're new to football." I admitted it. I was. I told him I didn't know enough about the game and that's why I employed people who do. I asked him about the plastic pitch. He opened my eyes. He said the club was able to host 330 games on it the previous year. We got 27, if we were lucky. It seemed a real revenue-maker and also a place for the whole community. He then showed me around their facilities. He took me into what I can only describe as a university lecture theatre. It was decked out with TVs, it was bright and airy. The CEO then says to me, "This is where the players come to analyse our games and this is where they come before games to analyse the opposition." All I could think was, "Fucking hell, we're a million miles away from this." At that time, we had our TV set in the old board room. A cramped, depressing room. Things needed to change.

'I wanted a plastic pitch because I'd learned a team with a plastic pitch has a ten per cent advantage when playing at home. If you've got a plastic pitch, you've got 12 players. However, my advisors said it would be a waste of money because, if we got promoted, we would need to remove it for English Football League rules. Harrogate had a plastic pitch and then they got promoted. Did they rip up their plastic pitch? No. They put a hybrid pitch on top of it. If they ever get relegated, they can remove that and use the plastic one again.

'I said, "That's where we need to be." My advisors, though, said, "Frank, could you kindly fuck off and let us deal with it?" I listened to them, and so, this season, we've had a new hybrid pitch put down. The local council gave us £1m to put it in place. A condition of the council's money was that we would allow rugby to be played on the pitch. I said, "Of course, rugby is as much a part of our town as the football is." We see Oldham Athletic as being a centre for both sport and community events for the town of Oldham, and that's what it will be.

'In fact, we don't have fans at Oldham Athletic now, we have only supporters. My family is *supporting* Oldham Athletic. Everybody who comes to a game is helping us *support* Oldham Athletic. That's what it's about.'

Retirement from his main business certainly hadn't quelled Rothwell's appetite for adventure. At the age of

70, he became the oldest person to row a boat solo 3,000 miles across the Atlantic Ocean - raising £1.1m for Alzheimer's Research UK in tribute to his brother-in-law Roger, who died with Alzheimer's aged 62. Rothwell's previous expeditions include spending five weeks on a deserted island for Channel 4 TV show *The Island* and he was the tenth person to circumnavigate North and South America by boat.

'When I was rowing across the Atlantic, I realised this was something that I could do that could make a difference,' he said. 'Not just to the street, the town or the county – but for all of mankind. I used my business contacts to raise funds for this very important cause. Alzheimer's is a condition that affects everybody – directly or indirectly. You can't compare that to running a football club. Yes, they're both adventures, but one is for mankind, the other is an ego trip, let's be honest.'

With one eye on the Rochdale derby, Frank added, 'My wife and I lived in a council flat in the centre of Rochdale when we first got married, back when I was 19. We could see the stadium from where we lived. I was sad when Rochdale got relegated. I'd much rather Oldham and Rochdale played each other in a higher division, as opposed to down here. Hopefully they will again, one day. This is a horrible division to get out of, and I do hope Rochdale manage it, along with ourselves.'

Ahead of the derby match, or the 'El Flat-cap Classico' as some locals affectionately called it, the moods in both camps could not have been more contrasting. Oldham, after an indifferent start to the season, had replaced manager David Unsworth with a much wilier operator at National League level in Micky Mellon, and the club's fans were buoyed by recent positive results, including putting National

League high-flyers Altrincham out of the FA Cup at the fourth qualifying stage.

Conversely, Rochdale had just bowed out of the competition at Hereford, making it five games without a win for head coach Jim McNulty. In addition, captain Ethan Ebanks-Landell was suspended due to a booking picked up against Maidenhead, which had taken him beyond the permissible threshold. This forced McNulty into pairing young George Nevett with Max Taylor at the centre of a back four, and, perhaps more interestingly, Kyle Ferguson at right-back over the more natural Kwaku Oduroh.

As to the match itself, the Dale players found themselves embroiled in a nail-biting seven-goal spectacle, ultimately succumbing to a 4-3 loss against a spirited Oldham side.

And it was the visiting players who started the game more like they were contesting a derby match, being quicker to every ball and looking to get forward as quickly as possible. The home players, conversely, seemed more ponderous with the ball in their own half, searching for options that simply weren't presenting themselves.

Tyrese Sinclair and Cian Hayes on the wings were failing to cut inside, and Kairo Mitchell was dropping too deep from his centre-forward position, condensing play and preventing Oldham from being stretched.

Max Taylor, especially, looked nervy in the Dale back line, seemingly overthinking his role and making critical mistakes that allowed Oldham to bear down on goal.

This was compounded when Adam Clayton's free kick met a wall of Oldham defenders, leading to a swift counterattack by the visitors. After a bit of pinball, Nathan Sheron took full advantage of the situation, unleashing a blistering strike from 20 yards to open the scoring.

Early in the second half, Oldham then doubled their lead when Devarn Green headed home a precise cross at the back post, which Moulden really should have kept out. McNulty reacted swiftly, making a double substitution. Sinclair was forced to exit the game due to an injury inflicted by a reckless tackle, being replaced by Jesurun Uchegbulam, and Clayton made way for the experienced Ian Henderson.

This produced an upturn in the Dale intensity. Henderson's presence allowed Mitchell to begin playing off the shoulder of the Oldham defenders, pushing them further back and creating more space out wide. Uchegbulam and Hayes used this to run at their men and the deficit was halved in no time when Hayes pulled the ball back for left-back Jimmy Keohane, who fired goalward for Mitchell to chest the ball past Oldham's keeper, Mathew Hudson.

Keohane himself then managed to level shortly after the hour mark, slotting the ball home after a corner from Ryan East fell invitingly to him in the crowded penalty area.

However, Oldham quickly regained the lead, with Hallam Hope delivering a masterful curling shot into the far corner of the net after being afforded generous room inside the box. James Norwood then put the game seemingly beyond reach for Dale, extending Oldham's advantage with a fourth goal in the 72nd minute, slotting calmly past Louie Moulden after latching on to a through ball that Taylor inexplicably let by him.

Yet there was still cause for optimism. Mitchell had a header deflected behind for a corner just before Keohane notched his second goal and Dale's third, slamming home the ball as it fell kindly to him on the right this time.

As the clock ticked down, the Dale players poured all of their energy into the game during 16 minutes of added time. Mitchell had a late header that went over the bar,

Dale captain Ethan Ebanks-Landell in an aerial duel against Oxford City.
Pic: Daniel Youngs

Rochdale's record goalscorer Ian Henderson notches yet another.
Pic: Daniel Youngs

Superb winger Cian Hayes is introduced to Rochdale's derby rivals Oldham Athletic. Pic: Daniel Youngs

Prodigious talent George Nevett enjoyed a fine debut season as a pro. Pic: Daniel Youngs

Ian Henderson, Kairo Mitchell and Tyrese Sinclair celebrate. Pic: Daniel Youngs

Full-back/holding midfielder Cameron John takes the game to FC Halifax Town. Pic: Daniel Youngs

Rochdale head coach *Jim McNulty inspires from the dugout. Pic: Daniel Youngs*

Kairo Mitchell and Ethan Ebanks-Landell wheel away in joy after netting against Aldershot Town. Pic: Daniel Youngs

Kairo Mitchell readies another missile against Gateshead. The striker finished the season with 14 goals. Pic: Daniel Youngs

Winger Tyrese Sinclair proving a menace against Kidderminster Harriers. Pic: Daniel Youngs

Jesurun Uchegbulam drives forward against Hartlepool United. Pic: Daniel Youngs

Ethan Ebanks-Landell, George Nevett and Jimmy Keohane find a rare moment of levity against Hartlepool. Pic: Daniel Youngs

Rochdale's player of the season Harvey Gilmour proved to be the engine in midfield. Pic: Daniel Youngs

Louie Moulden seemed to assist as many goals as he kept out. Pic: Daniel Youngs

Bromley manager Andy Woodman looking relaxed during a campaign that resulted in promotion. Pic: Dylan Clinton

Dorking's one-man-band Marc White sees his side succumb to a last-gasp winner for Rochdale. Pic: Steve O'Sullivan

while Keohane and Henderson both found their efforts thwarted by the athletic Hudson. However, despite their valiant efforts, McNulty's team fell short of finding the elusive equaliser.

Notwithstanding the electric atmosphere, the match had been marred by pockets of crowd trouble and allegations of racial abuse directed at Dale substitute Oduroh, which McNulty condemned afterwards.

'I think it spoiled the game,' he said. 'It's really quite shameful. I was made aware of an instance of racial abuse. It's the worst element of human behaviour. [Oduroh] is a young lad being exposed to men's football and it's the first time he has experienced anything like this. He shouldn't have to. No one should have to. The rest of what went on wasn't as serious as that, but it all added up. I love a derby game, I was caught up in the excitement of it during the key moments, but, with the nonsense that went on, I didn't enjoy it.

'As for the football, we showed tremendous fight again. You'd think every team would have fight in it, but they don't. I played football for 20 years and I was part of teams that didn't have the fight that these players have. I'm proud of them for that.

'The game was lost on moments of weakness. We showed too many of these moments to recover from. My heart breaks for the players at some of the mistakes we make because it costs us results. It's my job to pick them up from this.

'Added to that, Oldham have major financial clout when compared to us. They can replace like for like from the bench. They want to replace a number two? They can bring on a number two. A number nine? They can bring on a number nine. We're not there. The only business we can do right now is if another club can do us a favour. Not a lot of people want to do you a favour in football. If you're going to get a favour in football, there's probably a lot of compromise. We could go and get promising young players on loan, sure, but the National League is tough. It eats you up as a footballer. You need a lot of qualities to thrive here, qualities that, unfortunately, we most likely need to buy. Our board are trying to do all they can, I know that, and so we are where we are.'

In addition to Tyrese Sinclair, Kyle Ferguson also picked up an injury during the match.

'There's a fear about Tyrese that it could be something serious, but you never know, we won't know until Monday,' McNulty said.

'Kyle Ferguson, we think, has damaged a tendon in his groin, which isn't good. It's going to expose the wafer-thin nature of the squad, there's no doubt about it. Every injury we get hurts my soul. The players are giving me everything, but we're in a vulnerable state squad-wise. Everyone saw, though, that they will give their all, no matter what team we put out, whatever position they end up playing in for us.'

McNulty also issued an update on Devante Rodney after he disappeared from the squad completely having made substitute appearances in the previous two fixtures.

'It's not great,' the head coach said. 'At the moment, he is unable to train and compete. He's tried his best to come back, but he's simply not able to be on the pitch for us at the moment. It's tough for him and tough for us. If you take the main guy out of any team this season, they would be five places lower in the league than they are today. We've been without Dev all season.

'The way it looks right now, we may go the whole season without Dev, I just don't know. He can't train, he can't play, he's tried to give his all, but he can't do it.'

* * *

GATESHEAD, UNDER THE progressive management of Mike Williamson, had been making waves in the National League during the 2023/24 season. Despite not being one of the bigger-budget clubs in the division, Williamson had nevertheless crafted a team that played what the modern-day fan would brand 'attractive football' and blended it with what a pragmatic fan would call 'winning football'. The approach, in many ways, was most similar to that which Jim McNulty sought to achieve with his own charges, making this home fixture very much a mirror contest.

However, just seven days before the Heed were due to travel to Spotland, Williamson, and his backroom team, left the club to take up a vacancy at League Two side MK Dons, leaving squad goalkeeper Rob Elliot in charge on an interim basis.

Dale certainly made the most of any shell shock the Gateshead players may have been feeling at losing their mentor, racing into a two-goal lead under the floodlights on a more seasonably reflective chilly autumn Tuesday night. However, as had happened too often so far during the season, this lead was relinquished and the Dale players found themselves hanging on for a point as the match entered its death throes.

McNulty made four adjustments to the line-up following the Saturday defeat against Oldham. Ethan Ebanks-Landell returned from suspension, and Jesurun Uchegbulam, Kwaku Oduroh and Ian Henderson were included in the starting XI.

Max Taylor and Adam Clayton were relegated to the bench, while the injured Kyle Ferguson and Tyrese Sinclair were looking at four to six weeks in the treatment room.

The game got off to an energetic start, with both teams showing their attacking prowess in the first half. Nevertheless, it was Dale who carved the better opportunities.

Kairo Mitchell narrowly missed the target with a shot on the turn, assisted by Henderson at the edge of the box. Cian Hayes then embarked on a dazzling run down the right wing, cut into the penalty area, and had his shot saved, with Henderson sending the follow-up over the crossbar.

The opening goal came 16 minutes into the game with Uchegbulam scoring his first for Dale in some style. The ever-impressive Hayes saw his ball into the box deflected into the path of Jimmy Keohane, who collected and laid off for Uchegbulam to unleash a curling shot into the top corner with pace, leaving goalkeeper Archie Mair with no chance.

Dale then extended the lead just before the half-hour mark with a header from Henderson. Ebanks-Landell delivered a superb pass over the defence for Mitchell to chase. With Mair saving Mitchell's subsequent shot, the rebound looped towards Henderson, who rose highest to head into the net.

Gateshead had the National League's joint-top goalscorer in the ranks, and Marcus Dinanga was proving a menace on behalf of the visitors, hitting the underside of the bar with a powerful header.

The Heed did eventually pull one back after half-time, however, through Ed Francis, who struck a fine left-footed effort into the top corner from outside the box after being afforded too much space.

The visitors then had a chance to equalise shortly afterwards, with Moulden first denying Greg Olley's long-range attempts and then making a fantastic one-handed save to divert Dinanga's one-on-one effort away from the goal.

However, Moulden couldn't stop Kenton Richardson's equaliser, although he perhaps should have done; a low daisy-cutter from just outside the area beat his gloves midway through the second half.

Both teams pressed for a winning goal, with Uchegbulam coming close twice for Dale, including one saved effort and another narrowly missing the target after he cut in from the left. Nonetheless, neither side managed to find the game's fifth goal and it ended in a draw, leaving the home supporters to reflect on what it might take to see their team win again.

The answer seemed elusive. On the positive side, Rochdale had displayed direct and attacking football, similar to the second-half performance against Oldham. Hayes was beginning to stand out as an effective wide option, showcasing a real desire to take his opponents on. The team also scored a goal from a well-executed long pass from the back to Mitchell, highlighting the potential of McNulty's 'total options' playing style over ineffective ball retention.

However, there remained notable issues and concerns. Rochdale still struggled to prevent the opposition from creating chances. Even before the comeback, Gateshead could have scored in the first half, underlining the players' difficulty in defending within their own box. Again, a focus on closing down opponents higher up the pitch to limit crossing and shooting opportunities might have been a better approach. However, the lack of options due to squad size and injuries was clearly beginning to affect overall performance, and there was a tangible sense of desperation for help from the bench that simply wasn't forthcoming.

While McNulty praised his players' first-half performance, he cited fatigue for his side's second-half capitulation.

'On the balance of play, I'm probably pleased with the point,' the head coach said. 'I really like Gateshead, I think they're a very good team. Personally, I think they're the best team in the league, regardless of where they finish.

'A lot of the teams in the league have a solid identity. Gateshead are beyond two years into a project. They've evolved their group to really suit what they're doing, and I expected a really tough challenge tonight.

'To impose ourselves on them, and to go 2-0 up in the fashion that we did, was outstanding in the first half. However, I never felt fooled, even at 2-0, that the challenge wasn't real. They had their moments in the first half, too. I think there's real important moments in games – if Hendo's header goes in to make it 3-0, for example, it kills their belief that they can come back.

'Their first goal was an unbelievable strike, it couldn't be more in the top corner. They got good momentum from that and it was challenging. But, I must say, going to 2-2 and with momentum swinging in the game, I was really pleased with our resilience and character, and that we still carried that counterattack threat.

'As we really fatigued and struggled to find changes from the bench to help the team, the players dug deep and took a creditable 2-2 draw. The players were selfless and humble with their work. It's a big out-of-possession shift against Gateshead and the players felt it.'

* * *

FINALLY, IT WAS time to face Hartlepool United, Rochdale's stablemate in the 2023/24 season's fallen EFL clubs.

On paper, the north-east club had an edge over its north-west rival. Firstly, it boasted prior National League experience, having only been promoted from the division two seasons prior. Secondly, Pools boasted a manager with both EFL and National League experience in Jon Askey, who had most recently guided York City from National League North to the fifth tier.

Historically, Dale and Hartlepool, or even Hartlepools as the club was known before it declined all things plural in 1968, had met many times – 150 to be precise – with Dale edging the record by 59 wins to Hartlepool's 55. Pools had even been managed by the late, great Brian Clough during that time.

While Askey was no Ol' Big 'Ed, he was, nevertheless, an astute and experienced tactician, who had led Pools to 12th in the table prior to this fixture, one position above Dale.

As a player, Askey was known for his versatility as a winger and striker. He spent the majority of his playing career at Macclesfield Town, where he achieved noteworthy success, including multiple minor trophy wins, league titles and promotions. He became the club's record appearance maker and fourth-highest goalscorer, before his transition into coaching and management, through which he had also achieved promotion with Macclesfield and Port Vale.

Mercifully for the travelling support, Askey wasn't able to engineer success on this particular occasion as Dale bounced back to victory in a thrilling encounter, securing a 3-2 triumph.

Jim McNulty decided to stick with the same starting XI that featured in the Tuesday night game against Gateshead, but with Devante Rodney inexplicably returning to the bench, replacing Tommy McDermott.

Dale started the game the stronger outfit, displaying equal potency both playing through the lines and going long, all on a heavy pitch. Such was the visitors' mastery, they were able to move the Hartlepool players about the pitch, allowing the likes of centre-half George Nevett to join the midfield and offer further options.

As a result, the match got off to a perfect start as Hayes netted his inaugural goal for the club within three minutes. Louie Moulden played a crucial role once again, delivering an exceptional bullet of a long pass that found the winger. Hayes outpaced goalkeeper Joel Dixon and slotted the ball home with his right foot.

Dale maintained control of possession, with Hayes coming close again and Ryan East having a decent shot blocked. Hartlepool did manage to test Moulden sporadically, but he denied both Matt Dolan and Joe Mattock, and then Tom Crawford's curling shot that was bound for the top corner.

Dale's lead doubled in the 33rd minute when Jimmy Keohane scored his fourth goal of the season, continuing his knack of finding room in the box and capitalising on Kairo Mitchell's flick to hit the bottom corner from 12 yards.

With six minutes of stoppage time added by the fourth official, Dale secured their third. East found space in the centre of the field and fired off a shot from 25 yards, placing the ball neatly into the far bottom corner.

However, right before half-time, Hartlepool managed to pull one back thanks to Nicky Featherstone, who made the most of lax marking to connect with a cross from Joe Grey and place an effort past Moulden, narrowing the gap to 3-1.

Unfortunately the second half saw Dale revert to a pattern that was becoming all too familiar, failing to adapt to a shape and personnel change from the opposition and surrendering superiority to panic and pressure.

In the final ten minutes, it proved costly when Mani Dieseruvwe managed to further reduce the deficit by bullying his way to a cross to head past Moulden. Given the surrender in recent games of both tactical and goal superiority, the Dale fans were having their nerves shredded once again.

The home team increased the pressure, and Dieseruvwe had a golden opportunity to level the contest in the dying minutes, but missed his connection with the ball inside the six-yard box, with the goal wide open. On this occasion, however, Dale held on thereafter, enduring an additional seven minutes of stoppage time to secure all three valuable points.

'I'm pleased for the fans,' said McNulty afterwards. 'They sung their hearts out for us all day. They went through the whole challenge of the game with us and I'm really pleased for them.

'I'm pleased for the team, too, going into what is a most welcome week [of rest] for a depleted squad.

'I'm pleased with how they dug in, stuck together, weathered the storm, and showed some brilliant fight and traits of togetherness in the second half, which ultimately rewarded what was an outstanding 50 minutes for us. Regardless of any pressures in the second half, I feel it was a deserved win.

'We're an exciting team. Our squad isn't built to sit back; even when not at full strength, we aim to win games, score goals and play attractive football. The first half was a testament to that. It was enough to win the game alone. Despite conceding just before half-time, we showed character.

'We've often been pegged back when ahead, but our goal now is to maintain our attacking mindset and aim to win convincingly. We believe in our style of play and its ability to trouble any team in the league.'

This result would leave Rochdale ninth in the National League table to end October. While it was a slight disappointment that the play-off position of a month ago had been relinquished, the depleted squad might have fallen even further. To still be in touching distance of the top seven was a cause for optimism. Supporters were left wondering, however, how much longer McNulty's depleted side could continue to produce results without further reinforcements. Being out of the FA Cup would, at least, allow for fatigued limbs to catch a much-needed rest before November's leg of the league campaign got under way.

National League table as at 31 October 2023

	P	*W*	*D*	*L*	*F*	*A*	*Pts*
Chesterfield	17	14	2	1	43	22	44
Barnet	18	13	3	2	38	22	42
Bromley	18	10	5	3	28	18	35
Solihull Moors	18	9	7	2	27	19	34
Altrincham	17	7	8	2	31	23	29
FC Halifax Town	18	7	7	4	21	17	28
Aldershot Town	18	8	3	7	32	32	27
Gateshead	17	7	5	5	36	25	26
Rochdale	**18**	**6**	**6**	**6**	**31**	**29**	**24**
Oldham Athletic	18	5	8	5	26	27	23
Eastleigh	18	6	5	7	27	31	23
Woking	18	6	4	8	20	20	22
Hartlepool United	18	7	1	10	29	34	22
Southend United*	18	9	4	5	34	18	21
Dorking Wanderers	17	6	3	8	20	24	21
Boreham Wood	18	4	8	6	20	25	20
Wealdstone	18	5	5	8	20	25	20
Dagenham & Redbridge	18	5	4	9	18	24	19
Ebbsfleet United	18	5	2	11	23	34	17
AFC Fylde	18	4	4	10	28	36	16
Maidenhead United	18	3	7	8	18	29	16
York City	18	3	7	8	25	37	16
Oxford City	18	3	5	10	24	36	14
Kidderminster Harriers	18	3	5	10	12	24	14

* Southend deducted ten points for failing to pay an existing tax bill.

November 2023

ON 10 MARCH 2013, a phone-shot YouTube video went viral among and beyond the football community. It featured a middle-aged supporter shouting abuse at opposing players and then confronting an opposing supporter when challenged. Far from being a disturbing clip, the footage bordered on comedy, due to the fan's age and stature.

Dubbed the 'Wealdstone Raider', the 57-year-old Gordon Hill gained online recognition as a meme for his delivery of the phrases 'You want some?', 'I'll give it ya' and 'You've got no fans'. More interestingly, it put the team he was following, Wealdstone, firmly on the map.

Ten years on, the Ruislip-based club had climbed two leagues from the Isthmian League to the National League and had developed a whole new reputation as an inclusive family club, and one that played attractive football too – all while remaining semi-professional.

I caught up with Wealdstone's chairman Rory Fitzgerald (no relation) ahead of Rochdale's trip to west London to hear more.

'I was approached by the club about eight or nine years ago,' he said. 'At that point, they were looking for a main club sponsor. I own a number of businesses not a million miles away from the club, my main one being GPF Lewis plc, and I had some mutual friends and connections with the board at the time, so they reached out. We had a number of meetings and GPF Lewis became the main club sponsor.

'The club then asked if I wanted to be more involved, either financially or with my time, in terms of offering advice. I was a little bit reluctant at first, but only because I was already running a number of businesses and had a young family. If I do something, then I like to do it properly and that requires time and effort. So, I kept my distance for the next two or three years.

'I was then approached by the board of directors and previous chairman, Peter Marsden. There had been a falling out; a difference of opinion between him and the existing board. The board wanted me to see if I could help broker a better working relationship, for want of a better expression, between the existing board and the chairman and vice-chairman.

'I was asked to come in and be part of the new executive board and, finally, I agreed. I became vice-chairman, working under Peter. However, after a few months, it was clear that the board couldn't work with Peter. There was a difference of views on how the club should move forward, how things should be done, so they gave Peter a vote of no confidence.

'They asked me to step up full time. I was a little bit dubious and reluctant to do this, due to the time that would be involved. I agreed to do it until the end of the season and would then review it, subject to the club being happy, subject to me being happy.

'We got to the National League South play-off semi-finals that season and lost to Woking. I knew the club was capable of more and so I made the decision to stay on. We changed the management team and I got heavily involved.

We appointed a new manager in Dean Brennan and an assistant in Stuart Maynard, who's now, of course, first-team manager. Then, the next year, we went and won the National League South. I've been chairman ever since.'

Fitzgerald is a firm believer that Wealdstone is a key part of the local community, but admitted there was work to be done to compensate for a 'missing generation' of supporters.

'We spend an awful lot of time going into the local schools, because that's the next generation of our supporters,' he said. 'Unfortunately, Wealdstone didn't have a proper home for the best part of 15 years. As a result, the club lost a generation of supporters; probably two generations. When you look at the demographic of our support, and this is not meant disrespectfully, there are a lot of older supporters. There's such a huge gap. We're missing that 25-to-35-year-old element.

'So, in recent years, we've really committed to going into the community, going into schools with our youth academy and junior teams, really trying to push it and encourage kids to come to games, giving pre-season tickets to anyone under 16 and actively encouraging their parents to come down with them.

'We know we can't be everyone's first team because we've got a wealth of Premier League teams close to where we are in London. You know, Arsenal, Tottenham, Chelsea, Fulham, Brentford. There are just so many and it's really hard to compete. But if we can be everyone's second team, their non-league team, then that's the bonus and that's what we're trying to do. I've got three children, so I know how expensive football can be, especially at Premier League level. An afternoon at Wealdstone is much more affordable and, while the level of player may not be Premier League standard, it's still a high standard. There's very little gap between the National League and League Two these days.

'There's a good atmosphere, too, especially with the likes of some of the bigger clubs, such as Southend, Chesterfield and Wrexham, visiting. You can engage with the players in a way you just can't at a Premier League level. We have also just announced outline plans for a new 6,300-capacity stadium, with potential to expand further, following the decision by Hillingdon Borough Council to allocate us an 18-acre site.'

And while Fitzgerald credits the Wealdstone Raider for elevating the club in terms of the wider public consciousness, he believes it is all of the above that has cemented the club's modern reputation.

'Gordon, the Raider, raised the profile of the club, of course he did,' he said. 'But we've moved on from that. We're playing in a professional arena now, playing some good football and we're better known as a family club that is doing incredibly well in the National League. We've got more than 100 boys in our academy, training every day with a full-time education programme. We're a real community hub and that's down to the club officials, the players, the managers, ex-players, the supporters and all the people who volunteer and help make the club what it is today.

'Ultimately, we'd like to be an EFL club, but we're not naive enough to think it's going to happen overnight. When I took over, we said we want to become a National League team within three years. We did it in year one. When we got to the National League, I said the objective was to become established. We're now in our fourth season. I think as long as you're always moving forward, you can't ask for much more, so we haven't put a further timeline on what we've been doing. If we keep doing what we're doing, hopefully dreams might come true.'

Rochdale supporters' dreams certainly came true when it was announced, ahead of their first visit to Wealdstone, that Cian Hayes's loan period with the club had been extended by an additional month. However, fellow loanee Tommy McDermott, who had barely troubled the first team, had been recalled by his parent club Port Vale.

Unfortunately, the break afforded to the Dale squad due to a lack of participation in the FA Cup seemed to have had the opposite effect a rest should have inspired, and they suffered a 3-2 defeat, conceding a last-minute goal. Despite taking the lead twice in Ruislip, the fragility of mentality that had become all-too-familiar reared its head again to cost the side valuable points – and against part-time opposition, to boot.

The match saw one change from the Hartlepool game, with Adam Clayton replacing Jesurun Uchegbulam in the starting XI. Uchegbulam and Cameron John, who was returning from a six-week injury, were on the bench.

Dale started strongly, with Kairo Mitchell scoring his eighth of the season thanks to a decent through ball from Harvey Gilmour. Goalkeeper Louie Moulden was then forced to make crucial saves, while Mitchell and Ryan East tested Stones goalkeeper Jed Ward at the other end. The hosts equalised just before half-time, however, with a close-range effort from Jack Cook, after a failure by Dale to block the initial cross.

The Dale players began the second half as they did the first, and East made it count, scoring with a deflected shot after a quick break orchestrated by Hayes. However, the lead was short-lived, as all Dale leads seemed to be, with Sean Adarkwa scoring three minutes later. Another cross, another goal.

Hayes remained a threat on the right, but Dale couldn't regain control of the match. Despite further efforts from Gilmour, Hayes and Ian Henderson, Wealdstone stood strong and secured the win in the 95th minute with Cook's late header from a poorly defended free kick.

Head coach Jim McNulty expressed disappointment with the timing and nature of Wealdstone's winning goal.

'It's tough to take with it being such a last-minute winner,' he said. 'Truthfully, today, I think both teams could have scored more goals.

'We could have won the game. We could have been the team to get the third goal before they did. When they do get their goal, it ends the game. It's disappointing, the timing.

'Add to that, Jez [Uchegbulam] was ill. He'd missed a lot of training, so we couldn't start him. We had to work without him, so we changed it round a little bit. [Ryan East] got a goal for us from further forward – he played well.

'Even at 2-2, we tried to win the game. I'm disappointed with all three goals coming from elements of crosses. That's a disappointing factor and I'll have to look back at them. We have to take it on the chin today and move on to the next one.'

* * *

THE HISTORY OF Aldershot Town FC began with the establishment of a military camp in 1854. Football initially served as a pastime for soldiers there, with a football club for officers formally set up by 1863, the same year the Football Association was formed. However, it would take more than 60 years to establish a senior civilian club in the area.

In December 1926, Jack White, a well-travelled sporting journalist, and Llewellyn Griffiths, the town clerk, played pivotal roles in founding Aldershot FC. The club successfully applied for admission to the Southern League and played its matches at the Recreation Ground.

During its early years, many players were associated with the Army Physical Training Corps, and some played for Aldershot during the Second World War.

By 1992, Aldershot FC was a Football League side, but faced financial turmoil and was wound up in the High Court, ceasing all fixtures in mid-season. From this disaster emerged Aldershot Town FC, formed by a committee of fans and local businessmen, with the club relying heavily on the support of passionate fans, sponsorship and advertising. The club's crest featured a phoenix rising from the flames, symbolising its rebirth.

The new club began its non-league journey the same year, starting in the Isthmian Division Three, and quickly climbed the ranks. After finally achieving promotion to the Football League in 2008, the Shots seemed to be a stable addition to League Two until encountering financial difficulties once again in 2013 and, ultimately, suffered relegation back to the fifth tier. Aldershot were, at this point, taken over by a consortium led by former chairman Shahid Azeem, who has, ever since, sought to restore the club to former glories.

Now, with the first team under the management of Tommy Widdrington, who had guided the Shots into the play-off places in the National League table and the second round of the FA Cup at the time of their visit to Spotland, the objective had never looked more likely to be fulfilled.

'I first saw the National League as a player back in 2006 with Salisbury City,' Widdrington said when I caught up with him for a pre-match chat. 'We had come up two divisions very quickly and there was always one outstandingly bigger club than anybody else at this level. I think at the time it may have been Stevenage, but, now, when you look at the makeup of the National League, there are lots of big clubs here – your own club, Rochdale, Oldham Athletic, Chesterfield and so on.

'Therefore, I think the big gap is really between the National League and the National League North and South rather than the National League and League Two. I actually think there are more clubs in the National League suited to League Two than there are in League Two presently. I think the clubs that are going up a level have the stability of base for League Two and even higher.

'First you have to get there, though. In terms of achieving success at Aldershot, I have no philosophy or ideologies. I've got no "ologies" at all, in fact, just a few GCSEs. At the end of the day, it doesn't matter what level you're playing or competing at, you need varying ingredients, but, firstly, the biggest thing required, in my opinion, is a football club that is aligned with the football operation. I've worked at a club where the football operation was way ahead of the football club and then what happened was the elastic snapped because the club couldn't fund the success that the football team was delivering.

'So, straight away, the infrastructure and the backing from everybody involved is vital. There needs to be what I call a collective intention and that intention needs to be realistic. When I joined the club, the team had won just 12 home games in four seasons. That puts pressure on winning away from home just to survive.

'The first thing I said is that we need to get the team winning at home. Never mind anything else, let's just achieve that. I knew we had the fan base and they would get behind us and show us patience if we were sending them home happy more often than not. We've been proven right.

We've had, I think, 16 home games since I've been here and we've lost just one of them. The crowd hasn't dropped below 2,000. It doesn't bring ultimate success but it starts the wheels moving in that direction.

'The other stat I noticed was that the team hadn't won an FA Cup game for five seasons. So, the fact we got through the fourth qualifying round, and then we went to Swindon and did what we did in the first round proper, was incredible and another objective met. Listen, I'm not daft. I know that was a freak result [Aldershot beat the League Two side 7-4], but it was a worthy result. The town really got behind the football club and I believe everyone is now pulling in the same direction, be that the people who come to support the club or the people who put their money into it in the background.

'With that backing I then need to obviously make sure I have the right team to represent the club. I don't quote people very often, but I'll quote [former Arsenal manager] Arsène Wenger here: "There is untouched and immeasurable amounts of talent out there. What that talent needs is a platform." This is what I firmly believe in. The vast majority of my players have been at very high-level academies, but, for whatever reason, they have just not been able to burst through that final ceiling to get into the first team.

'This results in swathes of talented footballers leaving top-level clubs because the standard is so high that not every one of them is going to be able to make a squad of 30. This doesn't make them bad players. Technically, they are superior to so many others. They just need the right person to develop that for them from that point on. They've been with a big club for at least ten years and are suddenly faced with dealing with the disappointment of that familiarity being taken away from them.

'Managers at every level have to win games, so not many will put their faith in a kid at 16, 17 or 18 to play in their first team. But I've realised that my background over the past 15 years has been as much in recruitment as it has been in management. Therefore, my knowledge of the kids who are now hitting 22, 23 years old is strong. I've been following the progress of a lot of these lads and so I know what they are capable of. There's no doubt about them being technically good enough to play in the National League, but can they handle owning a first-team shirt?

'Now what I've got at my club is a lot of lads who are showing me, up to now, that they are owning the shirts, probably for the first time in their career. So, while I've given them the opportunity, I've got to give them praise for handling the fact that I've put my faith in them and they're repaying me. I'm not getting excited because it's not even Christmas yet, but there has definitely been an upturn in form and that is down to the recruitment over the summer. We have the right dynamic of players who are young enough, hungry enough and fit enough to see out 90 minutes.

'I told you I don't have a philosophy, but I do believe football should be entertaining. People come away from our games thinking both teams have had a right good go. We haven't had any 0-0 draws. In fact, we haven't had many nils at all in our scorelines. It seems to be working for us so far, though.'

Widdrington has three talented children – two sons and a daughter. One of his sons, Theo, is on the books at Aldershot. The other, Kai, is a professional dancer and a mainstay on the BBC show *Strictly Come Dancing*.

'Kai was in the Centre of Excellence at Port Vale when I was a player in the first team,' he said. 'He was one of these kids that was like a meerkat. Full of energy that you couldn't get out of him, even with football and karate and all the other things he was doing. You had to put him in the car and drive it to get him to sleep. Our neighbours at the time ran a dance school. They offered to take him for lessons a few nights a week, just to use up his energy. He had to concentrate on numbers and timings and music. It wasn't just running around kicking a football. It worked. He stuck with it from the age of seven to about nine or ten, before we then had to move to the south coast.

'He joined Southampton's academy down there, but kept up the dancing. When he got to about 12 or 13, he had to make a choice between football and dancing. He chose dancing and the reasoning was that he didn't want to be outside in the freezing cold and rain every morning but rather he wanted to be in a nice warm studio, holding on to a woman, where he was the main man and not one of 11. It's certainly proven to be a successful decision for him.

'Kai was the alpha child, if you like, being the first-born, but Theo could have been a dancer too, as he was dragged to many of Kai's classes and joined in. His scores in the tests they did were actually better than Kai's. However, football remained Theo's number one passion and he was at Portsmouth from the age of six to 19. He has played for a number of clubs I've been at, but he has always done so despite being my son rather than because of it.

'If you came to training and you didn't know which player was my son, you would leave the session still not knowing. At work, I'm his boss. He is great at respecting that and the other players would be quick to let me know if it was anything different. He plays for me on merit and merit alone.

'Then there's my daughter, Tia. She's 18 and at university. I think she will end up in sports science. I'm proud of all my children.'

Prior to the Aldershot match, Rochdale supporters were saddened by the news that chair of the Dale Trust, Colin Cavanah, had decided to step down from his second stint in the role after five years. The news was revealed at the trust's AGM, which also explored the fact the National League had refused the club permission to draw down the loan offered by chairman Simon Gauge and director Richard Knight earlier in the season. The reasons given were based on the loan being secured on the club's stadium.

The trust also revealed it had been unsuccessful in its application for a Community Ownership Fund grant that would have enabled it to take ownership of the Spotland pitch. With doors being closed on much-needed revenue streams at seemingly every turn, there was much on the table for further discussion.

On the pitch, Dale secured a somewhat surprising 2-1 victory, thanks to Kairo Mitchell's ninth goal of the season. Aldershot initially took the lead with Jack Barnham's first-half goal, but Jimmy Keohane equalised just before half-time. In the second half, Dale displayed dominance, culminating in Mitchell's 79th-minute goal for a well-deserved win.

Jim McNulty made strategic changes to his starting XI yet again, including Cameron John's return and Jesurun Uchegbulam replacing Ian Henderson. McNulty laid out his side in a 4-2-1-3, with Ryan East, as at Wealdstone, playing furthest forward of the midfielders.

John's return at left-back noticeably helped the team defensively. His natural inclination to cover centrally allowed him to assume a semi-sweeper role.

Cian Hayes, on the right, once again looked to go forward first and foremost, something none of the other wide options had demonstrated on a consistent basis by this stage of the season. Hayes's low centre of gravity was incredibly difficult to defend against and he was almost crawling underneath defenders at times.

However, it was, of course, Aldershot who took the lead when Barham received a low ball in the area before turning to finish into the bottom corner. Keohane quickly levelled when Uchegbulam saw a shot saved by Dutch goalkeeper Jordi van Stappershoef, the rebound from which hit Mitchell, who prevented the ball going out of play before back-heeling it back into the box, where Keohane was on hand to turn home via a deflection.

The second half saw Dale in complete control, with Uchegbulam and East missing chances and showing less inclination to recycle the ball backwards. A clever free kick from Adam Clayton to Mitchell almost added to the lead but Van Stappershoef made a crucial save.

In the final minutes, Dale executed another well-drilled set-piece routine, leading to Mitchell's decisive goal. A corner was played short into substitute Devante Rodney, who laid it back to Clayton. He clipped it to the back post where Mitchell stooped to head home clinically.

Afterwards, McNulty praised his players for their fight and said it was a deserved three points.

'It's been a long week reflecting on a last-minute loss in the last game, which, looking back at, we can't believe we didn't win,' he said. 'We should have been out of sight.

'But it was a deserved victory today. We had total control in the game and were more than value for the win.

'The team always fights. No matter what the circumstances or the feelings. They got the goal back before half-time, which was big, and it was a good goal. It brought us into half-time with a bounce.

'As the first half was growing, we were controlling huge parts of the game, it was just about whether we would be able to break them down. We were confident we would and, to be fair to the team, they kept their patience, and stuck to what they believe in over the course of the 96 minutes.'

* * *

WHILE ROCHDALE'S RELEGATION to the National League had already re-established some old local Football League rivalries, such as those with Halifax and Oldham, it would also bring about the inaugural league meeting against another relatively local side, whose animosity towards Dale seemed based solely on a perceived miscarriage of justice some 40-plus years ago.

As mentioned earlier in this book, Altrincham, historically considered to be one of the most progressive clubs on the non-league scene, missed out on promotion to the Football League in 1980 thanks to the idiosyncratic re-election system that stood in place of direct promotion and relegation. The team finishing bottom that season was Rochdale. The belief of all concerned at Altrincham was that no one in their right mind would vote to keep among their number a side which had finished well adrift, and had well-documented financial woes. As it transpired, they did (missing votes notwithstanding), and Altrincham's bid to become a Football League club would never come to fruition.

It seemed churlish that supporters of Altrincham should still hold Rochdale responsible for the votes of others, but it did add a touch of spice to what was already an historic encounter between the two clubs. In fact, the teams had only ever met competitively twice before, both in the FA Cup (1965 and 1982) and both with Altrincham proving the victors.

Away from historic events, however, the Altrincham of the current era was fully embracing modern football. In 2021, the club installed Phil Parkinson as its first full-time manager, the 40-year-old agreeing to leave his job as a sports science lecturer to take the reins.

Appointed four years prior on a part-time basis, after Altrincham had suffered successive relegations, Parkinson, with his assistant Neil Sorvel, sparked an immediate transformation, winning the Northern Premier League title at the first attempt and then promotion from National League North via the play-offs.

Despite the club's semi-professional status, they quickly established Altrincham in a National League dominated by full-time teams with far bigger budgets.

At the beginning of the season previous to this one, the club announced its move to become full-time professional for the first time in its 130-year history, to match its modern management team.

'As the most successful part-time club ever, we are always striving for success both on and off the pitch,' co-chairman Bill Waterson said at the time. 'We have bold and ambitious plans to grow and shoot for success.

'In Phil Parkinson and Neil Sorvel, we already have great leadership on the pitch. However, what we're asking our players to achieve on a part-time basis is becoming more and more challenging. With access to a high-level training facility from next season, we feel that now is the time for full-time football and this is a massive step in the right direction, not just for the club but also for our community as a whole.'

Parkinson had guided Altrincham into the play-off positions as his side visited Spotland on a cold November Tuesday night, but it was to be Rochdale who won through, securing a second win on the bounce and turning in a best defensive display of the campaign to date.

Ryan East scored a double, and Kairo Mitchell notched his tenth goal of the season, leading Dale to a dominant 3-0 victory.

Jim McNulty stuck with the same line-up from the previous win over Aldershot and Dale started the match brightly, with Cian Hayes and Jimmy Keohane, who had been named October Player of the Month, pushing forward and testing goalkeeper Ethan Ross.

On 15 minutes, Dale finally broke the deadlock through East. Harvey Gilmour initially won back the ball in midfield and Hayes reacted quickly to carry it forward. East then expertly slotted home from just outside the area, showcasing his confidence, once again, in playing further forward.

Despite the Altrincham players showing their own quality, with those such as former Dale man Alex Newby and Chris Conn-Clarke finding good areas, they were constantly denied by Louie Moulden. Moulden really earned his stripes after Ethan Ebanks-Landell was adjudged to have brought down Gerald Sithole in the area. Moulden made a superb save to his left from Conn-Clarke's resulting penalty, and the rebound was dragged wide.

After the break, Dale secured the crucial second goal through East again, who scored his fourth in four games by latching on to Cameron John's fine cutback from the left after a sustained build-up involving 23 passes. The attack persisted, and, shortly after Hayes had had a testing effort saved by the Altrincham goalkeeper, Dale extended the lead. Mitchell expertly brought down a curling ball into the area from Ian Henderson and, with his back to goal, managed to spin and score with a left-footed effort.

Despite one final opportunity for the visitors, with full-back Eddy Jones's low drive being saved by Moulden, the Dale goalkeeper earned a well-deserved clean sheet.

McNulty described his side's performance as ruthless.

'It's a good win against a good team, who are making serious moves in this league,' he said. 'For how good Altrincham were tonight, and have been this season, I thought that we did a great job at nullifying them down to having very few moments. It was a pretty ruthless performance from us.

'The clean sheet is a big bonus. Big credit to Louie Moulden tonight for saving a penalty for us at a crucial moment in the game. These things define games. They change games. You saw the way that the boys celebrated that save, that was really big. Ultimately, that gave us the strength to go on.

'Up until that point, I thought that we were playing amazing, certainly up until 1-0. We were great to watch.'

McNulty was also full of praise for Kairo Mitchell, who had now scored eight goals in his last 12 games alone.

'I'm really pleased for Kairo to get his ten goals for the campaign because, again, despite the fact that I love what he does for the team overall, I know how much goals mean to strikers. I know how that makes them feel. It's great to hear the fans singing his name. He deserves it. Ten goals right now at this stage in the season is certainly something to be proud of.'

* * *

DAGENHAM & REDBRIDGE are best known for their non-league exploits, yet Rochdale had become acquainted with them during their dalliances in the lower reaches of the Football League between 2007 and 2014, meeting 12 times in that period.

Formed in 1992 through the merger of two clubs, Dagenham FC and Redbridge Forest FC, the Daggers' most notable achievement came in the 2006/07 season when they secured promotion to the Football League by winning the fifth-tier title.

As the Rochdale wagon train rolled into the Chigwell Construction Stadium for the first National League meeting between the two, Dagenham were sitting 13th in the table, four places and five points behind the visitors.

Managed by former player and lower-division and non-league journeyman striker Ben Strevens, the Greater London side had won four of the last six games and were finding some kind of rhythm of form.

However, it was Dale who secured a third consecutive victory with a 2-1 triumph. Cian Hayes delivered a truly spectacular goal, complemented by an Ian Henderson classic chip, which even a late goal from the hosts could not take the shine off.

Jim McNulty made one change to the starting XI, bringing in Henderson for Kairo Mitchell, who had picked up an injury in training. Tyrese Sinclair returned to the matchday squad after a five-week injury absence.

Although Dale initially struggled to create clear-cut opportunities, the players turned the tide midway through the first half. Ryan East had a shot blocked and, on the half-hour mark, Hayes scored a sublime goal with a left-footed dipping effort from 25 yards after cutting in from the right.

Dale continued to press, with Henderson and Hayes having further chances before the break. In the second half, Dale doubled the lead as Henderson capitalised on a defensive mistake, surged forward and lifted the ball over the advancing goalkeeper.

However, the hosts pulled a goal back after the game entered the final ten minutes. George Nevett's attempted clearance hit Frank Vincent and fortuitously fell for him to slot home from close range. It wasn't enough, though, and Dale finished November in eighth position.

'We were outstanding,' McNulty said afterwards. 'I feel like we were maybe lower, in terms of productivity and pure chances, but we controlled the game so much today.

'We were always able to expose what they were willing to give us. In the moments when there was space to find through them, behind them, round them, we always did.

'The players were excellent with their execution. Everything relies on execution and confidence, so it fully is down to the players. They were in their groove today and I feel like 2-1 really flattered Dagenham.

'They're a really high-intensity pressing team, they want to take the ball off you. We faced a lot of challenges very close to our own goal today, but, with pure belief and great execution, we made a really challenging fixture look really routine.'

Any buoyancy the supporters were feeling after the Dagenham victory, however, was deflated two days later when sports journalist Pete O'Rourke announced via social media that Rochdale had 'failed to pay their players and staff their full wages for November. Players and staff have only been paid 25 per cent of their wages.'

A recent update from the Dale Trust regarding a meeting it held with the Rochdale board did suggest a route to external investment was progressing, but the statement alleged by O'Rourke indicated it was at a rate not nearly quick enough.

The listing of a new company at Companies House, JNG Capital Group Limited, only added fuel to the fire, as its directors had registered its address as Spotland Stadium.

The members of the Rochdale board, for now, remained tight-lipped.

National League table as at 30 November 2023

	P	*W*	*D*	*L*	*F*	*A*	*Pts*
Chesterfield	21	17	2	2	53	28	53
Bromley	22	12	6	4	36	23	42
Barnet	22	13	3	6	43	35	42
Solihull Moors	22	10	7	5	32	30	37
Gateshead	21	10	6	5	47	27	36
Aldershot Town	22	11	3	8	38	36	36
Altrincham	21	9	8	4	40	29	35
Rochdale	**22**	**9**	**6**	**7**	**40**	**34**	**33**
FC Halifax Town	22	8	8	6	24	21	32
Oldham Athletic	22	7	9	6	33	33	30
Eastleigh	22	8	6	8	34	37	30
Hartlepool United	22	8	3	11	36	42	27
Wealdstone	21	7	5	9	26	30	26
Southend United*	21	10	5	6	37	22	25
Dagenham & Redbridge	22	7	4	11	24	29	25
Dorking Wanderers	21	7	4	10	26	37	25
Boreham Wood	22	5	9	8	27	32	24
Maidenhead United	22	5	9	8	23	32	24
York City	22	5	8	9	31	41	23
Woking	22	6	4	12	24	30	22
Ebbsfleet United	22	6	4	12	30	42	22
Oxford City	22	5	6	11	33	42	21
AFC Fylde	22	4	6	12	33	44	18
Kidderminster Harriers	22	3	7	12	15	29	16

* Southend deducted ten points for failing to pay an existing tax bill.

December 2023

SOUTH-EAST LONDON CLUB Bromley was managed by the vivacious Andy Woodman, a former Crystal Palace academy goalkeeper who had spent most of his career enduring the peripatetic lifestyle of a journeyman footballer around the lower leagues.

Upon meeting him ahead of Rochdale's away fixture there, he revealed to me that a well-known friend he made as a scholarly footballer not only illustrated the contrasting fortunes presented by the game, but how that contrast also shaped his own desire and philosophy to succeed.

'I started off at Crystal Palace as a young schoolboy goalkeeper and then became an apprentice, as it was known then,' he said. 'That's when me and Gareth Southgate became good friends. You may have heard of him. We were like all young players who held aspirations and dreams of going on to bigger and better things. Gareth went on and did the bigger and better things, and I became a bit of a journeyman footballer, probably like 90 per cent of all footballers.

'I made my way around the various leagues as a player and then, at the end of my career, I got offered a coaching position at West Ham United under Alan Pardew. From there, I kind of followed him around – to Charlton, to Newcastle, to Crystal Palace.

'As a first-team coach, I amassed 16 years at various Premiership clubs before I found myself at Arsenal, as head of goalkeeping. I had a lovely first year there working with Arsène Wenger. He was a great, great coach. He stepped down, but I stayed on for another five years. I worked with some other really big names there, you know, Freddie Ljungberg, Steve Bould. It was a good gig, but then the opportunity came up at Bromley to become manager. I felt I was at a stage in my life where it was now or never.

'I'd worked with some big-name managers over the course of my career. I'd worked with some good ones, some bad ones and some indifferent ones. I just felt I had enough about me to do it. I felt I knew the score – what works, what doesn't. I know what players want. I know how players want to be treated.

'The game hasn't changed. Football's still football. But I think the way people are treated and the way that players react to you and respond to you has definitely changed. It's hard for me to talk myself up, but I do think I have the right personality for it, where I feel I can get the best out of players, and I believe I've proven that in my three years at Bromley. We've won a bit of silverware [the FA Trophy in 2022] and got to the play-offs twice, the highest-ever position the club has managed – and with probably one of the lower budgets in the league.'

Bromley finished seventh the previous campaign, enough to earn a play-off spot, where they subsequently fell to Chesterfield after seeing off Woking.

'I'm very lucky,' Woodman said. 'When I got offered the job by the chairman, I said I'd only take it if he was going to do things properly and professionally. In fairness to him, he has backed me in all my ideas. I wanted to make sure we had GPS, so we could track how hard the players work.

I wanted them to be treated like professional footballers. I wanted to make sure we had an auditorium, so we could do meetings properly. These were the changes that needed to be made. It was a non-league club when I came in and it was being run like a non-league club.

'All I've done is apply my 35 years of experience to how I believe a football club should be run and how people should be treated. I've gone from having no office, to a portacabin, to a nice office within the stadium, and all with good people around me, all heading in the same direction.

'Even with all that, I think the National League is the hardest level for a novice manager to start at. I would've loved to have started out in League One or League Two, with a bigger budget, to show people what I could really do, but you've got to be realistic with the opportunities that come up.

'I'm not one bit disappointed to be starting my managerial career at Bromley, because I've cut my teeth by being involved in every decision taken from top to bottom. I don't think there's a manager anywhere up and down the country that wouldn't want a little bit more on their budget. I'm no different from anyone else. But we really have to cut a cloak according to the material we have. I'm on top of that. All those people in the game I've worked with, they will ring me up and offer to help me out with players. I think that's been a real strength of mine. We get the best out of what we have.

'It might sound funny, but I run this club as if it was Arsenal. The players come in, they have breakfast, they do their activation session, then we have a meeting before training about what we're going to do heading into the next game. We then train, we have lunch, then we go out and do an afternoon session. That is pretty much the format I've worked off to make sure that we leave no stone unturned right across the board. The players who think that's too much? Well, they drift away. Players who buy into it will only improve themselves and get better, because that's what top players do. Top players work hard and anyone who thinks that players in the Premiership are lucky are delusional. They're there because they work hard.'

Bromley are typical of many clubs at non-league level in having an artificial playing surface at their home stadium. However, Woodman believed the advantages outweighed the negatives.

'The plastic pitch comes up a lot in conversation,' he said. 'First of all, it's of immediate benefit to the club. You can hire out the pitch all day, every day. We get people playing on it all the time, people doing training sessions. It creates revenue for the football club. On top of that, you get revenue from people then using your facilities – the bars, the restaurant.

'From a playing point of view, it was a problem at first, because the team I had didn't know how to play the pitch and that was something that we really worked on. You've got to make it an advantage. We worked on that and we got a system and style of football that helped us rather than hindered us. When the big guns come to town, we have ways of playing the pitch which are only going to help us and not them. It's a real tactical advantage in those bigger games.

'The other advantage is that we have no games called off. Postponements can be very expensive for clubs, especially at this level, so to negate that with the pitch is crucial. At the end of the day, we've a facility that doesn't need a groundsman, so we never miss a day's training either. We never have to water a dry pitch and we're never left with a muddy pitch. That's another cost saving. At Arsenal, they can afford a whole team of groundsmen. At your Rochdales and Bromleys, you're only going to be able to afford one man, two at the most, so the grass pitches are going to be a lot of work.

'The pitch is just another part of the overall preparation. It's the small margins that are going to make us a little bit better than everyone else. It's the one per cent here and the one per cent there. If you make the most of those, they all add up and, before you know it, you're ten per cent ahead of the opposition before a ball has been kicked. That's what I've modelled my career on as a player and now my managerial style too.'

Being best friends with the current England manager, Woodman must surely find it tempting to pick his brains from time to time?

'Yes,' he laughed. 'We have the same moans about football. He'll moan about issues in his squad, and then I'll be moaning about some issues in my squad. Basically, we're moaning about the same sort of thing but at different levels. Equally, we'll praise our players on certain things, too. It's the same principle for managers at all levels. It's just a different quality of player we're talking about.

'We still speak all the time. He'll be the first to phone me up and congratulate me on a win, for example. We usually catch up on a Monday night. That seems to be the time when we're both free. He's a great friend to have and has been a big help to me.'

Unfortunately, there was no Gareth Southgate on hand for Jim McNulty, as his charges looked to better the 2-2 draw they managed against Bromley at Spotland earlier in the season. A further hindrance was that they sought to do so without the magnificent Cian Hayes, who had been recalled from his loan by parent club Fleetwood Town.

It proved a crucial absence, as, regrettably, Dale's three-match winning streak was halted via a 1-0 defeat in the capital.

The visitors lined up in a 4-2-1-3 formation, with Ian Henderson moving out to the right to fill the gap left by Hayes, and Devante Rodney coming back into the team as centre-forward.

Despite controlling the first half, McNulty's men struggled to create chances. As usual, they displayed excellent ball retention and moved into the final third well, but with an ultimate aversion to the penalty area once there. For all the first-half domination it was yet another cross into the box that should have seen Bromley one up by half-time. Louie Moulden's save from Deji Elerewe's bullet header was held well.

The game opened up in the second half, with Dale coming close to scoring on several occasions. The players got down the flanks more often, at a tempo that was more threatening. However, the visitors failed to press this advantage and Woodman made changes that freshened up Bromley's own approach, going more direct.

This ultimately led to Olufela Olomola's fine strike in the 80th minute, which secured the win, after Harvey Gilmour opted not to clear his lines as the pressure built.

'I thought the minimum we were good for was a point,' said McNulty afterwards. 'I think, overall, it was a good performance, and Bromley were clinical. They had two moments in the game, and they took one of them.

'We dominated a lot of the game and, at half-time, I believed if we kept doing what we were doing, we would create chances. We had our moments, we just didn't score. If we play that game again, with those exact chances, I think we win the game with a cushion.

'It's football. I said to the team, I don't want them to be too down. If I look at it from purely a performance perspective, it was good. We were much better than Bromley, in my opinion, on the day. They hung in there and I thought the goal was coming.'

The head coach also confirmed that Kairo Mitchell would be missing for up to two months with an ankle problem.

'His situation is worse than we thought, after having the scan. It's testament to his bravery because he was trying to push himself for the last game. He's got some serious ankle ligament damage and we're probably going to lose him for eight weeks. It's a loss because he was in great form.'

* * *

A STATEMENT PUT out by the Rochdale AFC board of directors on 4 December indicated that the previously anticipated takeover of the club, described as 'imminent' by online sports journalist Pete O'Rourke at the end of November, had been abandoned. The announcement followed several days of intense speculation, triggered by a company, JNG Capital Group Limited, and three of its directors, registering its address as Spotland Stadium.

The club statement seemed to attribute the company's U-turn to fan speculation and scrutiny on social media.

'We recognise that supporters want what is best for the club and that this, at times, will result in speculation on potential investment,' it said. 'However, it should be acknowledged that a small percentage of this online speculation has made concluding investment deals more challenging.'

In response, the Dale Trust issued its own statement, shedding further light on the situation. It clarified that it had met these potential investors, which included intermediary Nick Brayne, former professional footballer Guy Branston, and a former lower-league chairman and club director, whose identity remained undisclosed.

The trust said this consortium had planned to join the club's board, offering to purchase unsold shares and those acquired by current directors from Morton House. Gary Strong, a finance broker not present at the meeting, also planned to join, with funding assured from an unnamed third party, and no financial burden on the club or its stakeholders. The group's strategy centred on potential promotion back to the EFL, with increased revenue enabling stability and a potential sale at a profit upon achieving League One status.

However, when the group registered itself as JNG Capital Group with Companies House, a certain James Lawrance was also listed as a director. The trust said Lawrance had not been discussed as a potential board member during its meeting with the group.

'The sudden incorporation of JNG Capital Group on 28 November took everyone by surprise, and scrutiny of its directors on social media led to the withdrawal of Lawrance and Strong from the deal by the weekend's end,' the trust confirmed.

More worryingly, it appeared that the club's need for investment had reached a desperate stage.

'As of today, the club remains in talks with numerous parties over minority and majority investment,' a club statement said. 'However, none of these talks are now at an advanced stage, and we are very much open to engaging with any interested party.'

The statement also revealed that chairman Simon Gauge and his family had generously provided funds to stabilise the club's finances while an investment partner continued to be sought.

'In order to assist with this process, some changes to the board of directors are expected to be announced in the coming days,' it added.

* * *

WHILE THE FA Trophy is not the most storied competition in English football, it does provide clubs who would never otherwise get a sniff of a Wembley appearance a realistic chance to play on the stadium's hallowed turf.

Much like the EFL Trophy, which provides the same opportunity for the two divisions above the National League, there are those who turn their nose up at the competition, especially those who may be embroiled in decisive factors at either end of the table and thus view it as an unwelcome distraction.

The FA Trophy was created in 1969 for non-league clubs that paid their players and couldn't enter the FA Amateur Cup. Since 2008, it has been open to clubs in tiers five to eight of English football, with FC Halifax Town holding the prize as of the start of the 2023/24 competition.

Much like the big guns do in the FA Cup, National League teams enter the Trophy at the third-round stage, and Rochdale's debut encounter here was to be a home tie against Gateshead, the two already having crossed swords at Spotland in the league, playing out a 2-2 draw.

The Tyneside club certainly had pedigree in the competition, having reached the final the season previous, and made it count here, seeing off Dale 5-1 on a wet Tuesday night after the game had been postponed the previous Saturday due to a waterlogged pitch.

McNulty had toyed with his first-team selection for this tie, hinting that he saw the forthcoming league game against York as the more pressing priority, but the manner of the defeat was still difficult to excuse.

Goalkeeper Brad Kelly made his professional debut for Dale in one of four changes from the Bromley game, with Max Taylor, Tyrese Sinclair and Kwaku Oduroh also coming into the first XI. There were debuts for scholars Luke Mann and Isaac Burgess from the bench too.

'Unfortunately, Devante Rodney has pulled his hamstring in training,' McNulty revealed of the striker's absence from the team sheet. 'It's a blow and a shame for Dev, having just got back. It's a shame for the team too, because it leaves us incredibly light now with Ian Henderson as our only striker at the club who is fit.'

And it was Henderson, captaining the team, who came close to scoring early on with a header that hit the crossbar. Adam Clayton's 25-yard strike was then saved by Harrison Bond, but it was Gateshead who were given a gilt-edged chance to take the lead from the penalty spot. Connor McBride blazed the ball over the bar, however.

McBride later redeemed himself with a goal at the end of the first half and Gateshead extended the lead in the second half with goals from Billy Chadwick and Callum Whelan. Although Dale's Sinclair pulled one back from the penalty spot, two late goals from Gateshead's Marcus Dinanga made the final score a poor read.

Despite a commendable work rate from the players, shaped in a 4-3-3, there were few positive aspects to take from the tie. They struggled without a direct tempo, often resorting to a predictable playing style. The absence of Hayes, who was effective in carrying the ball forward, was evident, as was Uchegbulam's reluctance to do the same.

Defensive vulnerabilities, particularly in the channels, were exposed. Standout performers included George Nevett, showing continual improvement on the ball, and Henderson, who remained an asset to the club, but the need for a more dynamic approach, irrespective of the personnel on the field, was painfully highlighted here.

'We just don't have the squad to compete in more than one competition,' McNulty conceded afterwards. 'Our squad is so small that I couldn't even protect all of the players I wanted to tonight. I had to expose some players that I didn't want to expose and I am relieved we got through the game with no more injuries.

'Gateshead have players all over the pitch that can hurt you and they have them in their squad too. When they make a change, it's seamless. We're not there yet and that showed tonight.

'I knew at the start of the season that we wouldn't progress too far in the cups. That's what I accepted with the budget and squad we have. I need to make sure the squad is ready for the league game against York now, as I see it as a winnable game.'

* * *

A CLUB STATEMENT on 13 December announced that Jamie Sarsfield had stepped down from the board of directors after two and a half years of service.

Much of Sarsfield's time with Rochdale, following his appointment in the summer of 2021, had been spent assisting the academy and creating business leads.

I caught up with Sarsfield – born and bred in Rochdale – to find out just how gruelling things had become behind the scenes, as his hometown club continually searched for investment.

'I know the statement that the club put out said I was stepping down to focus on my business interests, but that is only partly true,' he said. 'It's true that I sold my first business, which generated more than enough money for me to comfortably retire, but I had also set up an IT business for the care sector seven years ago that is now really taking off both here and overseas, so it does require a lot of my time.

'However, that is only part of the reason I have decided to step down. The other part is that I no longer agreed with certain others on the best way forward for the club.

'Of the current board members – Simon Gauge, Tony Pockney, Richard Knight, Guy Courtney, Jan Wormald and Murray Knight – I am the only one who actually solely owns a business. I like to think that is the expertise I brought to the table. I don't believe in sitting at that table and not contributing, which I felt, at times, I was. I visited other football clubs off my own back to learn how they do the commercial side of things. It was me who did the deal with brewery JW Lees, which put a significant amount of money into the club. It was me who did the O'Neill's kit deal, which involved them kitting out the whole club shop. It was me who recognised our insurance on the stadium would not even rebuild one stand if it burned down. I had great relationships with many of our existing suppliers too, and built great relationships with many others, in the way a business person should conduct themselves.

'Each director, who has paid for the opportunity to sit at that boardroom table and give their time to the football club for free, should save an expense elsewhere with their expertise. Jan, for example, works in HR. He saves the club money in that regard as he handles HR for the club. Guy, for example, saves the club money with his IT and media expertise. That's how it should work.

'I guess, in the end, I felt my opinion, based on my own expertise, was no longer carrying weight, especially with regard to potential investors. In my own business, I've always made the decisions I believe are right. I wasn't the sole decision-maker at the football club, and I am not one to go along with decisions I don't agree with, so I decided to step down.'

Jamie joined the board in 2021, along with Gauge and Richard Knight.

'I paid my £25,000 for my seat at the table as I wanted to help the club out in what was a transitional period,' he said. 'Pretty soon afterwards, it felt like we had all been thrown under a bus with the Morton House shenanigans. I was like, "What? A court case?" It cost all of us board members a further £77,000 each to get those shares back from them. That is money that we are all facing having to write off with the club's current predicament. It's a lot of money to lose – money that should go to our children.

'The most important thing is the future of the football club, though. I truly hope that is resolved for the best and I will continue to do what I can, even though I am no longer a board member.'

* * *

ROCHDALE HAD ENJOYED an August bank holiday win at York City in the pair's first National League encounter and now it was the turn of the Minstermen to visit Spotland.

That victory for Dale in the opening month of the season had cost then York manager Michael Morton his job. Now the team from the other side of the Pennines was managed by the much more experienced Neal Ardley who had, in recent seasons, transformed Solihull Moors into serious promotion candidates.

While Ardley hadn't quite sparked a similar revolution in the cathedral city, he had managed to arrest a serious slump and York was now a more formidable opponent than previously.

Rochdale's own woes were painfully evident. Jim McNulty, as he was forced to do in the midweek annihilation by Gateshead, named scholars Luke Mann and Isaac Burgess as part of his matchday squad. Ian Henderson remained the only recognisable striker among the 16 players on the team sheet.

As to the match itself, Louie Moulden made an early save, tipping over Olly Dyson's volley, but the home side went on to dominate possession thereafter. Despite this, Dale faced challenges in finding the final ball. Adam Clayton then suffered a knee injury, further adding to McNulty's anguish, and he was replaced by Kwaku Oduroh, leading to positional changes, with Jimmy Keohane moving to left-back and Cameron John stepping into the midfield.

Throughout the game, Dale continued to hold control, and Tyrese Sinclair had several attempts to open the scoring before Ian Henderson's chipped finish was ruled offside. Lennell John-Lewis's header was saved brilliantly in the final moments by Moulden to deny York what would have been an undeserved winner.

With the Dale squad depleted, and then having to adjust to a tactical reshuffle brought about by Clayton's injury, the goalless draw was a terrific effort, especially as there was so little on offer from the bench. The players retained the ball well and at least tried to play at a better tempo than the previous game, with Uchegbulam driving down his wing much more.

However, the lack of cutting edge up front, mainly due to the sole reliance on a club legend who should have been enjoying his twilight years, was a cause for concern.

'I thought we were very dominant in the game,' said McNulty afterwards. 'We controlled both halves. The players' fight in the performance? I can't ask for any more, especially with the situation they're in.

'Reflecting on it, York maybe thought it was going to be a difficult challenge to win it off us in our own half and that it would be dangerous for them to do so, leaving space in behind.

'They gave up the ball in that regard and we played almost the whole game in their half. When a team plays a real low block like that, you need your fans on side, because there has to be an understanding that the opposition's whole team is behind the ball. In games like that, it's very important not to get countered and sucker-punched. I thought we were unfortunate with the moments that we created in the first half, where we could have scored.

'The game really opened up in the second half and we had loads of chances – 15 shots. We were just unfortunate that none of the chances went in.'

* * *

ROCHDALE'S TRIP OVER the Pennines to FC Halifax Town, in an attempt to avenge the poor 1-0 reverse earlier in season, led to an entertaining 2-2 pre-Christmas draw.

Jim McNulty's side was buoyed by two early presents ahead of the fixture, with midfielder Ryan East's loan from Bradford becoming a permanent deal until 2024, and left-back Finlay Armstrong joining on a month-long loan from Fleetwood Town. The 20-year-old, a product of Burnley's youth academy, went straight into the starting line-up for the visit to The Shay, with Cameron John starting in midfield in place of the injured Adam Clayton, who was facing up to ten weeks on the sidelines.

Dale started brightly in poor conditions and grabbed the opening goal. Jimmy Keohane initiated the play by breaking into the area and passing to Jesurun Uchegbulam, who delivered a cross to the back post. Tyrese Sinclair, under pressure from two defenders, managed to nod the ball on, which fell to Ian Henderson, who scored his 144th goal for Dale.

The hosts responded strongly, forcing Louie Moulden into action with a couple of close-range headers, but he couldn't prevent Aaron Cosgrave from equalising as he converted a low cross from six yards, despite there being more than a whiff of offside about the finish. The Shaymen then took the lead when Moulden was judged to have fouled Max Wright in the area, and Jamie Stott successfully converted the penalty, completing the turnaround just before half-time.

The second period saw a few half-chances for both teams, but Dale managed to level midway through. Keohane disrupted the hosts' attempts to build from the back, stole the ball and drove into the area, eluding the defence before finishing with his left foot.

Dale then had a significant chance to take the lead when Harvey Gilmour, facing his former club, delivered a precise through ball to Uchegbulam, who crossed to Henderson. Although Henderson controlled the ball well, his shot hit the upright.

In added time, Moulden made a crucial save on the goal line after a low cross threatened to find the net, securing Dale a valuable point against the Yorkshire rivals.

'I thought it was an amazing game – very, very entertaining,' said McNulty afterwards.

'Both teams gave it a go using the different ways that they play. I've got massive respect for them and I think they have for us. It's a result that is difficult to take, though, based on what I've seen from the officials. Commenting on officials is something I try to avoid, but the first goal was one of the most difficult I've watched. He's not half a yard or a yard offside, he's six metres offside.

'It changed the flow of the game and, before I knew it, we were 2-1 down. There was an amazing travelling support which lifted us, but I have to commend the players, driven on by the fans, for finding the strength to come back.

'We lost bravery when we went 1-0 up and allowed Halifax back into the game. The players were wronged by a decision and lost courage and clarity, and I didn't like us at that stage in the game. We reset, found courage and took a point out of the game.'

* * *

AFC FYLDE, CHAIRED by businessman David Haythornthwaite, whose Tangerine Holdings veterinary science empire helped to fund the club, would provide Dale's festive double-header. With just 45 miles separating the two clubs, a home game on Boxing Day and a trip to Mill Farm on New Year's Day was a pleasant quirk of the National League fixture compilers, who sought locality for teams over the holiday period.

Having won National League North the season previous under the stewardship of manager Adam Murray, Fylde had started the 2023/24 National League campaign in poor fashion and it had cost Murray his job. It therefore had fallen to former Dale player, and caretaker and assistant manager, Chris Beech, to steady the ship.

Another chairman with lofty ambitions of reaching the EFL, Haythornthwaite's own association with Fylde started in 2007, when the club was still called Kirkham and Wesham and in the fourth tier of non-league. In 2008, the club changed its name to AFC Fylde, partly to better represent the Fylde coast area of Lancashire and to reflect its ambition to become a prominent football club in the region.

Infused with boundless ambition, Haythornthwaite's investment and strategic sponsorships led this remarkable transformation, solidifying his pivotal role in shaping the club's future as it ascended the leagues, with notable projects such as the Mill Farm facility unfurled along the way.

'Ever since I was six years old, I've been a Blackpool fan,' he told me when I asked how he first got involved in football. 'You will know the club was taken over by the Oystons in the 1980s and I think we can all agree that it ultimately didn't work out too well by the end. I tried to buy the club twice during the period of their ownership, but I was knocked back both times.

'In 2007, a friend of mine, Dai Davies, said that I would never own Blackpool, so suggested I thought about helping a team he was involved with called Kirkham and Wesham. I agreed on the condition that things would be done properly and that me and he would have total control.

'I remember the first committee meeting. We were there until 11pm with folk still arguing about who should have taken the corner flags to the previous match. The next meeting consisted of just me and Dai, and that's the way it has been ever since.

'I then set out a 15-year plan to get the club into the Football League by 2022 and, for a long time, we were on course for it. We were one game from getting there, but lost the National League play-off final to Salford City in 2019. A massive 90 minutes.

'A lot happened in the years leading up to that. We won the FA Vase [in 2008] and the FA Trophy [in 2019]. We are the only team in history to achieve that. All we're missing is the FA Cup. Dave Whelan did it with Wigan, so why not? With that said, I would swap those two Wembley victories for the one we lost against Salford.

'I saw the club's journey to the Football League as something that would run parallel to my own business. I was very confident in the way my business was growing and I knew it could finance the club. The two are intrinsically linked. Without the business, there is no club. I put about £1.5m into the club each year from my own pocket.

'The first thing I had to get my head around when I got to Kirkham and Wesham was a little thing called ground grading. In any particular league, you will have a set of officials who go around and look at your ground and decide if it's worthy to be in that division. There will be a set of rules that you have to comply with. Bizarrely, you could have a pitch that slopes yards from one end to the other and is unplayable, but, if you have got two ladies' toilets and two gents' toilets, you qualify. It was that kind of thing. Ludicrous stuff really.

'We were in the West Lancs League at the time, which is a decent standard, but to compete in the first natural rung of the football pyramid, if you like, we needed to be in the North West Counties Second Division. To do this, we needed floodlights. This is because, at that level, you play cup games midweek and at night. It may seem a minor thing, but it's a massive, massive thing to get floodlights. It costs substantial money.

'We played on a council pitch on Coronation Road, which effectively meant you had to go and pick all the dog shit off it on a Saturday morning to make it reasonable to play on. The local council was not interested at all in supporting Dai. I wanted to help him build this team, so I went and found some farmland behind a pub in Walton that was available for lease, which we could develop to a degree. We moved the team there. The funny thing was, you had to go through the pub car park to get to the ground. I'm glad the landlord never changed his mind about allowing us access, as that was the only way in, so we'd have been knackered if he did.

'That first year, we finished second in the North West Counties Second Division and won the FA Vase. It was brilliant. But one thing happened before the Wembley appearance which got me thinking. We had a shop in Kirkham where we sold tickets. We were going to Wembley for the first time and I was looking down a list of people who had bought a ticket. There was a chap I knew who loved football but wasn't on there. I called him up and asked if he was coming to Wembley. He said, "If you think I'm going to Wembley to support a team from Kirkham, you've another thing coming." He was from a village called Freckleton. It was then I realised just how parochial the Fylde area was. If I was to build this team, it needed to represent the whole area, not just two villages. That is how AFC Fylde was born.

'And so, we went up to the North West Counties First Division and I had to build some temporary stands, but, as our success continued, I knew we would have to move to a more permanent home with better facilities. In 2013, six or seven years in, I started looking for a site and found Mill Farm, which we have developed into the state-of-the-art facility it is today.

'We have grown the club from having no fans to around 1,200. I know other clubs' fans take the piss out of us for it. We'd obviously like to have more, but we have at least created a community. It is very hard in England to start a club and build a fanbase. In America, it's easy. I have an office in Atlanta. Atlanta set up a "soccer" team and had 10,000 season ticket holders right away. The reason? There is no competition for miles and miles. Here in Fylde, there are around 60 football clubs in a 100-mile radius, most of them big, successful ones, too.

'But I enjoy what I do. Nobody ever really buys a football club to make a return on investment. Sure, at the very, very top there is an opportunity to do that, but, for everyone else? No. I do this solely because it's my passion. I'm just like any other fan in that regard. You do, obviously, need a very understanding wife, and I'm lucky to have one. Another chairman I knew ended up in hospital. He gave power of attorney to his accountant and wife, so the cheques could still be signed. When the wife found out how much he was putting into the football club each month, she hit the roof! She went down to the hospital and almost finished him off.

'It can be soul-destroying at times. Just like any fan, you can think, "I'm not watching this shit any more." But then you're back the next Saturday because you're optimistic it will be better. It's like golf. You play a bad hole and you feel crap, but you don't walk off the course. You play the next hole because it might be better.

'I started this journey and it's a driving ambition for me to see it through. I still wouldn't claim to be a football expert. I mean, I know football, but there are too many people in the game that claim to be experts. It's a funny industry like that. Usually, the people claiming this are only interested in lining their own pockets. You do meet nice people along the way, but there are a lot of not so nice people in football too.

'One of the benefits of having a small fanbase is that the flack I get is equally small. People just tend to be grateful I'm putting the money in. I do read the message boards and social media – anyone who says they don't is lying. I know I have made some bad decisions. Manager Dave Challinor, now doing so well at Stockport County, was my worst. He was with us for eight years and I sacked him after a run of bad results. Not only was that rash, it damaged our relationship and he doesn't speak to me now. I regret that. If Dave had stayed with us, we would be a Football League club now, I know it. I then appointed Jim Bentley. He didn't work out. I appointed James Rowe, with all his controversy. Another bad decision. Adam Murray got us out of the National League North, which was fantastic, but was out of his depth at National League level. We almost got promoted out of this division last time we were here, now we are bottom of the league. That's how much this league has moved on in terms of standards.

'That's why I've now opted for the director of football route. I believe splitting that role and the coaching – as your Brentfords and Brightons do – is the best way forward. It's too much to put on one person and I am looking to implement this as we speak.'

The Rochdale marketing bods had elected to make the entry fee for the Boxing Day home leg of this festive double-header a mere £1. As a result, a crowd of just under 4,500 people descended on Spotland to see what Jim McNulty's depleted squad could muster against the National League's second-bottom side.

What they witnessed was a tired, but gritty and resolute, 2-0 victory for the home team, which left McNulty's men just a point outside the play-offs to see out 2023.

Ian Henderson marked his 200th goal in English football with a first-half strike, and Kwaku Oduroh secured the win with his maiden professional goal in the latter part of the second half.

McNulty maintained an unchanged line-up from the previous Saturday's draw at FC Halifax Town, with newcomer Finlay Armstrong making his home debut. Despite controlling possession in the first half, Dale created only a few half-chances.

The deadlock was finally broken just before half-time, however, when Louie Moulden's exceptional long pass found Henderson, who skilfully lifted the ball over the visitors' oncoming goalkeeper, Theo Richardson.

In the second half, Fylde had the better chances, with former Dale loanee Max Conway and Josh Kay missing opportunities, Moulden making the crucial saves, including two one-on-one stops.

With one last throw of the dice, Richardson joined an attack from a corner late in the game. Moulden claimed the delivery and quickly distributed the ball to Oduroh on the halfway line. Taking advantage of the absent goalkeeper, Oduroh skilfully navigated the final defender and calmly rolled the ball into the net from 25 yards, securing three points and igniting joyous celebrations for Dale.

It was a solid win for a team light on numbers and out on its feet. Cameron John, once again, excelled covering in defensive midfield, and combined well with the tireless Harvey Gilmour, giving the more advanced players the assurance that any mistakes would be mopped up behind them. This allowed Ryan East to play closer to Henderson up front. Under the radar, George Nevett probably had his best game from a defensive perspective, with excellent positioning allowing him to cut out numerous crosses.

'It was a good win, in difficult circumstances,' said McNulty after the final whistle. 'Assessing my players, live in front of me, truthfully, I thought they were out on their feet a little bit. Again, I felt like I couldn't really help them. Fylde made changes – most line-ups can freshen up. Our options for change are so minimal it's almost not even possible.

'I had concerns pre-game about how we were going to find the energy to bring a Boxing Day showpiece to the ground today. I don't blame the players one bit for being down on energy. They weren't down on fight, but they were definitely down on energy. You could see there was a loss of energy in the performance compared to what we've had recently.

'But how they found the fight to stay in the game and show enough, in the end, to get a victory against a really dangerous opponent, is really commendable. To take five points from the last three games and keep two clean sheets, in what was definitely our worst performance of those three games – in the other two we were excellent – was commendable.

'For [Kwaku Oduroh] to get that goal at the end was really nice for the squad and the fans. It was a nice moment for the ground. It was good that those people got to see a team that really fought for the town, and it culminated in an exciting goal and a great celebration.'

* * *

AS THE MISTLETOE and wine were swept aside to make room for party poppers and resolutions, I caught up again with Jim McNulty to find out how he felt the first half of the season had panned out.

The air was heavy with an understandable sense of disenchantment, yet beneath the surface lingered a stubborn optimism that refused to be extinguished.

'I'm at a point of reflection whereby all I'm really feeling, given the circumstances at the club, is pure and utter overachievement,' he said. 'I just see a group of players outperforming the circumstances they are having to work in. In fact, what they are doing is not helping them get what they need, if that makes sense? It's like the office worker who covers for his sick colleague and does a good job – then the bosses think they can get by with the one worker.

'It does excite me, what this group of players could do, but, without help, they won't achieve it. What we are doing, being just outside the play-offs, is not sustainable without help. We are winning games, somehow, but all I feel at the final whistle is relief because we got through another one without losing another player. I just want to be able to compete at this level but, at the minute, there is nothing I can do to help the players. I would never say that a bigger budget would automatically equate to success, because football just doesn't work that way, but I could at least assemble a squad that could compete over the entire campaign and provide the current players with some relief.

'Against Fylde, we had a drinks break around 70 minutes in. I could see the players were dead on their feet. They were in a state of paralysis almost – they'd stopped defending and they'd stopped attacking. I had to implore them to keep going because I had nothing to offer them from the bench. I can't rotate the squad from game to game either. Mentally, the players are finding that extra bit that is required at the moment, but they cannot continue to do so. They are human beings and you can't keep flogging them into the ground. I mean, we are playing with one centre-forward at the moment and he is 39 years old.

'I still don't feel like there is a true understanding of the circumstances at the club. It certainly isn't in line with expectations. I think there needs to be a bit more transparency from behind the scenes. The more opposition managers I'm seeing in my office, the more I'm realising other teams have more financial flexibility when compared to us.

'I'm now being told there is a need to strip this club back and run it based on the attendances we get. Also, because of reduced EFL funding, it means the academy will probably have to go. We won't have a scholarship programme but instead we will have a college B-Tech programme that will be looking to develop our young talent while making money. I think Bromley have a similar programme that has proven successful. Things like food provision may need to go too. While we wait for an investor, we are having to strip back the club's Football League legacy and are becoming a true non-league club. These are things people need to be aware of when they are giving their expectations of how Rochdale AFC should be performing. The bookies had us as second favourites for promotion at the start of the season. Based on what? Not our present circumstances, that's for sure. I just want there to be a greater transparency so that, externally, people are aware and are not getting irritated when the inevitable happens. It all needs to be aligned.

'Signing players is almost impossible at the moment, too. I didn't realise until now what a big deal accommodation is at this level. It was almost something that you just didn't have to consider in the Football League because salaries were high enough that the players didn't need accommodation to make a move possible.

'A lot of clubs at our level now have some kind of accommodation facility built into them, so they can offer accommodation for free when negotiating with players. That lets them explore the whole transfer market.

'We're offering guys salaries, but then they have to get accommodation on top of that and that needs to come out of their salary. It immediately puts us in a weaker position. Basically, at the minute, I can only sign a player from Fleetwood, Burnley, Bolton, Stoke City or Port Vale, and they have to live within a 45-minute drive of Rochdale or they won't join us because we can't pay for any accommodation.

'So, there are players I like presently from the south, from the east coast, some from Scotland, but I just can't get them. Essentially, I'm told, "Here are your five or six clubs, so focus on them." They've got to be free, too. They can't cost us any money – and we can't accommodate. That's what is going on behind the scenes.

'My worry is, if you pay bottom-end National League wages, or even National League North wages, where do you inevitably end up? That's my fear. So, yes, we are definitely overachieving at the minute.

'You ask why I put up with it? Well, for the same reason as you. I love Rochdale. I love working with the players. I love working with the team. I love the exciting moments. I love it when we play these guys out of position, and we work on things so hard, and they actually come together and we get wins. They're the best moments.

'But it is easier to destabilise a club and morale than it is to establish it. The players didn't get paid in November, as you are aware. People at the top of the club may have known this would get sorted eventually, but the players didn't and neither did their families. Things like this affect morale and it takes time to build that back up. I have to thank the players for keeping their levels up while going through that period.

'I'm aware the chairman is having to put his own money into the club at the moment until we can find an investor.

I have massive respect for that. Now, I don't know the chairman's personal wealth, but you need a lot of money to run a football club, even at this level, and it isn't worth jeopardising your family's future for. No club is. I don't know how long this is sustainable for. For that matter, I think Simon and his family deserve a great deal of appreciation for keeping the lights on at our football club. We tried the fan-owned approach, but it just hasn't worked. It never does, in my opinion. Someone, at the end of the day, just has to have lots and lots of money. It's frustrating, but we have to accept it.'

McNulty also said the lack of finance and bodies was affecting the way he wanted his team to play football.

'I'm a system-based manager,' he said. 'You know that, you've watched all the games, I've seen your social media. It's what I believe in. In implementing this, you learn and realise so much. You begin to fully understand why Pep [Guardiola] at Man City, or [Roberto] De Zerbi at Brighton bring in players who you then don't see for months. They're good players but they need to be fully immersed into the system. I am trying to do that here at Rochdale. It's not always easy though. We had Max Conway on loan from Bolton and we were really working with him to get him ready. Just as I felt he was there, Bolton recalled him and sent him on loan to Fylde. These are the challenges I have to manage while sticking to doing things the way I believe they should be done.

'It's not always an ideal way of doing things, though. Those players who are ready to step right into your system, such as Cian Hayes, perform well, get noticed, and then recalled or poached by another club who can pay more.

'It's highly frustrating. You coach them and prepare them for the situation, but you do so knowing they could vanish at a moment's notice. This also affects the other players too, in terms of morale. It's a difficult model to replicate over and over. I'm also having to play certain players on the front line who should be more of a project.

'Despite all the challenges, I still go into every game believing we can take something from it. These players give their all. If we can just get them a bit more help, then we can push on.'

Interestingly, Rochdale chairman Simon Gauge issued a New Year's Eve message of his own to supporters.

The need for investment in the club was emphasised, with challenges highlighted due to the club's share structure. Even so, further share purchases by supporters were encouraged by Gauge, with 50,000 made available for acquisition.

'We were fully aware that this season would bring a lot of challenges as we transitioned from an EFL playing budget to a National League one,' he said. 'Although our budget is competitive, with some of the playing contracts carried over from the EFL, it means that we have not been able to build a squad as big in numbers as we would have liked. However, we are certainly not short on quality within our squad.

'There will be tough times throughout the season when injuries bite. We are suffering from that now, but the quality, spirit and fight among the players, shown no more than during the two Christmas fixtures so far, has been incredible. With one or two of those injured players returning from injury, there is cause for optimism on the horizon. We will try to support Jim the best we can to freshen the squad where we can, but that will be strictly within the financial parameters already set out.'

Gauge also mentioned the academy, which McNulty feared was soon to be downgraded.

'Our academy continues to perform admirably in difficult circumstances. As many of you will know, academies are largely externally funded. Upon relegation from the EFL, clubs continue to receive 100 per cent funding in the first season post-relegation, and 50 per cent in the second season post-relegation. In the third season post-relegation, clubs are no longer permitted to operate an academy in the Premier League/EFL games programme and are therefore not permitted to draw down funding. Against this backdrop of uncertainty, the emergence of George Nevett, as well as the senior debuts of Brad Kelly, Isaac Burgess and Luke Mann, is a superb achievement and a huge credit to each and every person involved.'

National League table as at 26 December 2023

	P	*W*	*D*	*L*	*F*	*A*	*Pts*
Chesterfield	24	19	2	3	58	31	59
Bromley	26	15	7	4	44	28	52
Barnet	25	15	4	6	52	36	49
Solihull Moors	25	12	7	6	38	34	43
Gateshead	24	11	7	6	50	31	40
Altrincham	24	10	9	5	45	34	39
FC Halifax Town	25	10	9	6	30	24	39
Rochdale	**26**	**10**	**8**	**8**	**44**	**37**	**38**
Aldershot Town	25	11	4	10	42	45	37
Oldham Athletic	25	9	9	7	40	38	36
Eastleigh	25	10	6	9	42	45	36
Wealdstone	24	9	6	9	34	34	33
Maidenhead United	26	7	10	9	28	35	31
Dagenham & Redbridge	25	8	5	12	29	33	29
Southend United*	24	11	5	8	40	27	28
Hartlepool United	25	8	4	13	41	50	28
Boreham Wood	25	6	10	9	30	40	28
Woking	25	7	6	12	26	31	27
York City	25	5	11	9	33	43	26
Dorking Wanderers	24	7	4	13	28	43	25
Oxford City	26	6	6	14	38	50	24
Ebbsfleet United	26	6	6	14	34	49	24
Kidderminster Harriers	26	4	8	14	19	33	20
AFC Fylde	25	4	7	14	35	49	19

* Southend deducted ten points for failing to pay an existing tax bill.

January 2024

TO BRING IN 2024, Rochdale's unfortunate streak of losing the inaugural match of every month persisted as they were defeated 2-0 by AFC Fylde on New Year's Day. The match was also overshadowed by a distressing injury to Jesurun Uchegbulam.

There was a lengthy stoppage when the winger collided with advertising hoardings in the second half. He was treated by medical staff, before being stretchered off and taken to hospital. Thankfully he was discharged later that evening.

Jim McNulty made two changes from Boxing Day's win over the Coasters. Max Taylor replaced the injured George Nevett, who, it was revealed, was facing eight weeks on the sidelines due to an ankle injury. Kwaku Oduroh came in for the suspended Tyrese Sinclair.

With options limited, the head coach named just three substitutes. The fact McNulty chose not to fill his bench with additional scholars seemed to be a stark message to the board of directors about the first-team's plight.

On the field, McNulty opted to return Cameron John to left-back, with Oduroh in at right-back and Finlay Armstrong on the left of midfield. Jimmy Keohane played behind Ian Henderson up top, with Ryan East playing a deeper role than he had been. This was further complicated by Henderson dropping deeper during stages of the game, often leaving Dale without a centre-forward.

Despite the effort put in by all those on the pitch, and McNulty trying to keep Fylde guessing with in-game tactical shuffles, the lack of numbers in the squad told in the end.

Dale fell behind in the 58th minute when Danny Ormerod's clinical finish put the hosts ahead, and the young striker doubled his tally four minutes later after a scramble in the area fell kindly and he stabbed home from close range.

While Uchegbulam's injury dominated thoughts in the immediate aftermath of the game, concern soon turned to the unsustainability of McNulty's limited options.

'Jez's injury is all that matters to me right now,' said McNulty after the match. 'Whatever else I talk about today, my mind goes back to Jez.

'As to the team, though, there is no other team in a situation like ours in the National League. The togetherness we felt with the fans today made me proud. That togetherness is the only silver lining I've got. I'm not playing games when I say this, but I am in disbelief at our current situation – one pro and two scholars on the bench today! We're so short on numbers that it is almost dangerous.

'We're all humble enough to accept there will be days when we don't play well. We can't batter everyone. When days like today happen, we just march on to the next one together. Without that togetherness, we don't have anything.'

* * *

AHEAD OF THE home match against Kidderminster Harriers, Jim McNulty was finally able to add another defender to his squad by picking up free agent Kyron Gordon. The 21-year-old had come through the Sheffield

United academy and had most recently held a contract at AFC Fylde.

'He's a bit of a hybrid full-back/centre-back,' McNulty said. 'We believe we've needed some help in that area of the squad, and we think he can certainly help us.

'All the references I've had from people in the game suggest that he's a good pro, he's a winner and he plays from the right place, which is his heart. So, he's a good addition to the group in that regard as well.'

But the plight of a diminished first team was perhaps no more worryingly underlined than when McNulty himself revealed he had re-registered himself as a player in order to help the squad.

'We all know where we are situation wise,' he said. 'In any other situation it's not something we'd be considering, but the squad needs some help.

'Although this is a measure that we will hopefully not have to use, my players have been willing to play in any position at any time for me so far. So, when they need the help now, I think it's important that I show I am also willing to make the same sacrifices for them.

'It's ultimately my appreciation of the players' efforts so far. I am showing them I am willing to stand side by side with them, like the fanbase has. Any little thing that can help, I am willing to do it.

'This is more of a short-term emergency type measure while we assess the market, to get the type of players that we want, and think can help us. There are players out there right now that we could take immediately on a free, but we want to be certain that they can join us and be the type of people and players that can help to amplify what is already good here.'

The Dale Trust, also well aware of the first team's depleted numbers, launched a 'Squad Builder' initiative, whereby it sought to raise funds from members and supporters alike that would be ring-fenced for sole use by McNulty for the purpose of signing players.

On the field, once again, the current group dug out a result in the face of adversity. Tyrese Sinclair and Ian Henderson reached their tenth goals of the season each, guiding Dale to a 2-0 triumph over the Harriers.

Making his debut, Kyron Gordon stepped in for Kwaku Oduroh at right-back, while Finn Armstrong sat at left-back. Sinclair returned after serving a one-match suspension, filling in for the injured Jesurun Uchegbulam on the flank. Cameron John moved back into his defensive midfield role, with Ryan East moving further forward as a result, and Jimmy Keohane was perched on the left of the forward line. Kyle Ferguson also rejoined the squad after a lengthy two-month absence due to injury.

During the first half, both teams struggled to create significant goalscoring opportunities. Ashley Hemmings had the best chances for the visitors, putting one attempt wide and another straight at Louie Moulden. Despite dominating possession, Dale couldn't break through Christian Dibble's goal, with blocked shots from Ryan East and Cameron John.

The deadlock was finally broken 15 minutes into the second half when Sinclair scored a remarkable goal, arguably the best of Dale's season. Max Taylor delivered a well-placed ball for the winger, who, with his back to the goal, skilfully chested it down outside the box, turned and executed a looping volley over Dibble.

Just ten minutes later, Dale increased the lead. East's free kick into the Kidderminster area found Taylor, who stretched to stab the ball towards goal and Henderson ran in to turn it home from close range.

The victory secured a third consecutive home clean sheet for Jim McNulty's men, positioning them in seventh place in the National League standings, the final play-off spot.

It could have been easily overlooked in such difficult times how Dale had improved as a defensive unit over the recent weeks. Personnel put to one side, the team had looked much more solid and compact when defending its box and much better at covering space. The biggest compliment that could be paid, perhaps, was that, other than in terms of reduction in numbers, the side wasn't missing George Nevett in defensive situations.

The commitment from all of the players to constantly shift position and see out the full 90 minutes was as admirable as anything seen from any Dale side in recent years and both they, and McNulty, deserved all the praise they were getting for this.

'It was a game in which we had to generate our own energy,' McNulty said after the game. 'In moments where it's flat, you need a spark, some quality, something to go for you.

'We were on the edge of doing something good all the time, but it always broke down. I have to be mindful of what I'm asking the players to do at the minute, because they're in very tough circumstances.

'There were some minor tweaks and small points where we could help at half-time, and we found a bit of a spark in the second half. I thought it lifted the ground and got us what was a very pleasing result.'

McNulty also gave an update on Dale's injured players.

'The great news on Jez [Uchegbulam] is that it's nothing major,' he said. 'The fear from the ambulance guys at first was a suspected hip fracture, which was really concerning. That was ruled out, so hopefully it's just an impact injury, but who knows? Fingers crossed for him being available for the next game.

'Kairo Mitchell is still some time away. Devante Rodney and Adam Clayton are the same. George Nevett is out for eight weeks and Brad Kelly is out for the season.'

* * *

ROCHDALE'S LACK OF participation in the FA Trophy fourth round allowed the players a much-needed breather.

However, any thoughts the supporters themselves had of relaxing were quickly dashed when news broke that goalkeeper Louie Moulden had been recalled from his loan by parent club Wolverhampton Wanderers, whereby he was then duly dispatched back out on loan to League One side Northampton Town until the end of the season.

The 22-year-old had made 29 appearances for Dale, remarkably assisting five goals and keeping six clean sheets. He had been an integral part of the team and its function to this point. To describe his departure as a blow would have been a gross understatement.

Jim McNulty clearly felt it. However, the head coach couldn't afford to feel sorry for himself and moved swiftly into the market to bring 21-year-old Tiernan Brooks in on loan from Notts County until the end of the season.

Brooks, who had won promotion from the National League with the Magpies the season previous, also possessed two Republic of Ireland under-21 caps.

'I'm very happy to get Tiernan in,' McNulty admitted. 'He's got the whole skillset to come into the team and amplify our qualities. He is a goalkeeper that we were very interested in during the summer, but he already had a loan move to the League of Ireland sorted.

'I think we've signed a very good young goalkeeper and I'm really thankful that it has all come together.'

McNulty also took the fortnight's break to assess the rest of his squad, and chose to send Kwaku Oduroh back to his parent club Derby County. The full-back had joined Dale on loan from the League One side in the summer, making 22 appearances to this point.

'It's with a heavy heart that Kwakes [Oduroh] returns to Derby,' said McNulty. 'He's had a brilliant loan for us and contributed greatly towards all of our efforts on the pitch.

'But beyond being a good player, he was an amazing team-mate to the rest of the squad and a good person who will always remain on the journey with us.

'His goal, his first in professional football, on Boxing Day will live long in the memory of all of us and was a really special moment for him to cherish, and for us too.'

McNulty then used the freed-up loan spot to bring D'Mani Mellor back to the club. The 23-year-old forward had spent the second half of the previous season on loan at Dale from League One side Wycombe Wanderers, starting all eight of McNulty's games in charge at the end of the campaign.

'D'Mani has the attributes and qualities that we look for in a player, in an area of the pitch that required reinforcement,' McNulty said.

'He produces good versatility and tactical understanding, with the ability and willingness to play in any of the attacking positions. D'Mani has already demonstrated to me last season, as a team-mate and during my period as interim head coach, that he possesses the values that are aligned with those that matter most to this team. He is highly regarded by his team-mates, and he always puts the team first.

'We believe our current environment will enable D'Mani to reach the potential that we all believe he possesses, and kickstart what has been a stuttering season for him thus far.'

With the reshaped squad now eager to take on a Wealdstone side that had just lost its entire coaching team to Notts County, the elements would prevent the players from testing their mettle against the unsettled club as the Spotland pitch succumbed to freezing temperatures the day before the match was due to take place, leading to a disappointing postponement.

The chance to avenge the last-minute winner Dale had conceded down in Ruislip earlier in the season would now need to wait until February.

* * *

PREVIOUS TRIPS TO the Altrincham area for this writer had involved a walk around the ancient parkland at Dunham Massey followed by a bite to eat at the Axe and Cleaver. For the first time, I was hoping to throw a football match into the mix, too, but the fixture compilers' choice of a cold, dark, stormy Tuesday night in January put paid to that, with a consecutive disappointing postponement the outcome.

After seeing the Wealdstone game frozen off three days earlier, a late pitch inspection deemed the Moss Lane playing surface waterlogged and, having now not played for more than a fortnight, the well-rested Dale squad was keen to get back on the field in a bid to avoid any rust setting in.

* * *

A LENGTHY TRIP to Aldershot would finally see the Dale players return to action after 21 days of inactivity, where they faced a side that had suffered a slight wobble since the two clubs met at Spotland in November.

While Rochdale had been victorious on that occasion, it had been against the form book, with Aldershot occupying one of the play-off places at the time. Since that encounter, however, Tommy Widdrington's side had slid down the table slightly, sitting in ninth position at this juncture, with Dale in seventh.

You wouldn't have known by watching, however, as Aldershot ran out comfortable 3-1 winners on this occasion. Dale looked, for the most part, ineffectual by comparison.

Tiernan Brooks made his debut in goal, and D'Mani Mellor, on loan from Wycombe Wanderers, commenced his second stint at the club by making the starting line-up also.

Despite falling behind within six minutes due to Jack Barham's scuffed shot, which fortuitously found Lorent Tolaj to tap in at the back post, Dale quickly levelled. Ethan Ebanks-Landell's precise long pass set up Ian Henderson, who expertly brought the ball down on his chest and calmly finished, marking his 147th Dale goal.

Shortly after, there were appeals for a penalty when Tyrese Sinclair was brought down, but the referee dismissed the claims. Tolaj had further opportunities for the hosts, with Brooks making crucial saves.

However, Dale conceded a penalty just before half-time when Max Taylor fouled Stuart O'Keefe in the box. Cian Harries stepped up to convert the spot-kick, giving the home team a 2-1 lead.

Despite Dale's efforts, including a close call with a Sinclair curling free kick, the hosts extended their lead in the second half, Barham slotting the ball home off the inside of the far post.

Although Brooks made notable saves thereafter, denying Barham and Tolaj, Dale couldn't mount a comeback. The hosts held on to secure victory as Dale disappointingly struggled to create clear-cut chances in the closing stages.

'I just thought we weren't very good, to keep it in its simplest form,' said McNulty afterwards.

'It's been a difficult three weeks with not playing, and, in that time, we could never treat it as a break. We were always preparing for a game that kept getting called off, so I was very mindful, leading into this game, that we couldn't prepare the players as we would have liked to, load-wise.

'Putting the postponements to one side, our skills and techniques with the ball, I didn't think were very good, that's all. It affected the players' confidence as the game went on and went against us. But I didn't see them give up.

'I saw lots of grit to try to stop their onslaught at times. Three-one flattered us to a degree. Tiernan Brooks made some excellent saves – it could have been a much bigger score.

'I've seen Aldershot get some big scorelines this year and they make the game very much like a basketball game.

'You have to be in your rhythm and, when you get the ball, you need to be ready to control the game. Today, because we weren't in our rhythm, when we got the ball back, we lost it too quickly, which is really not like us.

'We weren't able to be what we have been and we weren't able to make the game how we wanted to make it. I looked at the players when they were suffering and the fight and the effort was there, so I can't go too deep on them.

'We just need to take our medicine and move on to the next one. It's unfortunate that we had to lose that game to get into a better place, but I think we *are* in a better place for having a game again.'

National League table as at 27 January 2024

	P	*W*	*D*	*L*	*F*	*A*	*Pts*
Chesterfield	29	24	2	3	72	34	74
Bromley	31	16	10	5	52	33	58
Barnet	30	17	4	9	58	44	55
Altrincham	28	12	10	6	53	38	46
Solihull Moors	28	13	7	8	44	39	46
Oldham Athletic	29	12	9	8	45	39	45
Aldershot Town	29	13	5	11	51	53	44
Gateshead	28	12	7	9	52	40	43
Rochdale	**29**	**11**	**8**	**10**	**47**	**42**	**41**
FC Halifax Town	29	10	11	8	32	31	41
Eastleigh	29	10	8	11	50	58	38
Hartlepool United	31	11	4	16	47	57	37
Wealdstone	26	10	6	10	36	36	36
Maidenhead United	29	8	11	10	30	37	35
Southend United*	28	13	5	10	44	31	34
Boreham Wood	30	7	13	10	39	51	34
Dorking Wanderers	29	10	4	15	35	47	34
Dagenham & Redbridge	29	9	6	14	36	41	33
York City	29	7	12	10	39	47	33
Woking	29	8	6	15	29	38	30
Ebbsfleet United	31	8	6	17	38	56	30
AFC Fylde	29	7	8	14	42	52	29
Kidderminster	31	7	8	16	26	39	29
Oxford City	30	7	6	17	42	56	27

* Southend deducted ten points for failing to pay an existing tax bill.

February 2024

AFTER WHAT SEEMED an eternity, the Rochdale players would set foot on home turf again by hosting Dagenham & Redbridge.

In the days leading up to the game, Jim McNulty was able to further add to his squad, albeit via the loan market, by bringing back instrumental winger Cian Hayes until the season's end. The signing was made possible thanks to a sizeable contribution from a long-standing supporter, directly to the club, and with help from the Dale Trust's Squad Builder Fund.

'It felt like a loss when he returned to Fleetwood,' said McNulty of Hayes. 'He was in a good vein of form and was really enjoying his football here. His first loan was exactly what he needed, and he produced exactly what we wanted as well.

'He's one that we've obviously monitored since he returned, and the moment he became available we were always looking to make that a possibility again.'

Hayes was, however, unavailable against Dagenham due to injury.

'He is at the back end of a medium-term injury that he sustained in his time back at Fleetwood,' McNulty explained. 'That may have helped our chances of getting him back again, because, off the back of his first loan here, there were EFL clubs keeping their eye on him.'

Winger Sam Mather and midfielder Sam Murray, both players from Manchester United's under-21 squad, also signed with Dale for the remainder of the season. The collaboration was a result of a unique loan initiative crafted by the coaching staff at United's academy, enabling young talent to gain valuable experience in non-league football.

Throughout the remainder of the season, the players would have the chance to engage in training and matches with United's academy as well as for Dale, striking a balance between non-league challenges and elite-level development.

'With where we're at numbers-wise, the two players will be a definite help to us, as much as we'll be a help to them,' said McNulty.

'We won't have access to those players all of the time, that will be at United's control, which it should be. Initiatives like these are really useful for clubs in situations like ours, whereby we are extremely tight on numbers.

'We've had to be incredibly flexible with the guys we do have so far, in terms of playing players out of position, who have done an amazing job. Any niche initiatives from big clubs like this can only be helpful to us.'

As to Dale's opponents, Dagenham had made steady progress in the National League since they were defeated by McNulty's men in November.

Led in the dressing room by former striker Ben Strevens, they were one of many clubs at this level looking to restore EFL status at the earliest opportunity.

Strevens himself boasted a decent playing career from which he could draw experience. Starting with non-league Wingate & Finchley, he netted 28 league goals in the

1998/99 season, guiding his team to promotion and putting him on the radar of clubs higher up the food chain.

'I was in Watford's academy when I was a young boy, from about the age of 9 to 16,' Strevens explained when I met him ahead of the match. 'I left because they said I wasn't big enough to make it as a pro. I found that rejection tough. I was in my last year of school, and one of my good friends was playing for Wingate & Finchley, and he said they've got an under-18 team that plays midweek. He said, "Why don't you come down and play for them?" So, I spent about a year playing in the under-18s. The following pre-season, the first-team manager said he wanted me to play for him. I went on to score lots of goals for the first team and that's when the interest from higher up the divisions started.'

A move to Barnet followed, where Strevens continued his scoring streak.

'I went on a few trials, got offered a few academy forms, but I wanted to try for a first-team environment, and John Still, the manager at Barnet, offered me a three-year contract. It was an amazing opportunity for me at a club close to home. So, I grabbed it with both hands and that was my first chance at professional football.'

Loan spells at Slough Town and St Albans City preceded his tenure as a regular first-team player at Barnet. Despite amassing 41 appearances in the 2005/06 season, Strevens finally bid farewell to Barnet, having scored 42 goals for the club.

'I couldn't have had a better first manager as a pro than John Still at Barnet,' he said. 'He has given so many players a career. He really made sure that, as a forward, I knew I had to work hard and not just be able to put the ball in the back of the net, but hold the ball up and run the channels, too. I think that probably landed me the chances I got.'

After stints with Crawley Town and Dagenham & Redbridge, where he earned that historic promotion to League Two, Strevens had spells at Brentford and Wycombe Wanderers, helping them to League One. Further moves included Gillingham and returning to Dagenham.

'I have to be honest, I think my drive, based on being told I wasn't big enough to be a professional footballer, got me to the level I ultimately reached more than raw talent did. I had been at college with my friends, and I was working with my uncle, doing gardening, when the opportunity to go into the professional game presented itself, so I really wanted to prove myself.

'Do I think I could have gone higher than League One? I'm not sure. Maybe I could have. But, I think if someone had said to me when I was right down the lower end of non-league I'd get up to League One, I would have taken it.'

Eastleigh became Strevens' next destination, where he excelled as both player and coach. His leadership qualities were evident when he briefly took on a joint-manager role at Whitehawk. Returning to Eastleigh, he eventually assumed the permanent managerial position, guiding them to the play-off semi-finals.

'I'd gone to Eastleigh at the back end of my playing career as a part-time player when, pretty quickly, we were promoted up into the National League and went full time. Chris Todd took over as manager. Towards the end of that season, the assistant manager left and Chris asked if I could help until the end of the season, while still playing. I did it on a sort of interim basis and then it carried on into the start of next season. Unfortunately for Toddy, he lost his job four games into the next season and I was sort of stuck there as caretaker manager, but still wanting to be a player. A new manager came in, and there was no fall-out or anything, but I ended up moving on, as I was seen as part of the old guard, so to speak.

'I had a little spell at Whitehawk before coming back to Eastleigh as assistant to Andy Hessenthaler. Andy then got offered the job at Dover Athletic and went there. I didn't want what happened to me the last time to happen again, so I threw my hat in the ring to take the Eastleigh manager job permanently.

'I didn't get off to a good start as caretaker, losing the first game, but, thankfully, the interview process was lengthy, and results picked up under my watch. The players all wanted me to get the job, too. I ended up getting it and I took the team all the way to the play-off semi-finals, unfortunately losing on penalties, but that was a good group of lads I had and a good first opportunity to become a manager.'

Despite his achievements, Strevens parted ways with Eastleigh in January 2022. However, his managerial credentials were soon recognised by the Daggers, leading to his appointment as their new manager in March 2023.

'The first time being sacked as a manager, I'm not going to lie, it hurt me. I was like, "Do I want to go back into it? Is this something I want to do?" I was working for the academy at Luton Town and really enjoying my time there, but the opportunity came for me to interview at Dagenham & Redbridge, and I'd probably say that's where I had my most enjoyable time as a player, so it obviously was a draw to go there. I won the National League there as a player and secured EFL football for the first time in the club's history. The chance to go back and be the first person to achieve that as both a player and a manager was too good to turn down.

'The risk is, obviously, if it doesn't go to plan, then it tarnishes my time at the club as a player, because people may more readily remember my spell as a manager.

'The National League overall is getting better and better each year. There are very few part-time clubs left in it. I feel like there is a real influx of top-quality players who are dropping down the leagues sooner than they would have done previously. This allows teams to play very competitive football. I would say, for me, even from my time being a player and my first spell as a manager at this level, the standard has gone through the roof.

'I want my players to be on the front foot. I want them to play with a bit of freedom. I try to give them a structure to work from, but I also want them to go and enjoy themselves. Importantly, however, I think you must treat every club you come up against differently.

'The most important factor is that this club represents the people who come to support it. It's a real hard-working area. There isn't a lot of money in Dagenham and everyone that comes to the games, well, they've worked hard throughout the week and they want to see a representation of themselves on the pitch. They want to see hard-working people who care about playing for the football club and they will forgive you for giving the ball away if they see you trying to do the right things and work for the team. I think that's probably more what I focus on at Dagenham rather than a playing style or philosophy. Yes, we want to play a certain way, but I think we really have to show the characteristics of the people that we're representing.

'We've had some good moments and we've had some tough moments over the season, but I feel we're in a good spot at the moment where the fans know what the boys are trying to do.'

Unfortunately for Rochdale, Strevens' characteristically hard-working side ensured a maintenance of the trend of losing the first game of the month by inflicting a 2-1 defeat. Inih Effiong scored a double for the visitors while Tyrese Sinclair netted a fine curling strike for the home side. Despite Dale controlling possession in the second half in pursuit of an equaliser, the players were unable to break through, and the visitors held on for the win.

McNulty made two changes to the starting XI from the previous weekend's defeat at Aldershot Town, as Kyle Ferguson and Jimmy Keohane came in for Max Taylor and Finlay Armstrong. Cameron John reverted to left-back, while Kairo Mitchell returned to the squad after two months out through injury. Also on the bench was under-16 academy player Mateus Mane, who had been a regular for the youth team and was courting attention from clubs higher up the football pyramid.

Sadly, the team displayed a similar unavailing approach to its play as the previous weekend, much to the home crowd's chagrin. The resistance, or inability, to mix up play led to this encounter probably being the worst home performance of the season.

The players just didn't get the ball forward quickly enough and, when they did make the final third, the ball was then retained rather than put into the box.

Record-goalscorer Ian Henderson played in a deeper role, which didn't work because his movement on the shoulder of defenders was something that allowed the whole side to be more direct. D'Mani Mellor's effort, unfortunately, didn't make up for his lack of threat to the opposition either.

Ryan East's impact was also stifled by playing deeper, illustrated perfectly on the rare occasion that he found himself in a more forward role when he provided an assist for Sinclair's goal.

All of these positional irregularities, alongside the absence of Louie Moulden and George Nevett, both of whom contributed to how positively progressive the team could be, were the main reasons supporters got what they saw against Dagenham.

McNulty had previously demonstrated he had found a way of having his players play multiple passes at the back, set their shape, draw the press, then hit it long. They had now simply ceased doing this anywhere near enough in games.

'What I trust in is the culture of this group, their togetherness and their humility,' said McNulty by way of defence of his players post-match.

'They accept when we haven't done well, and I think that's the reason this is the first time we've been beaten back-to-back in 30 league games.

'I back the fact that this group of lads will be on the training ground again this week with the attitude of, "We need to be better than the last game," and not with an arrogant attitude that it was everyone else's fault. Because it wasn't, it was ours.'

McNulty did admit, however, that Dale didn't have the required cutting edge.

'It's a disappointing loss,' he said. 'We struggled – a lot of the performance was sluggish. The timing of the main actions in the game were not good for us.

'We didn't start the game well. We were slow out of the blocks when we wanted to be quick at home. We know we've had very good home form – that's the first game we've lost at home since October [in the league].

'The first ten minutes was us trying to wrestle back control of the game. We had to battle to get that control and, I think, after the ten-minute mark, we did that. We got into better areas.

'It was just quality in the cutting-edge end of the pitch. We were low on it. We were able to get the ball around

Dagenham into the key areas but the final pass, cross, one-two, shot, all eluded us.

'For me, we struggled with a lack of maturity and focus on what was important. The scuffles and things don't matter, getting the ball back in play and moving is important for us. That's what the real elite teams do against a team that plays slowly.'

The fact McNulty was once again forced to name an academy player on the bench also served to highlight the financial plight of the club. In the crowd at Spotland during the game was Azhar Ali, the prospective Labour MP for Rochdale. Following the match, chairman Simon Gauge engaged in what he described as positive discussions with Ali and his team, as well as Rochdale Borough Council leader Neil Emmott.

During the meeting, Gauge emphasised Dale's significant contributions to the local community and economy while addressing the club's severe financial challenges. The atmosphere of the meeting was described as constructive, with all parties said to show a willingness to explore sustainable solutions for the club's long-term survival. It was agreed that urgent talks would continue between the club and the council.

* * *

WITH SCHEDULED INACTIVITY for both Rochdale and Altrincham due to a lack of participation in the FA Trophy, it was agreed the pair would instead contest the National League fixture that had fallen foul to stormy weather the previous month.

Jim McNulty led his charges the short distance to Moss Lane in Cheshire to face a side in magnificent form and sitting fifth in the table. Altrincham manager Phil

Parkinson had described his side's promotion assault as 'unexpected', but this writer felt he was doing himself a disservice, as he had assembled a talented and well-drilled squad that had adapted exceptionally well to a full-time training model.

When the pair met at Spotland in autumn, the Dale players turned in their best performance of the season to that point, running out 3-0 victors. Unfortunately there would be no repeat here, with the result very much following the form guide, and McNulty's men found themselves on the wrong end of a 3-0 reverse.

Justin Amaluzor's close range-finish separated the sides at half-time, before a quickfire second-half double from Regan Linney and Chris Conn-Clarke ensured Altrincham picked up all three points.

The result, and performance, had, perhaps for the first time, uncaged discontent among many Dale supporters, who were now questioning the points return of their team since the turn of the year, which stood at three from a possible 15. Any hopes held of snatching a play-off place also seemed to be fading with each passing game.

It certainly wasn't pretty, despite several quality players returning to the first-team squad in the shape of George Nevett, Kairo Mitchell and Adam Clayton, with Cian Hayes also making his second debut.

Bafflingly, the so-far unimpressive D'Mani Mellor started the game over the much more assured Jimmy Keohane, and it was perhaps choices such as this, as well as in-game decisions, that attracted some supporter criticism towards the head coach.

'I think Altrincham deserved to win,' Jim McNulty said afterwards to the assembled media. 'We've shared two 3-0 scorelines with them now. Truthfully, I don't think we deserved to beat them 3-0 at our place, I thought they deserved to score at least one on the night. I remember [their manager] saying the same after that game, and I'd be surprised if he doesn't say similar after today [about us].

'Altrincham were more clinical than us, but I would say that's all they were. We were in the game, we got around their goal a lot and had loads of opportunities and shots. We hit the post and had loads of one-v-ones deep into their box, which are the ones you want. I don't think it was a 3-0 game. Like the one at home, the scoreline doesn't necessarily reflect the game.

'For the first 25 minutes, I thought we were really good, on top in the game. They were in their groove, and they have a real self-belief right now with where they are as a team.

'We didn't show the same cutting edge and conviction that they did. We're trying to re-find our rhythm and having a lot of players back on the pitch will help that. We will stutter in the meantime, but, with performances like today, we will win games. I've no concerns about this group winning games.'

* * *

FOOTBALL IS THE home of many a cliche and, if any stock is to be put into the one about a week being a long time in the sport, then six of them must seem like a millennium.

In just that space of time, the Dale faithful had regressed from an optimistic bunch anticipating a top-seven National League finish to an anxious collective looking towards the bottom end of the table.

Such had been Dale's form since the turn of the year that the gap between the club and the top seven had grown, and the gap between the club and the relegation spots had shrunk.

As the in-form Solihull Moors rolled into town, sitting fourth in the table, hopes of Dale's plight improving seemed dim.

And so it proved. Despite McNulty finally being able to field something resembling his combined strongest starting XI and bench, and a promising first-half showing, his side slumped to a 2-1 home defeat.

The visitors seized an early advantage when Callum Maycock finished off a swift move, but, despite Cian Hayes's goal bringing Dale level at half-time, Solihull managed to score shortly after the break through Tahvon Campbell, which ultimately proved to be the decisive goal in what had become increasingly horrendous weather conditions.

McNulty opted for two alterations to his line-up compared to the previous Saturday's match against Altrincham. Jesurun Uchegbulam and Ian Henderson came back into the team, replacing Tyrese Sinclair and D'Mani Mellor. Additionally, Devante Rodney returned to the matchday squad for the first time since December after recovering from injury.

The visitors were visibly the stronger team, however, with everyone knowing their role well. The mobility of Campbell – who Dale had sold to Moors in January – was key to allowing other players to join him and cause issues defensively. The Dale players seemed to struggle with runners all afternoon.

Jimmy Keohane's ongoing exclusion also deprived the team of not only his own versatility, but the flexibility of others who could play elsewhere when the Irishman was in the starting XI. As an observer, this writer felt Cameron John alongside Harvey Gilmour, with Ryan East in a role nearer the opposition goal, would have played to the strength of all players.

Perhaps more worryingly, the defensive stability that was on display six weeks earlier seemed to have deserted the team once again. Hayes and the returning Rodney did give cause for optimism, with their directness and willingness to engage in a foot race providing a difference going forward, but the oppressive nature of the side's form dominated all post-match chatter in the town's hostelries.

McNulty praised the supporters for their in-game backing, which, to be fair, remained consistently buoyant throughout the match itself, if not afterwards.

'The first thing that comes to my mind, and what I felt at the side of the pitch in the second half, was a massive respect for our fans,' he said. 'After consecutive losses, the fans were still singing away all second half. I thought they were absolutely amazing.

'I don't think we can say too much else at the moment, when we've just lost four on the spin. We need to be humble and accept that we've done things wrong, or that things have cost us from our own doing.

'I feel like a draw would have been a fair result, and the half of the pitch that we played in in the second half was a swamp. They kicked the ball into it and we couldn't get out of it.

'That said, we've conceded too many goals in the last few games, we've conceded too many chances. So, we have to go away and look at ourselves, including me. We just have to take our medicine, be what I've asked this squad to be all season and be humble. When we win, ignore any noise, and when we lose, take any noise we deserve.

'It's uncharted territory. Thirty games in before having the whole squad available, is unbelievable. I'm glad it's been the hard way in my first role of management. It's been amazingly challenging at times and a learning experience.'

* * *

AS THE SPOTLAND turf continued to resemble a defective sponge in the face of persistent inclement weather, Rochdale's scheduled Tuesday night home fixture against Boreham Wood was postponed. With the majority of the other National League matches going ahead that evening, Dale found themselves, despite dropping only three places to 13th in the table, just three points above the relegation places.

This stark turnaround in fortunes since January would have been enough to occupy the thoughts of any terrace stalwart, but another bombshell had landed just a few hours earlier that paled the declining on-field endeavours almost into insignificance.

In December, Jim McNulty said he wished the board of directors would communicate with more transparency regarding the true plight of the club. On 20 February, chairman Simon Gauge did exactly that. He issued a public statement that the club *had* to be sold by the end of the next month, or face a 'very real threat' of liquidation and closure.

Gauge, who had been striving to secure fresh investment for the past 14 months, had been using his family's capital to keep the club going in the meanwhile.

'My family has now reached its credit limit and cannot continue to do this,' he said. 'An investor needs to be in place by the end of March.'

He went on to state that the board was seeking an investor to inject £2m and was 'in discussions with interested parties'. However, he contended that the club's ownership structure was dissuading potential investors who 'wish to acquire up to 90 per cent of the club in a single transaction' and desire the funds 'to be directly invested into the club, rather than outside of the club, to individuals, through private share purchases'.

He therefore stated he had convened an EGM for Thursday, 7 March, where he intended for shareholders to approve an emergency restructuring that would generate nine million new shares.

'I am willing to convert my debt into equity and negotiate with any investor a gradual acquisition of those shares if necessary,' Gauge added. 'If this resolution is not passed, the risk of liquidation at the end of March is very real. The passing of this resolution does not ensure the club's survival, but it will certainly provide it with a fighting chance. To be clear, the existence of Rochdale AFC is at stake. The opportunity to give a long-term future is now in the shareholders' hands.'

As Gauge then embarked on something of a media tour to further outline this stark message, the Dale Trust's interim chair, George Brigham, sought him out in a bid to put all supporters in the picture.

In a subsequent trust statement, it was revealed Gauge had shared names of potential investors confidentially, allowing discreet due diligence by the trust to take place.

The trust reported that initial investigations indicated positive credentials for these potential US-based investors in terms of finance, sports-related business track record, and reputation.

'The trust finds these potential investors more credible and long-term focused compared to past experiences,' Brigham added. 'The proof of the pudding, of course, is in the eating. Nevertheless, we were grateful for the opportunity to start the "Dale fans will have you on toast procedure" only to find we could actually be part of a decent banquet.'

* * *

WITH THE THREAT of oblivion hanging over Rochdale, it was a wonder that Jim McNulty could focus on the club's primary business of winning football matches.

He doubtless could have also done without a trip to the runaway National League leaders with which to next conduct that business. Yet it was a trip to Chesterfield that awaited both him and his charges and, despite the Spireites having lost their previous two fixtures, there was to be no complacency as they took to the field at the SMH Group Stadium.

If there was any pre-match concern among the Dale support that events off the field would negatively impact the players, this was dismissed at the full-time whistle as they displayed a dogged determination to claw back a two-goal deficit to leave Derbyshire with a point.

McNulty made four changes from the previous weekend's defeat at home to Solihull Moors. Adam Clayton and Devante Rodney made their first starts since returning from injury, with D'Mani Mellor and Finlay Armstrong also coming back into the XI. Armstrong had extended his loan stay from Fleetwood Town for a further short period, while defender Dan Sassi, who joined from League One club Blackpool on a one-month loan deal just a day earlier, was added to the squad.

After a goalless first half, in which Dale displayed a more direct approach to play than of late, supported by some strong-willed defending, the hosts eventually scored twice in 15 minutes after the break.

A corner that had been partially cleared found its way back into the area, where Tom Naylor redirected it forward. The ball rebounded off the inside of the post, hit Armstrong on the line, and then rolled into the goal.

Shortly after the hour mark, the Spireites extended their lead when Will Grigg scored from close range after connecting with Ollie Banks's whipped cross. However, a battling response saw Mellor and Rodney grab their first competitive goals of the season, and earn a draw for Dale.

Ryan East, brought on as a substitute, delivered an exquisite through ball into Mitchell's path, leading to a shot parried by Harry Tyrer. Mellor capitalised on the rebound, calmly slotting the ball home from six yards out.

Despite Chesterfield then having a goal disallowed for offside, and Liam Mandeville volleying wide in an attempt to regain a two-goal lead, it was Dale who struck next. Rodney scored with a splendid left-footed shot into the top corner after a sequence initiated by another substitute, Tyrese Sinclair, and Armstrong.

The point was greeted at full time with rapturous jubilation from the travelling support, as it represented the never-say-die attitude that was required off the field, too. The players had embodied that spirit not just with the goals, but with the countless blocks and last-ditch challenges that had kept the hosts at bay for most of the game.

'I'm really proud of the team,' McNulty told the assembled media afterwards. 'I'm proud of all the players that were out there, those sat behind me, those that weren't with us, and all of the staff that were involved too. We only took a point but we feel like we could have won.

'We were feeling a bit disappointed at half-time that we weren't ahead. We had good chances, we looked menacing, we looked secure, even though we came under a lot of pressure from Chesterfield, which is to be expected. They are the soon-to-be champions.

'The game plan was to make us competitive. We were making chances and looking fairly solid. We conceded two goals from nothing really – they were set-piece moments. To be honest, I've got real sympathy for the team because

Chesterfield have scored so many goals this season. One big aspect of that is set pieces – they've produced so many set-piece goals in moments of sticky times. They did that again today.

'I told the players after the game that, at 2-0 down, I didn't have a problem with them, because I knew they'd given everything. The fact that they found the belief, hope and character at 2-0 down, off the back of recent results that we've had, and off the back of the news around the club this week, it was an amazing comeback.'

McNulty also confirmed that defender Kyle Ferguson would need surgery on a thigh problem and therefore miss the remainder of the season, but displayed optimism that he, and goalkeeper Brad Kelly, were his only injury concerns.

'Kyle has, unfortunately, had a real significant injury in training, which we're devastated about. He gives everything. He's got the perfect attitude, and he wants to help the team.

'For the first time ever, though, I've been able to rotate my squad. I've been able to bring players out that have needed a rest. I've been watching performances and, when you get to that 30-game stage of a season, people do plateau.

'They can feel flat and they do need a bit of inspiration to find the best version of themselves again. But we've not been able to do that, we've had to bat on, no matter how those players have been batting.

'There were guys not part of the squad today in Jesurun [Uchegbulam], Cameron John and Max Taylor. I've got to keep my eyes on them and look for the guys out there that need help and a rest.

'None of them will want to rest because they want to help us and they're desperate to fight. I'll have to fight with my own players to sometimes tell them what I think is best for them.

'We've got a monstrous schedule coming up. We're a good few games behind teams. Having a healthier, deeper squad gives us the best chance of coping with that schedule and the run-in.'

* * *

WITH THE FUTURE of Rochdale AFC anything but certain ahead of the club's forthcoming EGM, the football on the pitch came thick and fast at least.

There was little time to reflect on the draw away at league leaders Chesterfield as Dale hosted Wealdstone just three days later. Having succumbed to a late winner to the part-time outfit in Ruislip back in November, the home faithful were hoping for a different outcome on this occasion, given the Stones had since lost an entire coaching team to Notts County.

Now managed by former Arsenal midfielder David Noble, Wealdstone had gone on to struggle for consistency and it showed on a chilly Tuesday night, with Dale turning in one of the best first-half performances of the season to date, ultimately emerging 3-0 victors.

Jim McNulty made three changes to his starting XI from the previous match, bringing in Jimmy Keohane, Cameron John and Ryan East.

Despite an initial spell of possession for Wealdstone, Rochdale quickly asserted control. D'Mani Mellor and Kairo Mitchell had early attempts on goal, with Mitchell particularly unlucky not to score after a series of chances.

The home side did finally break the deadlock when Ryan East delivered a precise cross, allowing Ethan Ebanks-Landell to score his third goal of the season, side-footing home at the far post. Dale soon extended the lead just before half-time, too, when Cian Hayes capitalised on a rebound after Mitchell's neat header had come back off a post.

Hayes wasn't done yet, however, and he struck again three minutes later, this time with a sublime lofted chip into the far top corner from the right-hand side of the box.

The Wealdstone players had a few chances of their own, notably with a shot from Tarryn Allarakhia hitting the post, but Rochdale's defence held firm.

In the second half, Rochdale continued to create opportunities, with Keohane and Mellor going close to adding to the score. Despite Wealdstone's late efforts, Rochdale professionally saw out the game with a clean sheet and a comprehensive victory to give a small glimmer of light in the darkest of times.

The tactical acumen displayed was perhaps the highest point of McNulty's tenure, with Keohane's role critical throughout. Keohane starting as a right wing-back with Kyron Gordon tucked inside left the visitors visibly confused. They were then further befuddled as the Irishman quietly slipped into a midfield position, which changed throughout the match. Both part of a midfield three and a roving football equivalent of an NFL tight end, Keohane was creating space all over the pitch for others.

With him occupying an inside-right station for a lot of the time, it inevitably led to gaps elsewhere down that side, which the brilliant Cian Hayes capitalised on to devastating effect.

Even with the predictable 'after the Lord Mayor's Show' second half, Dale committed to keeping the opposition out while still creating opportunities themselves.

The performance provided evidence that McNulty's team still had the capability to be anything but one-dimensional.

'I feel I don't need to do too much talking tonight, as the team did its talking on the pitch,' said McNulty afterwards. 'Offensively and defensively we were brilliant. That came from the commitment, expression and a brilliant work ethic from the players. It could have been an even bigger score. There were so many leaders on the pitch.

'I now have options in team selection and that brings a freshness to our play, which was definitely another factor in tonight's performance. It's normal for players to plateau and I now have the options to give these players a rest. I now know what it feels like to have squad depth.'

* * *

AHEAD OF A scheduled fans' forum on the final day of the month, the board of directors issued a statement that World Soccer Holdings LLC (WSH) had officially signed a Letter of Intent (LOI) to acquire the club.

However, the statement stressed that the agreement was contingent upon shareholder approval of the resolutions to establish new shares at the EGM scheduled for 7 March.

WSH, based in Texas, already had a foot in European football, owning a sizeable percentage of Dutch club MVV Maastricht, mid-table in the second tier.

Chairman Simon Gauge expressed satisfaction, stating, 'We are thrilled to have received the LOI from World Soccer Holdings. Securing investment is crucial for our club's sustainability, and WSH aligns closely with the criteria we've been seeking in an investor. Their history of successful sports investments, coupled with a comprehensive long-term plan for our club, demonstrates their expertise in the field. We eagerly anticipate collaborating with them, shareholders, local officials and suppliers to fulfil the necessary conditions for finalising the club's sale.'

In response, World Soccer Holdings CEO Scott Dyer remarked, 'We are genuinely excited to embark on this investment journey with Rochdale AFC. We hold deep respect and admiration for the club's rich history and culture, acknowledging the dedication and sacrifices made by both the staff, board and supporters' trust to facilitate this partnership.

'We are committed to engaging with the Dale Trust to address any queries they may have regarding our investment, and we seek to garner support from local politicians to bolster our investment in RAFC. Preserving a century of legacy is paramount, and we believe that, through collaboration, we can propel the Dale to surpass its previous achievements.'

As predicted, this news dominated the conversation at the fans' forum that evening, where Gauge once again outlined a terminal diagnosis for the club should the proposed resolutions not be approved by shareholders at the March EGM.

He once again pointed to the share model, established a couple of years prior with his support, as being a deterrent to the potential investor. Initially championed as a fan-owned model, where supporters were encouraged to buy shares in various amounts, Gauge said this fragmented approach was now deterring investors who preferred direct acquisition from the club.

The proposed solution involved the issuing of millions of new shares for direct purchase from the club, albeit at the expense of diluting the shares held by thousands (when considering the Dale Trust) of fans who invested in the fan-owned model.

Murray Knight, the Dale Trust representative on the board, reiterated the fact that the supporters' body had conducted due diligence on names given to them by the chairman, which had returned positive results, but that the body's vote at the EGM would be guided by its members. It was later revealed that the persons upon which the Dale Trust had carried out due diligence had no obvious link to WSH at that time.

So, as uncertainty gripped the club, clarity and accountability from the top table was on display at least, leaving supporters and shareholders under no illusion as to which way their support should go as they filed out of the building.

Later that evening, the result of the Rochdale by-election was announced, pertinent to the football club as Gauge had been meeting with various candidates in terms of ascertaining how they might help the club if elected.

The night was won resoundingly by George Galloway (yes, he of *Celebrity Big Brother* cat pretence fame) after polling 12,335 votes, nearly 6,000 more than any other candidate. From the winner's podium, the Dundonian claimed to be an MP 'for all Rochdalians' as he promised to 'make Rochdale great again'. The veteran campaigner, who took his House of Commons seat for the Workers Party of Britain, took almost 40 per cent of the vote.

During his campaign, Galloway had said the decline of Rochdale AFC was a symbol of the town's wider decline, along with the loss of essential services, and that he believed, with the help of Rochdale Borough Council, he could help save it.

Azhar Ali, who had attended a game at Spotland with Gauge earlier in the month, won the contest to be Labour's candidate and appeared as their candidate on the ballot paper, but was disowned and suspended by the party over remarks widely alleged to be antisemitic. He finished sixth.

National League table as at 29 February 2024

	P	*W*	*D*	*L*	*F*	*A*	*Pts*
Chesterfield	35	27	4	4	86	44	85
Bromley	35	17	11	7	59	42	62
Barnet	35	19	5	11	65	50	62
Solihull Moors	35	16	9	10	54	47	57
Gateshead	34	16	8	10	66	46	56
Oldham Athletic	35	15	11	9	54	45	56
Aldershot Town	35	16	6	13	60	66	54
FC Halifax Town	35	14	11	10	42	39	53
Altrincham	34	14	10	10	61	48	52
Hartlepool United	36	14	9	17	57	64	47
Rochdale	**34**	**12**	**9**	**13**	**54**	**51**	**45**
Eastleigh	36	12	9	15	61	71	45
Southend United*	34	16	6	12	52	36	44
Boreham Wood	35	10	13	12	47	56	43
Dagenham & Redbridge	36	11	9	16	50	50	42
Maidenhead United	36	10	12	14	38	47	42
Ebbsfleet United	36	11	8	17	48	59	41
Wealdstone	32	10	9	13	43	49	39
AFC Fylde	35	10	9	16	56	64	39
York City	35	8	15	12	43	53	39
Kidderminster Harriers	36	10	9	17	32	44	39
Woking	36	10	8	18	37	46	38
Dorking Wanderers	34	11	5	18	39	57	38
Oxford City	36	7	7	22	47	77	28

* Southend deducted ten points for failing to pay an existing tax bill.

March 2024

SINCE ROCHDALE HAD first crossed swords with Ebbsfleet United at Spotland on the opening day of the season – an encounter the home side lost via a solitary goal – the south coast club had dispensed with the services of enigmatic German manager Dennis Kutrieb and had replaced him with Danny Searle, a coach who boasted both domestic and overseas experience.

Under Searle, Ebbsfleet had pulled away from the league's bottom four and welcomed Dale while enjoying a spell of good form. It was also the first game of a new month, which could only mean one outcome – a Dale defeat! And the visitors did indeed suffer a 2-1 reverse, despite Kairo Mitchell scoring his 11th goal of the season either side of a Dominic Poleon opener and a Dominic Samuel clincher in the 92nd minute.

Head coach Jim McNulty made two changes to his starting XI from the Tuesday night win against Wealdstone, with Devante Rodney and Adam Clayton returning from the start.

Jesurun Uchegbulam and Finlay Armstrong returned to the Dale bench with Manchester United loanee Sam Mather making a first squad appearance since his arrival in February.

McNulty confirmed that D'Mani Mellor and Tyrese Sinclair were sidelined due to injuries. Mellor had suffered a hamstring injury during the previous game, ruling him out for approximately five weeks, while Sinclair had rolled his ankle, with the extent of his absence not determined. Additionally, midfielder Harvey Gilmour was unavailable due to a two-match suspension following his accumulation of ten yellow cards.

As to the match itself, it was a flat display in truth, aeons away from the urgent tempo Dale had displayed in midweek against Wealdstone. This allowed the Ebbsfleet players the comfort of pressing the visitors around their own box. There were also defensive errors from the Dale players, which helped their opponents' cause. On the 15-minute mark, one such was a loose pass across his box from Tiernan Brooks, which Poleon picked up before firing the ball into an empty net.

Dale did find an equaliser five minutes before the break as Kyron Gordon's long pass put Jimmy Keohane in behind the defence on the right. His low cross found Mitchell, who tucked home from close range and, in the second half, with just three minutes remaining, Cameron John found himself unmarked inside Ebbsfleet's penalty area as a cross came in from the right. Despite meeting the ball cleanly, the full-back could only watch in dismay as his attempt struck the top of the crossbar.

In the dying moments, however, Samuel, who had been substituted on for the hosts, seized his opportunity when a deflected ball fell to him at the edge of the penalty area in acres of space. With a precise strike, he secured all three points for Ebbsfleet, leaving Dale 13th in the table.

'I can't believe we lost, to be honest, looking at the game in its entirety, based on chances,' McNulty said afterwards.

'We have to take our medicine and accept it. We gave them two goals today. We feel disappointed.

'My challenge to the players now is how focused can we remain to try to surprise people. Can we remain tunnel-visioned on winning the next game? Unfortunately, we couldn't replicate the last performance today.'

* * *

HAVING SPENT 106 years at Underhill, Barnet relocated to the Hive Stadium in 2013. Initially planned as a site for a new ground for Wealdstone, Barnet took over the project when Wealdstone faced financial difficulties. The man behind this project was Anthony Kleanthous, who became the youngest club chairman in the Football League when, aged 28, he bought the Bees in 1994.

Born in London to a Cypriot family, Kleanthous began his career in the motor trade before venturing into petrochemicals. Later, he successfully founded a telecommunications company, and his business portfolio expanded to include property, leisure and medical ventures. With more than 30 companies under his belt, his empire, at the time of writing, boasted a staggering worth of £250m.

In the world of football, Kleanthous had held prestigious roles as the youngest director of the Football League and the Football Association. He played a pivotal role in launching the FA Women's Super League and contributed significantly to the growth of National League broadcasting.

Not only a football enthusiast, Kleanthous had also left an indelible mark on the medical sector. Collaborating with Toshiba Medical Systems, he pioneered the UK's first medical imaging academy and invested in various medical scanning and diagnostic companies. At the Hive, the state-of-the-art imaging centre offered top-notch sports medical scanning services, catering to elite athletes and the local community alike.

It's a wonder the man had any time for running an actual football club, and yet, 30 years on, he was still at the helm. With his other pursuits taking him overseas numerous times throughout the year, he had entrusted Dean Brennan to oversee first-team affairs and the Bees' promotion charge for the 2023/24 season.

The Irishman had been at the club since 2021 after leaving a positive legacy at nearby Wealdstone. Firstly, Brennan arrived at Barnet as head of football, with Harry Kewell occupying the role of head coach, and, since September of that year, in the role of head coach himself, following Kewell's subsequent departure.

'I was approached by the chairman to manage Barnet earlier than that, actually,' Brennan explained when I met up with him. 'I turned it down at the time as I didn't feel the group of players was strong enough to get out of the division. They had about 40 players on the books, too. It was a bit of a mess.

'When I finally accepted a role at Barnet, it wasn't as head coach, it was as head of football, but the club *had* sorted itself out a bit. However, Harry [Kewell] didn't get the results he needed as head coach, so I stepped into that role when he left. I had vowed never to be a first-team manager again, as I had a bad experience at Wealdstone at the end of my time there, but I found, quite quickly, that I enjoyed it at Barnet.

'When I took over, the team was 23rd in the National League. We managed to get to 18th and so avoided relegation. I then evolved the team from there and got fifth place last season and, this year, at the minute, we are second in the table.

'We needed to get our supporters to buy into what we wanted to do. So, I created an open-door policy. I opened every door in the building, literally, and I had lots of cups of tea with the supporters. I wanted them to see the personality of everyone at the club and show them that we are all in it together. They are a very hardcore and loyal bunch of supporters at Barnet.

'That said, we're not a massive club. We're averaging only 1,900 home fans this season. In fact, we only got 1,000 on the gate the other night, which is poor. Our geographical location is an advantage when it comes to recruitment, you know, north London, lots of clubs to tap into. But this is a disadvantage when trying to attract supporters, for the same reason. You've got Arsenal and Spurs on your doorstep, and people prefer the Premier League to the National League, that's just a fact.

'Therefore, our budget isn't the biggest in the division. It's £800,000 for this season. The chairman has spent more in previous seasons, I know, but, as I always point out to him, it's his children's inheritance and it's up to him how he spends it. He knows, at the end of the day, that 1,900 paying supporters alone is not enough to create a competitive budget, so he dips his hand in.

'I've got a very good personal relationship with the chairman, thankfully. He's self-made and it's a family business he has created. So, you must appreciate that he's not a corporate man or anything like that.'

Brennan, like many managers in non-league football, made the transition from part-time to full-time.

'It's about how you manage the step up,' he said, when asked about the challenge of conversion. 'You go from it being just two of you doing everything at a part-time club, and seeing the players three times a week, to having a full staff and seeing the players almost every day. You've got coaches, a medical department, a physio, a recruitment department. If you're a good coach, which I believe personally I am, that extra time with the players is invaluable. You also get the benefit of analysing games with the players. Seeing how and why you won or lost.

'The biggest factor, though – whether you're part-time or full-time – is recruitment. The coaching is only ten per cent of any team function, the rest is on the players. You have to get the right players. And listen, budget is important, but, as I tell my chairman, you can still get nice wine from Aldi and Lidl. The challenge and skill is knowing where to shop with the money you have.

'We're most likely going to contest the play-offs this season. If we get promoted to League Two, I know I'll need to recruit a lot of players. That's not because I don't rate my current players, it's because of the transfer windows, which we don't have in the National League. Clubs stockpile players in the EFL because they only get two opportunities to sign them during the season. That's part of the new challenge.

'I don't fear promotion to League Two, though. I'd say the harder gap is National League North or South to the National League. I'd say confidently that's the biggest gulf in English football other than the Championship to the Premier League. So, promotion holds no fear for us, should we achieve it.'

Rochdale's own head coach, Jim McNulty, and his players, travelled to the Hive just three days after having made a similarly lengthy journey to Ebbsfleet, with the game having been postponed on its original date of 10 February.

He made three changes. Ian Henderson returned to the starting XI over Devante Rodney. Finlay Armstrong, who had his loan extended once more, this time until the end of the season, also started, while defender Dan Sassi made his first start for the club.

Any travelling supporters hoping for a repeat of Dale's scintillating 4-2 demolition of the Bees at Spotland in September had them immediately dashed when Ethan Ebanks-Landell was robbed of the ball in his own box in the first minute, leading to Barnet's opener, Callum Stead tapping home the following square ball easily. What followed was undoubtedly Dale's worst performance of the season to this point.

Far from the mistake acting as a wake-up call, Dale's rearguard continued at funereal pace, failing to provide Kairo Mitchell and Henderson with quick balls with which the forwards might create overloads, and instead they dallied in possession, inviting pressure on themselves from the Barnet attack. The right flank seemed particularly problematic, with Stead enjoying acres of space with which to employ his trickery.

A whole host of balls fed across from the right channel created chaos in the Dale box and it was only some form of divine intervention that kept the score to one. One such cross led to Jimmy Keohane being penalised, perhaps harshly, for a handball, but goalkeeper Tiernan Brooks made a terrific save to keep out the resultant penalty from Zak Brunt.

Dale, therefore, somehow, made it to the break only one goal down.

Perhaps a rousing half-time team talk would inspire more urgency in the second half, mused the watching Rochdale support. Sadly not. The game continued much the same, with Barnet mopping up second balls and dictating the play. There were flashes of chances for Dale, but it was no surprise when Stead scored his second of the match for the hosts. Brooks got down well to deny a first effort, but he could only push it as far as Stead, who had the simple task of placing the ball home.

The defeat left Dale 14th in the National League table, having picked up only seven points since the turn of the year.

'Ethan [Ebanks-Landell], being the way he is, instantly put his hand up and wanted to apologise to the changing room before he even allowed me to say anything,' said McNulty afterwards, of his captain's costly opening-minute mistake.

'That's the kind of man he is. Those are the types of characters we want in the team. People that ultimately have humility and are accountable for when they make mistakes. We can all make mistakes, even me.

'Ebanks, from that moment, gave everything to keep the ball out of the back of his net. He must've headed a thousand balls from right under his crossbar. Excuse the exaggeration, but it felt that way.

'It was a deserved loss, though, definitely. We weren't good. We weren't what we expect to be as a team. I don't think our performance warranted us having any chances tonight. Barnet could have had double what they scored. Every time they had the ball, they put pressure on us and we didn't do that to them. Every time we got the ball back, we were hopeless. It's only because we fought so hard to keep the ball out of the net that Barnet only scored two.'

* * *

AFTER CHAIRMAN SIMON Gauge's January statement, issuing new shares to provide a cash injection into Rochdale AFC, I got together once more with my close friend and fellow journalist Mark Hodkinson, the Dale Trust and other like-minded supporters. We had initially united upon learning of the attempted Morton House takeover in 2021. This time, we scoured our contact books, seeking wealthy entrepreneurs who might be interested in investing in the club.

We reached out to many potential investors, from prestigious former football managers to billionaire entrepreneurs, including one particular wealthy philanthropist with strong ties to the town of Rochdale itself. It was Mark who contacted this individual, following a steer from the Dale Trust, and his chance appeal ultimately bore fruit.

After reading Mark's plea, Sir Peter Ogden asked his representatives to contact Rochdale AFC and the Dale Trust to see how they could help take the club forward in as benevolent a way as possible.

Born and raised in Rochdale, Sir Peter had maintained strong ties to his hometown throughout his life. He was widely recognised for his philanthropic endeavours, particularly through the Ogden Trust, a charitable organisation he founded with £22.5m of his own money.

Sir Peter's philanthropic efforts primarily focused on supporting education, with a special emphasis on promoting the teaching and learning of physics in underrepresented groups. The Ogden Trust had spearheaded numerous initiatives aimed at enhancing educational opportunities for young people.

Knighted for his services to philanthropy and education in 1999, Sir Peter had made notable contributions to the business world, too. After a high-school education in Rochdale, he obtained a PhD in theoretical physics from Durham University and an MBA from Harvard Business School. He then embarked on a successful career that saw him rise to the position of managing director at JPMorgan.

However, it was his entrepreneurial spirit that truly defined his legacy.

In 1981, Sir Peter co-founded the computer services company Computacenter PLC and, in 1982, the financial software company Computasoft, which was subsequently renamed Dealogic PLC. Under his leadership, Computacenter flourished, becoming the largest privately owned IT company in the UK by 1994. Its success culminated in the company floating on the London Stock Exchange in 1998, with Sir Peter transitioning to a non-executive director role. He still retained a substantial 6.5 per cent stake in the company.

The timing of the Ogdens' approach couldn't have been more vital as, by this juncture, Gauge had already called the EGM with the club's plight now a lot more perilous than it had been in January.

The five resolutions at the EGM on 7 March were passed by shareholder vote, the primary one being the ability for the club to create a volume of shares that would allow a single buyer to own 90 per cent of Rochdale AFC.

While Gauge had initially publicised the interest of World Soccer Holdings in acquiring the club, and the Ogdens had made initial enquiries privately, another investor latterly signalled its own intent – a ten-strong consortium by the name of The Football Club LLC (TFC), a collective of professionals from the US and UK, which claimed to possess 'diverse expertise'.

Led by New Yorker Justin Corrado and Lancastrian David Dwyer, TFC said, in a press release, that it aimed to rejuvenate Rochdale AFC in partnership with the fans and community. The proposal included financial investment, support for players and coaches, and a strategic football and business plan. TFC also said it planned to return five per cent of the club's shares to the Dale Trust and grant it a golden share for protection.

This meant the football club now had what appeared to be three very credible investment options. Choosing the right one would be paramount.

* * *

OXFORD CITY, STILL under the stewardship of the genial Ross Jenkins, sat rock bottom of the National League when they travelled to Spotland on a sunny March Saturday afternoon.

When I spoke to Jenkins back at the start of the season, he couldn't have outlined in terms any more plain just how far behind his team was from the other clubs in the fifth tier in terms of resource. The season had certainly gone on to reflect that for the Hoops.

It seemed a reasonable expectation then, that Rochdale would, at the very least, match the 1-0 win achieved in the reverse fixture and restore some on-field pride for what was rapidly becoming a nightmarish second leg of the campaign.

It wasn't to be, of course, and, despite taking an early lead, Dale were 2-1 behind at the break, having to then fight tooth and nail to achieve the 2-2 draw that offered a solitary point at the final whistle.

Jim McNulty opted for significant alterations from the squad that faced Barnet on Tuesday. Harvey Gilmour's return from suspension, along with the inclusion of Jesurun Uchegbulam and George Nevett in the starting line-up, chief among them. Additionally, loanee Sam Mather earned his maiden professional start following an impactful performance off the bench earlier in the week.

Meanwhile, Devante Rodney found himself back among the substitutes, with Finlay Armstrong and youthteamer Corey Edwards omitted from the matchday squad altogether.

The game kicked off with both sides displaying a cautious approach, but it was Rochdale who seized the early initiative. Eleven minutes in, Kairo Mitchell demonstrated his scoring prowess yet again, notching his 12th goal of the season, muscling his way to a clinical finish from a well-placed long ball by Ethan Ebanks-Landell which beat the visiting back line.

However, Oxford City rallied strongly, capitalising on defensive lapses to overturn the deficit. Harvey Greenslade and Josh Parker exploited Rochdale's returning vulnerabilities at the back, scoring crucial goals to give their team the lead heading into half-time.

The second half witnessed a determined Rochdale pushing for an equaliser and they eventually restored parity in the 77th minute. The excellent Cian Hayes showcased his skills on the right flank, driving towards the byline before delivering a precise cross into the box. Sam Mather, seizing the opportunity, calmly slotted the ball home from close range, registering his first goal for Rochdale in only his second appearance for the club.

Despite late chances for Dale to snatch victory, including a missed opportunity by substitute Devante Rodney, the game concluded with both sides sharing the spoils, much to the vexation of the home support.

While Rochdale showcased glimpses of their attacking prowess and resilience, there were evident areas of concern highlighted in the match. The middle period, characterised by poor decision-making and a lack of leadership, saw the players' confidence waver, particularly in ball retention within their own third. Criticism was also directed towards team selection, with questions raised over the inclusion of out-of-form players ahead of potentially more impactful alternatives. The absence of Ian Henderson, Adam Clayton and Jimmy Keohane, who could offer tactical flexibility and stability, raised eyebrows among fans and pundits alike. Furthermore, the tactical approach, particularly in continually inviting unnecessary pressure, drew continued scrutiny from supporters.

'We're disappointed overall, if I'm being honest, with the goals we conceded,' said McNulty after the game.

'From our point of view, we expect diligence from ourselves in those moments, to know exactly what we're doing. In a game, when you go ahead and you're having chances, you feel like the second goal is coming.

'We had to battle against the flow of how the game then started to go, and I think the one shining light is the competitiveness that remained from us, in that we did not run away from that battle when it was looking and sounding tough.

'We fought to try to produce the moments that we practice, to get back to ourselves, in a game that had become a struggle, and, I think, in the second half, there came a moment, with about half an hour to go, where we wrestled control of the game again. Fortunately, we got a second goal, had chances to get a third and ultimately we came away disappointed with a point.'

* * *

STILL SMARTING FROM the Saturday performance against Oxford City, Jim McNulty and his players needed to wait only three days for an opportunity to make amends in front of the Rochdale support when Spotland Stadium welcomed Woking for a Tuesday night fixture under the floodlights.

Having lost the reverse meeting 3-2 in August, McNulty would find this Woking side a different proposition as they had gone on to struggle thereafter, form that had eventually cost manager Darren Sarll his job. Former Sheffield United midfielder Michael Doyle had taken over and had steered the Cardinals to three straight victories ahead of this tie – results that suggested Woking had regained some of the rhythm that made them play-off participants the previous campaign.

Despite Woking taking an early lead, and adopting a somewhat rudimentary approach to protecting it thereafter, moments of individual skill from Cian Hayes and Devante Rodney papered over Rochdale's overall lacklustre performance, securing their first victory in four games.

Finlay Armstrong reclaimed his spot in the starting XI for this one, replacing Cameron John, while Rodney stepped in for Jesurun Uchegbulam.

Woking initially dominated the game but failed to convert early chances. Charley Kendall eventually broke the deadlock in the 15th minute after dispossessing Ethan Ebanks-Landell, who was once again caught in possession after receiving a needless back-pass. However, the visitors' lead was eradicated just before half-time. Hayes embarked on one of his trademark runs down the right wing before cutting across the edge of the box and unleashing a beautiful curling strike into the far top corner.

The second half saw the game sink to a slower pace until Woking's Dion Kelly-Evans was shown a straight red card in the 66th minute for a two-footed lunge at Hayes. Despite being a man down, Woking continued to press, but it was Dale who found the breakthrough in added time. Rodney, presented with a free kick on the edge of the box in a central position, smashed a powerful strike low into the bottom right of the goal. Sadly, the celebration was marred by a red card for substitute Ian Henderson who, it appeared, used his arm to fell a Woking player while retrieving the ball from back of the net.

Woking then pushed hard for an equaliser in the dying minutes, but Dale's defence held firm.

Post-match, McNulty described it as 'a really tough game'.

'When I was doing my research and reconnaissance on Woking,' he explained, 'I became very aware they are riding the crest of a wave, and that they're a really challenging team to play against. In two of the games I watched recently, against two very good footballing teams in Altrincham and Gateshead, Woking managed to take the football away from both of those teams. I would also consider ourselves to be one of the football-playing teams in the division. I think Woking did a good job against us tonight, and I expected them to.

'With that said, in the first 15–20 minutes, Woking were completely different from what I expected based on my prior viewing of them, and it caught us by surprise. Those initial moments were really difficult for us because we needed to reorganise, to reshuffle. I hoped to accomplish that while the game was still 0-0. But, at the point when we attempted to make changes, they got their noses ahead, and, from that moment on, it became a fight and a battle against ourselves, against the emotions of being 1-0 down at home.

'Woking are obviously fuelled by the desire to survive, and, yes, consecutive wins have made them a formidable force to contend with. We felt that this evening. But, once again, from being behind, we showed unbelievable guts and character after we made it difficult for ourselves with moments that we are disappointed with. But to find the guts and the character is something I'm really grateful for game after game, win or lose, great performance, poor performance. I've always been able to call on that character, and it's a great sign to come from behind to win a game.

'Two individual moments of brilliance won it for us, ultimately. [Devante Rodney's] celebration was a moment for us all. It symbolised his feelings towards his team-mates, towards us as a group, as a staff. Dev has an appreciation for how we've handled his rehab, the patience we've shown him. He knows he's felt wanted here throughout, despite the torturous season he's endured. To come back at Chesterfield and score such an important goal, have that moment with the fans, and then face further setbacks down the line when he thought he was over it … it's really tough. Then, at Ebbsfleet, Dev was feeling like he let the team down on that day, and he didn't mean to. These circumstances are unforeseen sometimes, and Dev's still learning about himself and the issues he's had. He's still recovering from that. But tonight was a good night for him, a brilliant moment when he scored.'

Watching the match from the comfort of the directors' box was World Soccer Holdings CEO Scott Dyer, along with representatives of the Ogden family. Prior to the match, the board of directors issued a statement that the club had entered a period of exclusivity with WSH in relation to the proposed acquisition of the newly created shares in the club, following the recent EGM.

The Dale Trust issued a statement of its own soon afterwards, claiming, 'Whereas we recognise the need for a speedy resolution to the club's need for funds, we have yet to meet with WSH, this meeting is scheduled for tomorrow afternoon.'

The following day, the Dale Trust chairman, George Brigham, met Dyer for what he termed a 'lively discussion', covering various topics related to potential investment in Rochdale AFC.

Dyer was said to have initially expressed interest in the club due to its community-focused location and unique ownership of its stadium. He emphasised, according to Brigham, the importance of elevating individuals and organisations in communities, reflecting his charitable approach to opportunity development, inspired by his own Christian beliefs.

While WSH itself was not directly involved with any US football franchises, Dyer claimed to have strong connections with various organisations engaged in sports-related endeavours.

Dyer went on to outline that WSH operated with two partners and typically delegated most tasks to consultants. The future management structure of Rochdale as a business remained uncertain, he said, but the importance of maintaining continuity in personnel was acknowledged, with plans for additional staff to alleviate current workloads and drive revenue growth.

Dyer, acting as a liaison for investors, said he sought to attract both passive and hands-on investors. In the event of a sale, the owning company would be disclosed. Investors being courted included a group of Formula 1 drivers, who, he said, understood the necessity of patience and long-term commitment given the club's financial challenges and the competitive landscape.

However, he did admit that the initial purchase funds going into the club would simply not be enough to fund it beyond a short period and that he was 'working on this'.

Justin Corrado, the American who was co-fronting The Football Club LLC interest in acquiring the newly created Dale shares, expressed disappointment via his own statement, over what he called the chairman's 'decision to enter into exclusivity [with WSH] without an open process'.

Corrado shared TFC's letter of intent within his statement, which he said had been submitted to chairman Simon Gauge, and highlighted 'a lack of feedback' and the 'absence of a chance to respond to a competing bid'.

* * *

WHEN ROCHDALE FACED Eastleigh at Spotland back in August, the players enjoyed their easiest game of the campaign to that point. The 2-0 victory should have seen more goals scored for the home side, such was the visitors' listless approach to the contest.

However, the Eastleigh that Dale travelled to face for the corresponding fixture at the Silverlake Stadium had gone through something of a metamorphosis. The Spitfires had taken ten points from their previous four games, and, having had 14 days without a match, they were expected to be raring to go under new manager Kelvin Davies. They also possessed within the ranks the league's top marksman in former Dale loanee Paul McCallum, who had scored 29 goals in 31 games by this point.

It was a pleasant surprise, then, that Jim McNulty's men would turn in their best performance since Christmas to secure an emphatic 4-1 victory on the road – and a first away win since November.

McNulty made two changes from the side that started Tuesday night's win over Woking. Cameron John replaced Finn Armstrong, who dropped to the bench, while Jimmy Keohane came in for Sam Mather, who missed out entirely.

The vocal visiting Dale support was rewarded from the first whistle, with McNulty's charges dominating play and stroking passes about on the Silverlake's carpet-like surface with purpose and accuracy. Ryan East was proving a useful pivot at the base of the midfield allowing play to proceed up either flank, while Kairo Mitchell and Devante Rodney were linking up well at the top of the pitch.

This was expertly demonstrated when Rochdale seized a well-earned advantage after 28 minutes. Rodney initiated the play by catching George Langston in possession high up the pitch, before then surging towards the penalty area. With precision, he delivered the ball to Mitchell on his right, who calmly slotted it into the bottom corner of the net for his 13th goal of the campaign.

Perhaps the only blip on what was an otherwise masterful exhibition of McNulty's preferred style of play was the allowance of Eastleigh to level things up almost right away, McCallum heading home a Scott Quigley cross just three minutes later. Two former Dale loanees combining to do the damage a little too easily.

Rochdale regained the lead in the 45th minute, however, courtesy of a well-executed sequence. Cian Hayes threaded a ball into space for the advancing Kyron Gordon, whose low cross narrowly missed Mitchell but reached the back post, where Keohane was positioned perfectly to calmly dispatch it into the net from ten yards out.

After the break, Dale continued to dominate the hosts with sequence after sequence of forward-thinking football.

Ethan Ebanks-Landell initiated the move that led to Dale's third goal, delivering a precise pass down the line to Hayes. Demonstrating skilful footwork, Hayes manoeuvred past a couple of defenders before delivering the ball to Mitchell. Mitchell's quick flick found Rodney, who displayed remarkable composure as he navigated two defenders before unleashing a shot that rattled the underside of the crossbar before nestling into the net.

Rochdale extended the lead with a fourth goal 11 minutes from the final whistle. Mitchell started a forward run, and, with perfect timing, received a through ball from Hayes. With a powerful strike, Mitchell directed the ball towards goal. Despite Eastleigh keeper Joe McDonnell getting a hand to it, the shot looped in off the far post, doubling Mitchell's tally for the match.

'It was an excellent result, but, more importantly, an excellent performance,' McNulty remarked afterwards. 'We've been chasing good performances, believing they'll bring the outcomes we desire. Today was a culmination of diligence, confidence and execution from the players. They brought a week of training to life with a very good performance.

'We showed courage, establishing not just control, but dominance. The players have bought into our vision for success, showcasing their strengths. Days like today, it all came together. They were top goals, and we are capable of those moments as a team. I've got the utmost belief in them.

'Even when Eastleigh responded, we continued playing good football with hunger. Seven points out of a possible nine, showing guts, courage and resilience. I'm proud of the team today.'

* * *

IN THE DAYS leading up to Rochdale hosting Alan Devonshire's Maidenhead United for the reverse National League fixture, Jim McNulty faced something of a dilemma between the posts.

On-loan goalkeeper Tiernan Brooks had received a call-up from the Republic of Ireland under-21s for their UEFA European Championship qualifier against San Marino. With backup goalkeeper Brad Kelly out for the remainder of the season as a result of injury, McNulty had to scour the market, within his usual parameters, to find a replacement.

He did so in the form of Jacob Chapman, a 23-year-old from Huddersfield Town, who joined on a loan deal until the end of the season. A native of Australia, Chapman began his career with Sydney United 58 before making the move to Huddersfield Town in 2019. His journey in the UK had included loan spells at Ossett United and Gateshead, as well as appearances for Salford City.

McNulty faced a further selection setback as defender George Nevett, who had already garnered international recognition for his outstanding debut season, was also unavailable. Nevett received his second call-up to the Wales under-19s, following his initial selection in October. He was set to contribute to their squad for a friendly double-header against Belgium at the Proximus Basecamp in the city of Tubize, further solidifying his promising career trajectory.

These two enforced changes from the previous Saturday's 4-1 win at Eastleigh didn't disrupt the flow, however. Devante Rodney's first-half header was enough to secure a 1-0 win on a wet and churned Spotland pitch. The forward's third goal in as many games came seven minutes before half-time to ensure McNulty's men ran out with the three points their dominance deserved.

Chapman himself had a fine debut in goal, composed and commanding, and Dan Sassi fared equally well as Nevett's understudy. In fact, the defence as a whole was steely and resolute, protecting a lead that in previous games it may have helped to fritter away.

Harvey Gilmour's influence all over the pitch was also vital to the victory, putting in blocks on the edge of his own box while providing the clear link in almost all of Dale's attacks. Jimmy Keohane's recent return had also increased

Dale's threat, which made it all the more mystifying why he hadn't been utilised more during the poor run of the previous two months.

Once again, the Dale players looked to shift 11 men, sitting deep, around the pitch, while looking for space to create their own heroics. For the most part they managed to make the correct call as to when to go forward and when to go back. The main issue was not getting the ball into the Maidenhead box often enough. On one of the few occasions they did achieve this, with a straightforward ball by Ethan Ebanks-Landell, it led to the only goal of the game. The defender found Mitchell, allowing the striker to latch on to the ball before seeing his shot saved by goalkeeper Craig Ross. The parried ball looped up into the air with Rodney powering above a defender to head home from the edge of the six-yard box.

The only real downer, other than the lack of further goals for the home side, was an injury to Cian Hayes. The influential winger had to be substituted in the second half as a result.

'It was a pleasing win,' a content-looking McNulty commented afterwards.

'Home has been a good place for us. There was a connection again with the players and the fans – the Sandy Lane end were singing their hearts out throughout the game. I'll always mention it because it's so powerful for us when we find that connection and push towards getting the outcome that we want.

'We did that today against a team that are desperate and fighting for their lives, and desperate is dangerous. Maidenhead are a dangerous outfit. I've seen their victories, like the 3-1 win at Altrincham. They're capable of those performances.

'They sit and watch you do what you want to do, then, bang, they're on the break and have a chance. They very nearly did it to us in the opening exchanges as well. But it didn't surprise me.

'I wanted us to continue to have more courage, more belief and break them down. We scored a brilliant goal and, in the second half, we really went on to turn them over.

'There was a period before the inevitable pressure that always comes in the National League, where we put together some real nice moves that we didn't quite finish.

'I thought we could have put the game to bed. The players are actually disappointed, in a way, that they didn't win it by more because they felt like it was there for them.

'I'll make sure they're respectful of the opponents we've played and respectful of the result, which was a very good one. The fact we made 70 minutes of that game look clinical is impressive.'

* * *

FOLLOWING THE EXPIRATION of a period of exclusivity with World Soccer Holdings LLC on 24 March, Rochdale AFC instead announced the Ogden family as its preferred investor in the club.

The Ogden family said it would make 'sufficient funds available to the club to enable it to operate for the next 30 days' in order for the family to complete due diligence and present an offer so that investment could be concluded before the end of the season.

The family statement also said that their medium-term ambition was to assist the club to become financially sustainable 'regardless of football success'.

'We were made aware of the club's difficulties in recent weeks, and we held constructive initial meetings with the club and the Dale Trust,' the statement said. 'We have since been monitoring the situation while the club has been in exclusive discussions with WSH LLC. We were informed that the exclusivity period has expired and have since stepped up our discussions and diligence efforts.

'In our view, the club (and the Rochdale AFC Community Trust which is so closely associated with it) are community assets of immense value which need to survive. We intend to make an offer to the club, but we need some time to ensure that our diligence is completed, and our offer can be properly formulated. Perhaps, most importantly, we would like to ensure that all stakeholders have sufficient chance to review and consider our proposal. However, given the club's severe financial difficulties, time is not on our side.

'We will use this period to actively engage with all stakeholders, including the town's political figures, creditors and sponsors to ensure they are prepared to play their part in ensuring the survival of the club. This period will also be used to formulate our future plans for both first-team and academy operations.'

Rochdale chairman Simon Gauge described the proposal as a 'different type of football investment'.

'It is primarily driven by the recognition of, and motivation to preserve, the significant community value that clubs like ours provide,' he said. 'The Ogden family recognises the history that our football club has and are motivated to help us achieve sustainability so that we will be at the heart of our community for another 100 years and beyond.

'We hope that the government, along with the Premier League, EFL, National League and other stakeholders, also recognise the value that clubs like ours provide to communities up and down the country.

'If this is the case, they must agree on a distribution model that allows us and others to run in a sustainable way and create a proper pyramid with three up and three down from the National League to the EFL.

'A system with only one automatic promotion place available encourages clubs to gamble on promotion and operate in an unsustainable manner. This must be scrapped.

'I would also like to put on record my thanks to Rochdale Borough Council and the mayor of Greater Manchester, Andy Burnham, for their support to this point and I look forward to continuing to work with them as we strive to complete the best outcome for the club and community.'

The club stated it would make no further comment on the proposed investment while it assisted the Ogden family in carrying out a further period of engagement before a purchase of shares in the club was completed.

The Dale Trust, too, issued a statement reiterating its support of the Ogdens as the preferred investor. 'This is a great day to be a Dale fan, and once again the birthplace of co-operation springs into action,' it said.

* * *

FOOTBALL AND TYNESIDE evoke immediate thoughts of Paul Gascoigne, Kevin Keegan and Alan Shearer. The commonality here being that they are all synonymous with one club, Newcastle United.

However, the National League boasts its own little north-east football treasure in the guise of Gateshead. With its grandiosely named International Stadium, housed just on the other side of the Tyne Bridge from Newcastle itself, it's a fan-owned club with lofty ambitions.

The path to fan ownership had been anything but smooth, though. Hong Kong-based Indian owner Dr

Ranjan Varghese, and his Italian adviser Joe Cala, took on the club in 2018 and a period of turbulence followed, with Gateshead hit by numerous league sanctions, even being evicted from their own stadium at one point. In 2019, former Rochdale chairman Chris Dunphy unsuccessfully tried to buy the club from Varghese, before local serving military attaché Neil Pinkerton and a five-man consortium managed to wrest ownership of the club.

Their first challenge was dealing with a demotion from the National League to National League North, a legacy punishment handed to the club during the governance of the previous regime. Not only did Gateshead return to the National League following two Covid-hit seasons, they did so by winning the title and scoring an incredible 99 goals into the bargain. During the 2022/23 season, their first back in the National League, they reached the FA Trophy Final, losing narrowly by a solitary goal to FC Halifax Town.

I caught up with Pinkerton, intrigued by the club's story, to learn how he had made a success of the fan-ownership model at Gateshead where Rochdale had not.

'Gateshead is in my blood,' he told me. 'My grandfather used to take me to games from a young age. I was always involved with football and played it when I was young. It was instilled in me. I enjoyed going. I know watching Newcastle would have been the easier option, but I like being different and I'm very loyal to the town where I come from.

'I was deployed overseas when Varghese bought the club, and I understand he bought it because the chief financial advisor that he used, Joseph Cala, actually couldn't pass the owners' and directors' test, but it was Cala who turned up to run the club. Things then started to go quite wrong off the pitch when the club was doing very well on the pitch.

'Steve Watson was the manager at the time and he had a good young side, supported by experienced quality loan players such as Luke Armstrong and Luke Molyneux. Getting to Christmas time, we were right up in the play-off spots of the National League.

'In the January, things started to go wrong. We were hearing payments were being made late to local businesses and so on. Then the club was put under a transfer embargo because an HMRC bill wasn't paid.

'I came back from overseas at this point, but was based down south, getting ready for my next role as an assistant defence attaché to Estonia for the UK. A fans' group had formed called the Gateshead Soul. Being a lifelong supporter myself, I knew a good few of them. They asked if I would help facilitate the sale of the club with potential buyers they had sourced.

'Boy, did I not know what I was getting myself in for! It was a very complicated process and consisted of lots of calls in the middle of the night, due to geographical time differences, with the owner. You know, two in the morning, four in the morning. Then there was Cala himself, who was a very difficult person to deal with. I'm not joking when I said the club was literally 72 hours from going out of business.

'Your former chairman, Chris Dunphy, was one of the potential buyers engaging with the fans' group, and another potential buyer was Trevor Clarke, a local businessman.

'Chris got cold feet and I think that was largely down to the amount of debt that was coming out of the woodwork. Trevor was trying to buy it for himself at first, but I think he realised too, that it was too big for one person, so he came on board with us fans and other local businessmen and we formed a consortium.

'I was very blind, and was trusting a lot to those who understood business. I've been in the military for 21 years and, other than having a GCSE in business studies, that's as close as I've got to any business. It was myself who took on all the dealings with the FA and the National League, though, and I effectively bought the club to start with.

'We took the demotion from the National League on the chin, which was all to do with the previous owners, and then myself and Trevor had to unpick the ownership, which was another difficult and lengthy process – but we got there. Then we had to get a team together on and off the pitch. We persuaded Mike Williamson to step up as first-team manager and what a job he did. We were devastated to lose him [to MK Dons] in October, but he deserved the chance to step up.

'We are looking to keep growing the club year on year. The borough of Gateshead has got more than 200,000 people living in it, so it's not inconsequential, but it's always been difficult to attract fans and you always think, when you're a fan and not involved with it, "Oh there's lots you could do to attract more fans," but it's difficult. We've grown steadily each year and hopefully we'll see an upturn again this year.'

Rather than seeing his illustrious neighbours across the Tyne as rivals, Pinkerton hoped to tap in to Newcastle United supporters when they were stuck for something to do.

'Newcastle's St James' Park can only fit so many people into it, and they were playing in the Champions League this season, so that means they didn't play a lot of Saturday games, meaning we saw a few more on our gate. There are thousands of Newcastle season ticket holders this side of the Tyne, so hopefully they'll see us as a way of getting a Saturday football fix in the future too.

'We don't compete with fellow non-league club South Shields, either, as they're 12 miles away and in a different borough altogether. They actually tend to get a lot of Sunderland fans going to their games.'

With Gateshead progressing on the pitch, what is the ultimate aim for the club?

'Our ambition is to ultimately return to the Football League,' Pinkerton said. 'People will forget now that Gateshead was ever there. There's no time frame put on this, though. Just win the next game and then the next one. One game at a time. When it happens, it happens. That's the mentality. We're quite bullish this season, but never over-confident. Achieving what we have up to now, we have every right to be.

'As I say, we are fan-owned to a percentage and the rest is local businessmen. We don't have a rich sugar daddy putting all the money in, so we are realistic with salaries. What we do is offer players something they won't get elsewhere. The way we look after each other off the pitch and the way we play. We ask them to buy into what we're trying to do. It's not Moneyball, either. There's a lot of thought goes into these players that we have signed. In the past, the team played a certain way and it was hard to attract players. The management team now has us playing in a way that's attractive to a player. Even though we lost one manager mid-season to a bigger opportunity, his replacement has kept that continuity. Players are willing to come to us for a bit less money because they know they're going to get an opportunity and we won't stand in their way when it comes to progressing their own career. Just look at Macaulay Langstaff at Notts County as a prime example.'

For now, Pinkerton is happy to continue giving his time to the club he loves on a voluntary basis.

'I can do a lot of this job remotely,' he said. 'This fits in with my military career. However, I'm hands on when I can be. In the summer, I was moving furniture into a new clubhouse for the loan players and permanent signings – lifting and shifting in 20°C heat. The next minute, I'm sat in meetings with our partners – the council and local college – discussing various things, and then it's planning what we're doing the week ahead, doing the payroll, you know, it's everything! We're a growing team, but I still take on a lot myself. Until we can generate a better income, that's the way it is.'

Pinkerton also had a word or two about Gateshead's elaborately named home.

'OK, so there's a bit of a stigma attached to our stadium,' he said. 'I've been going there since the late 1980s, when I first started following the football club, so I've known nothing different. When the stadium is full and there's a good atmosphere, it's cracking. But, yes, you've got a running track around the pitch and people will pick up on that. In the main stand, you have a really good view. It's unobstructed, so you get the full length of the pitch. You can see everything that's going on. I was at Wembley for the FA Trophy Final last season and I was further away from the pitch than I've ever been. It's all subjective. I've heard people say they need binoculars at our games, but you've got St James' Park where you can be sat right up with the gods, miles away from the pitch. Again, I think people can be harsh because it's deemed a non-league stadium.

'The stadium was built in the 1970s as an athletics stadium. It was never meant for football, but it's our home and we love it. In the winter, it's one of the coldest places ever because it doesn't get the sun. The main stand is freezing. It's all part of its charm.'

By the time the Rochdale players made their bow at the International Stadium on Good Friday, they had already hosted Gateshead twice – a 2-2 draw in the league and a 5-1 hammering in the FA Trophy third round. Even more concerning was the fact the Heed had dispatched nearby rivals Hartlepool United 7-1 at the venue just three days earlier.

While it was certainly no hammering for Dale on this occasion, Gateshead still won out as the better side over the piece, with the visitors setting up to contain their hosts rather than impose their own game. For the most part, the Dale players held their shape well, attempting to force Gateshead into a mistake by employing a high line and pressing their players in their own half, but, a solitary goal in the first half proved decisive, allowing Gateshead to manage the game out in the second period with Dale failing to make the home goalkeeper break a sweat.

Jim McNulty opted for a single alteration to his line-up following the previous weekend's 1-0 victory against Maidenhead United at home. George Nevett, who had recently earned his second Wales under-19 cap, returned to the starting XI, replacing Dan Sassi, whose loan from Blackpool had been extended until the season's conclusion earlier that week. Additionally, Tyrese Sinclair made a comeback from injury and secured a spot on the substitutes' bench.

Despite Dale's tactics seemingly frustrating Gateshead during the early exchanges, the hosts finally took the lead in the 27th minute when Ed Francis's lofted ball over the top found the brilliant Dajaune Brown who, in turn, lifted it over Jacob Chapman, who was perhaps a touch too sharp off his line.

That goal was enough to disrupt the visitors' rhythm, while helping inspire the home side's own. The Gateshead midfield found its stride thereafter, stroking the ball about as if the opposition were mere ghosts at times, while Dale offered next to nothing in the way of a threat, Cian Hayes's odd menacing run aside. Chapman did redeem himself by clawing a goal-bound effort off the line in the latter stages, but it did little to alter the outcome.

McNulty was a little more reflective after this first defeat in five games.

'I thought it was a very close game,' he said. 'I heard Rob [Elliot, Gateshead manager] saying in the week that it's two of the best football teams in the league playing against each other. It very much was that. It was a cagey, tactical, possession-based affair.

'Truthfully, I don't think either team threatened the other team's goal that much. The only moment that we got done by was one of direct play straight over the top. I thought we would be able to cope in that moment and we didn't.

'I thought we were slow in the first half in terms of our performance. I don't think we started at our best and didn't play with the verve that we've had recently.

'I think that definitely improved in the second half, which was a reaction to what was expressed in the changing room at half-time. We began to become the team that pushed the game. Our line management got a lot better, we dealt with the direct stuff that Gateshead do play when you do get pressure on them.

'We grew into the game and all it needed was some personality, confidence, courage and ability with the ball. I think we showed more of that in the second half, whereas first half we didn't. Ultimately, over the 95 minutes, it was very tight.

'There wasn't a lot exchanged in terms of punch power on the other team's goal. But I'm not really surprised by that given both teams want the ball and the principles that both teams play to.'

National League table as at 31 March 2024

	P	*W*	*D*	*L*	*F*	*A*	*Pts*
Chesterfield (C)	42	30	5	7	101	57	95
Barnet	41	23	6	12	79	55	75
Bromley	41	20	13	8	64	44	73
Gateshead	41	20	9	12	83	57	69
Altrincham	42	19	10	13	80	59	67
Solihull Moors	42	18	13	11	66	59	67
Aldershot Town	41	19	7	15	69	74	64
FC Halifax Town	40	17	11	12	50	45	62
Oldham Athletic	41	15	15	11	58	53	60
Southend United*	42	18	12	12	61	40	56
Rochdale	**41**	**15**	**10**	**16**	**64**	**60**	**55**
Dagenham & Redbridge	42	14	11	17	62	55	53
AFC Fylde	42	14	10	18	71	75	52
Hartlepool United	41	15	7	19	61	74	52
Eastleigh	41	13	11	17	68	81	50
York City	42	11	16	15	52	66	49
Woking	42	13	9	20	42	50	48
Maidenhead United	41	12	12	17	48	58	48
Ebbsfleet United	40	13	9	18	56	67	48
Wealdstone	39	12	11	16	51	60	47
Boreham Wood	41	10	14	17	50	69	44
Kidderminster Harriers	42	10	13	19	36	51	43
Dorking Wanderers	41	12	6	23	47	75	42
Oxford City (R)	42	8	8	26	52	87	32

* Southend deducted ten points for failing to pay an existing tax bill.

April 2024

HARTLEPOOL UNITED HAD their second manager of the season in charge as the club travelled to Rochdale to contest the pair's Easter Monday National League fixture.

Former Sunderland striker Kevin Phillips had taken over from John Askey, who had failed to inspire the kind of promotion charge that had been expected of the other of the EFL's two fallen clubs.

Eight points clear of the relegation places on the day of the contest, Hartlepool had recovered from a 7-1 chastening at the hands of Gateshead to earn a creditable 1-0 victory over play-off chasing FC Halifax Town. Phillips, whose previous management stint had been a successful spell at South Shields, seemed to have his players well-drilled against teams that propelled the ball through the air, with Luke Waterfall and Tom Parkes particularly dominant there, but saw them struggle against the type of football that Jim McNulty had instilled.

In fact, it was in the reverse fixture in October that McNulty's men arrested a mini slump of their own, passing Pools off their own park, albeit Phillips wasn't at the wheel at that point. The game here started in a similar fashion too, but, after Kairo Mitchell was sent off in the first period, Dale had to rely on a Devante Rodney equaliser in the 96th minute to rescue a point. Still, it meant this was the first match of a new month that Rochdale hadn't lost during the entire campaign.

McNulty made three changes from the side that started on Good Friday at Gateshead. Dan Sassi, Finlay Armstrong and Sam Mather all returned to the line-up, replacing George Nevett, Cameron John and Jimmy Keohane.

Dale, wearing the yellow away strip due to both of Hartlepool's kits comprising blue, saw a lot of the ball early on and hit the woodwork inside the opening ten minutes when Cian Hayes's cross came back off the crossbar.

The best chance of the first half, however, fell to Mitchell after a superb passing sequence led to Devante Rodney squaring for his partner, who could only fire over when he really should have scored.

Just two minutes later, the striker was sent off. On first viewing, it seemed Mitchell succumbed to a rush of blood to atone for his miss, sliding in recklessly to win the ball from Tom Parkes. However, on second viewing, it was clear Mitchell was in control and won the ball without endangering his opponent. Sadly, referee Richard Eley deemed the challenge to be serious foul play and issued a red card. It was the kind of challenge that 20 years ago wouldn't have attracted a furore, but such is the modern game.

The dismissal served to highlight that, prior to the dismissal, the Dale players should have taken more advantage of the possession they were enjoying by quickening the pace. The ground staff were in danger of having to clear slug trails off the pitch at half-time, such was the lack of zip on display on too many occasions.

Tactically, the 4-4-2 formation employed, which often became a 4-2-4, appeared to be an attacking way to play, but it was negated by the fact the midfield two of Ryan

East and Harvey Gilmour seemed more mindful of keeping the ball rather than immediately looking forward, leaving them often caught between two stools. It also became all too obvious how left-footed the team was in that area, leading to reduced options, with both players often reluctant to play the way they were facing if the ball couldn't be shifted to their left foot first.

Going wide to Hayes often provided the team's only route into the final third, where it should have been the intention for everyone as a first option.

After the break, the visitors, with their one-man advantage, saw more of the ball, leading to them taking the lead when Joe Grey flicked home from a corner. There were other chances to follow, too, but all were wasted.

Substitute Tyrese Sinclair then sent a couple of efforts off-target from distance for Dale, before Rodney sent a free kick way over the bar from just outside the area. There was one more chance for Dale, however. When Chay Cooper attempted an inexplicable back-heel instead of killing the ball, it allowed East to send forth a long pass that dissected the Hartlepool defence for Rodney to run on to, and he rounded the goalkeeper before turning home from close range to send the Sandy Lane end wild. Once again, proof that a quick, direct and determined Dale side could put anyone to the sword on its day.

'There was a real togetherness shown and a real will to survive,' said McNulty afterwards. 'One of the things that was said at half-time, from myself to the team, was that I wanted to see a willingness to embrace suffering. We had to suffer to have any chance, and I thought that a chance would open up late in the game. It turned out that way. Through brilliant fight and togetherness, an unreal willingness to run, knowing that we were going to suffer without the ball, on a real heavy pitch that takes it out of your legs, we got the goal we needed.

'I had my concerns for the team, but I always believed that they were willing to sacrifice themselves for the greater good – that greater good being a potential result. We had to try to break the will of Hartlepool, to try to send a message that, in open play, they weren't going to break us down. I felt like they would want the ball in our box and would potentially be impatient, given where they've been at recently.

'I felt like we had the skills on the pitch to cope with that and that we could counter-threat. I think the fact that they only scored from a corner, when numbers don't matter as much and it's a physical match-up, was a shame. I thought that could be a challenge to our will.

'My focus thereafter was on the players individually. Was I seeing fight from them, a commitment to the game plan, and did they truly believe we could get something? They kept that belief and achieved a point, after what was a very disappointing decision from the referee.'

On the match official's decision to send Mitchell off, McNulty said, 'I'm mindful of these interviews being monitored, so I need to be careful as to what I say and how I say it. To give you a clue, it's only the second time this season I've been to see a referee after a game, the other being Halifax away, following the most disgraceful onside call I have ever seen.

'Today, I felt the referee maybe had in mind Kairo's tussling to get back on the ball before the challenge was made. I felt he may have been led by the Hartlepool fans, in front of who the challenge happened. These guys [referees] have difficult decisions to make in the moment, I respect that, but, after watching the incident back, it is one of the only times I have firmly believed that we will have a decision overturned on appeal. It's a clean, safe, low tackle, in my opinion.'

The club did indeed confirm after the match that it would appeal the red card for Mitchell.

* * *

THE AWAY LEG of the 'El Flat-cap Classico' was always an eagerly anticipated affair for Rochdale fans, whatever the competition. A trip to Boundary Park promised atmosphere and local bragging rights in abundance, with this occasion being no different, even if there was slightly more riding on the outcome for the hosts than there was for the visitors.

Oldham Athletic, following a thrilling 4-3 victory in the reverse fixture at Spotland, had been in and out of the play-off places ever since. The Latics now sat just five points off those positions ahead of this meeting, with four games remaining. Rochdale, by comparison, sat nine points adrift and a mid-table finish seemed inevitable.

Unfortunately, this derby failed to live up to the pair's previous encounter, with a 1-1 draw being a fair outcome in what was ultimately a dire game of football played in blustery conditions on a bobbly pitch.

McNulty made one change from the team that started Easter Monday's draw with Hartlepool, with Cameron John coming in for Finlay Armstrong. The appeal against Kairo Mitchell's red card picked up in that game had also been successful and so he started against the Latics.

Sadly, the limitations of the 4-4-2 employed by McNulty over the past few weeks were laid bare in a display that failed to act on the obvious. Dale needed a link between midfield and attack. Whether modern enthusiasts would call it a 'number ten' or an advanced role, Dale were clearly missing a player in the huge swathes of grass between the front men of Devante Rodney and Mitchell, and Ryan East and Harvey Gilmour behind them.

The other weakness noted in the early exchanges was that playing a front two of Mitchell and Rodney seemed only to work if Dale were looking to break quickly and go directly into, or behind, the opposition back four. Here, the players weren't doing either.

With Ian Henderson as an option on the bench, but ignored until far too late (though it could be seen even in that cameo how he could have influenced the game), or the failure to put Cameron John into midfield, allowing East to push on, there were opportunities missed. John's presence in the middle, on what was such a blustery day, would have given more security when Oldham were looking to go long, too.

The passing about at the back, when done without urgency, was costing the team goals far too regularly to be ignored also. When done quickly – one – or two-touch – it proved effective, but, when slowed down, which had become *de rigueur*, the danger meter started to rise at a rate of knots. Playing balls into players who weren't already on the half-turn, or aware of what was behind them, was proving self-destructive.

The hosts took the lead in the seventh minute in just such a fashion when Josh Lundstram won the ball high up the pitch and fed Hallam Hope, who fired into the roof of the net.

It was hard not to sympathise with players such as Ethan Ebanks-Landell. Once again, I found myself wishing they would insist on not receiving a pass unless they had a clear idea of their immediate next option.

There were, however, some good displays in an otherwise dire game, with Kyron Gordon the standout, looking more and more composed at full-back. It was also important to remember, with all of the above considered, that Dale didn't lose, with the Oldham players exhibiting as many flaws in their own approach.

Sam Mather had an effort deflected wide. From the resulting corner, the Manchester United loanee was involved again as Dale equalised. A corner was sent to the front post where Mather got a slight touch before the ball hit an Oldham defender a couple of yards out and trickled over the line. You can only imagine the red mist that must have descended over manager Micky Mellon at the ball-watching on display from his players.

'I thought it was a commendable effort from the team, to be honest,' said McNulty after the game. 'To go behind early, in a disappointing fashion for us as a team, it could have gone a lot differently, but I thought the team rallied and I thought we showed real bravery.

'With the wind out here at pitch level, and the dryness of the pitch, the ball just wouldn't settle on it, which made it challenging for the players. A lot of them have commented on that. It's a bit bobbly and the firmness of it was just a bit of a factor in trying to settle the ball down.

'That was a factor that affected the game a little bit for us with the style that we try to play, not so much for Oldham because I thought they were much more direct than us with their strategy for the day, which is football. You have to face a lot of different types of strategy. The ball doesn't bobble in the air, but it does on the ground, which made it tough for us to try and play the way we want to play.

'But taking all that into account, I think we were really brave, we stuck to our plan and there was a belief from the team that they could keep going. As the game grew, I thought we were the team that became more dangerous, other than a couple of breakaways [from Oldham] and they hit the post.

'When we reflect on the game, I think some of our final-third choices, we probably will regret and definitely learn from, because I think the game was there for us. There were moments where, once we got to the final third, we just needed a calmness and to make a better decision. I think the game could have been totally different for us.'

* * *

A HOME MATCH with Marc White's Dorking Wanderers would mark the first of Rochdale's final three National League games of the campaign.

While the home side's mid-table obscurity was all but assured before kick-off, the resulting 1-1 draw relegated the visitors back to National League South. It was a sad note for the likeable White but, to pluck a silver lining, the outcome meant he wouldn't need to worry about his coaching badges for another two seasons at least.

On a much more poignant note, both sets of supporters participated in a round of applause on the 15-minute mark in respect of former Rochdale player Joe Thompson, who revealed earlier that week that he was battling cancer for a third time. Thompson wore the number 15 on the back of his shirt during his time at Dale and this was respected by the current squad, who all wore the same number on the back of their own shirts before the game.

As to the game itself, Jim McNulty made two changes from the previous weekend's outing at Oldham. George Nevett and Jimmy Keohane returned to the starting line-up, replacing Dan Sassi and Cameron John, who both dropped to the bench.

With no visible change to the formation, the return of Keohane, whose ability to find space in different areas of the pitch, did at least give rise to more options during play.

However, in the first half, while Dale spent a lot of the game in the final third, the main issue was that shots were either delayed in favour of another pass, or blocked by resolute defending. Breaking down teams that played this way had become a conundrum for McNulty and not one that could be said to have been suitably solved.

After the half-time break, play did open up a bit more. Ryan East had a shot blocked and Devante Rodney was denied by Dorking goalkeeper Slavomir Huk, before the visitors took the lead when Alfie Rutherford's shot was deflected into the path of Charlie Carter, who smashed home off the inside of the post.

However, Dale were level within five minutes. Some patient build-up play led to Kairo Mitchell finding Rodney, who shifted the ball on to his left foot and shelled his effort into the top corner.

McNulty then rolled the dice in search of a winner with some unpredictable substitutions. Forwards came on at full-back and others came into the midfield, which visibly confused the opposition and saw Dale create chance after chance late on. Sadly, none could be converted, and another part-time team escaped Spotland with a point.

'We had a multitude of chances as the game went on,' McNulty said afterwards. 'I think Dorking came here to fight and to try to give the travelling fans the best effort they could. They were sitting in a low block at times, which we had to take our time to break down, which we did better and better as the game wore on.

'Ultimately, we have to get the ball in the goal, though. It's not just about how many times you can get it close to the goal. That counts for nothing if you do nothing with it. Today, for whatever reason, we just didn't manage to do that. Our profligacy meant that we only drew a game that we could've been out of sight in. The score certainly didn't reflect the performance. We completely controlled and dominated every other area, even when we went a goal down against the run of play.'

After the game, Rochdale's end-of-season awards took place, and Harvey Gilmour was the standout recipient. The midfielder clinched an impressive four accolades, headlined by the Dale Trust Player of the Season prize. Additionally, he secured the Players' Player of the Year title and the Brent Wilkinson Club Player of the Year distinction. His accomplishments were further underscored by his recognition from the South Manchester & Cheshire Supporters' Club.

Since arriving from FC Halifax Town in the summer, Gilmour had featured in 44 matches across all competitions in his first season at Dale.

In other recognitions, George Nevett claimed dual honours. He earned distinction as the Wilson Family Most Improved Young Player of the Season and also received the Dale Dragon's Community Trust Player of the Season award. The Goal of the Season accolade was clinched by Cian Hayes for his extraordinary strike against Dagenham & Redbridge in November. Hayes's spectacular effort narrowly edged out Kairo Mitchell's 30-yard goal in the home game against Eastleigh, securing victory by a mere two votes.

* * *

LUKE GARRARD cut a dejected figure as he led his Boreham Wood players out on to the Spotland turf for the reverse Tuesday night National League fixture.

When I last met Garrard, prior to Dale taking on his side in Elstree in September, he was full of optimism for the future, having led the Wood to the play-offs the season previous. Since that 1-1 draw, however, they had slid into the relegation places, leading chairman Danny Hunter to announce that his manager would be leaving the club at the end of the season.

'Luke and I have both recognised that, come 20 April, whatever the outcome of our season, it is the right time for us to say our goodbyes for now,' he said. 'I feel, for nearly a decade, we had the greatest chairman/manager collaboration in non-league football, but we both recognise this last period as one of huge regret.'

On the surface, it seemed Garrard had become a victim of his own success, of his own high standards and overachievement. For now, however, he still had a job to do, knowing a win would lift his team out of the relegation zone. In the event, neither his nor Dale's own players could find a goal in what was ultimately a drab stalemate that proved less fun than standing in a lengthy pharmacy queue.

Jim McNulty made three changes from Saturday's game against Dorking Wanderers. Tyrese Sinclair, D'Mani Mellor and Dan Sassi came into the starting XI, in place of Jimmy Keohane, Cian Hayes and Sam Mather.

The visitors had the ball in the back of the net after six minutes, although it was ruled out for offside, and Ryan East came closest for Dale when he crashed a 25-yard effort off the face of the crossbar. That was about it in terms of entertainment.

Kairo Mitchell's ability to run the line was seemingly stifled once again by having a strike partner in Devante Rodney who was presumably expected to do half of that job. The result was a player with potential not doing what he was best at, and his shortcomings – first touch, holding up the ball – being exposed. Mitchell, as a lone striker, had caused more issues for the opposition during the season when he was running in behind their defence. Here, both he and Rodney seemed much more static.

East's shot in the first half was an example of how simple the game is, but Dale simply failed to take such chances anywhere near enough. During the course of the season, when the players had gone long into space for willing runners, the goals yield spoke for itself. It personified the 'total options football' that McNulty coined at the beginning of the season. Again, this approach seemed now only the preserve of desperation.

McNulty acknowledged the game wasn't the prettiest when he spoke to the media afterwards: 'I think we controlled the game in its entirety and I don't say that with any degree of arrogance because Boreham Wood are obviously in a desperate situation and they were scared to give up anything.

'I was trying to bring an edge to the game, despite the fact we've got nothing to fight for in terms of the league table. Since the news came out that Luke [Garrard] was parting ways with the club at the end of the season, there's been a freeness and a freshness to Boreham Wood's performances. They've looked really physical, powerful, dangerous and competitive and I knew they would be all of those things against us.

'We had to be very, very good with the ball, and the stuff that may have looked very simple and very basic tonight, I can promise you it wasn't. There's a lot of stuff where I can sense the crowd wants us to do a bit more, but we needed to be patient in order to get into the parts of the pitch where we could have chances. I think we did that part really well.

I just think when we got around their box, we didn't get enough purchase for the amount of ball control, domination and territory that we had.'

McNulty tried George Nevett on the left of the defence for this game, and praised the youngster's performance there.

'With regard to all the things I just said about how much of a physical handful Boreham Wood were, I thought George was outstanding. I thought his awareness and his ability to confidently travel with the ball was outstanding for someone his age. He showed the quality that he's got, which is why we've had such a young boy playing so many games for us all season.'

* * *

ON THE EVE of the final day of the 2023/24 National League season, the Ogden family made official their landmark offer to purchase shares in Rochdale AFC. With plans to invest up to £2m for a 68 per cent ownership stake, the family said it aimed to secure the club's future while ensuring community involvement in key decisions.

Key terms of the offer included introducing a 'golden share' to be held by the Dale Trust, safeguarding the club's heritage and grounds. Existing shareholder loans, namely those of chairman Simon Gauge and director Richard Knight, were set to be exchanged for new shares, bolstering the club's financial position.

'These loans have kept the club afloat but repaying them would not be the best use of the club's limited funds, and converting them into equity significantly improves the club's balance sheet,' the family said. 'We would like to acknowledge that agreeing to exchange these loans for equity is a generous gesture on the part of Simon and Richard, as the shares they are acquiring have no immediate value, and only a very distant prospect of ever providing a return of their money.'

Post-investment, the focus would shift to achieving financial stability and long-term sustainability. The Ogdens said plans included establishing a shared sports facility to streamline club activities and the exploration of innovative youth development models beyond Premier League Elite Player Performance Plan limitations.

Support for the first team remained important, the family said, with a budget aimed at securing a play-off place in the 2024/25 season.

'While it is not our primary focus (because it cannot be guaranteed), we recognise that promotion to League Two would be the quickest way to revive the club's financial fortunes (as well as bringing joy to its supporters),' they said. 'We feel we should make it clear that we will not be taking a reckless approach to player budgets. However, we do intend to ensure that the first team budget is sufficient to give the club a fighting chance of achieving a play-off place.'

Continuity at board and management levels was also emphasised to 'ensure focus on delivering key initiatives', while additional expertise would be sought to join the board over time.

'The club has had a tumultuous few years,' the family said. 'In our view, now is not the time to make material changes at a board or management level. There is a significant amount of work to be done to deliver on the priorities highlighted above and we would like 100 per cent focus on those initiatives. As incoming majority owners, we will need to rely on the knowledge and experience of existing key personnel and we feel strongly that maintaining a level of continuity will give the club a much better chance of success than material disruption.'

The Ogdens' commitment to purchase shares following their advertised period of due diligence was met with universal delight and relief from the Rochdale supporters. From a landscape painted as bleak as any Lancastrian winter just a month earlier, the club's future seemed now fit for a Mediterranean summer.

* * *

THE FORTUNES OF Southend United had vastly improved since the club met Rochdale in the reverse league fixture at Spotland at the end of September.

A consortium fronted by Justin Rees, an Australian entrepreneur, had started the process of assuming control of the Shrimpers from Ron Martin, thus fending off the very real threat of the club being wound up in the High Court.

Prior to his involvement with Southend, Rees had worked at Liquid Capital Group Derivatives Trading, before founding Eighty20 Solutions in 2018. His consortium, comprising local Southend businessmen, made available £2m to settle the outstanding debts owed by the club to companies involved in legal proceedings.

On the pitch, the team had flourished under Kevin Maher and had more than overcome the ten-point deduction put upon it by the National League, to the stage where the Shrimpers were sitting above even Rochdale in the table going into the final day of the season, with a shot at the play-off places very much alive following an unbeaten run of 15 games which stretched back to February.

Jim McNulty made three changes from the midweek draw at home to Boreham Wood for the visit to Roots Hall. Tiernan Brooks replaced Jacob Chapman in goal, with Cian Hayes and Sam Mather replacing Tyrese Sinclair and D'Mani Mellor. First-year scholar Corey Edwards was named on the substitutes' bench and went on to give a good account of himself when brought into the fray following an injury to Harvey Gilmour.

Southend started the game like an invading force in Dale's third, understandable given what was at stake, but the visitors didn't half make it easy for them when trying to play out from the back while under intense pressure from the press. Possession was therefore turned over far too easily and there was a real sluggishness in closing down the wide players. This led to the home side taking the lead within just eight minutes.

A brilliant Southend move from one end of the field to the other ended with Jack Bridge checking back on to his right foot and delivering a precision cross to the far post for Gus Scott-Morriss to slide home.

Despite being second best for much of the first half, with no clear link between midfield and attack centrally, Hayes out wide on the right was making things happen for Dale at least. He hit the underside of the bar on the half-hour mark before he levelled things in the 41st minute when Ollie Kensdale conceded possession, allowing the winger to waltz clean through on goal. He showed great composure to round Collin Andeng-Ndi before firing home.

After the break, Dale improved and became more cohesive, meaning Southend's incisiveness was blunted somewhat. Even so, the Shrimpers carved enough chances to win the match, but it was to be Dale who provided the sucker punch.

Substitute Ian Henderson, whose introduction provided that missing link between midfield and attack, played a superbly weighted through ball for Devante Rodney to run on to, and the striker finished coolly underneath the advancing Andeng-Ndi in the final minute of stoppage time.

The 2-1 victory meant Dale finished a maiden National League campaign in 11th place and Southend missed out on seventh, the final play-off spot, although results elsewhere went against the club regardless.

'That's a great way to finish the season,' McNulty said afterwards. 'Southend have had a similar storyline to ourselves, in terms of adversity and the real threat of going out of business, so I have a lot of respect for them.

'They also still had the play-offs in their sights before the match and we had nothing tangible to play for, but the players found a brilliant performance and, once again, the character of this group showed, as it has all year long. To go one down and then turn it round is a complete credit to them. When you go one down, you can really see who has that commitment and desire for the team.

'We had some very young players on the pitch today – Corey [Edwards] at 16 years old, Sam Mather, who is 18, and George Nevett, at 18 years old. It's easy for young players to shirk that commitment when under pressure but not one of them did. That bodes well for their future.'

* * *

AFTER A COUPLE of days of reflection, the Dale support began to vocalise their appreciation of just what Jim McNulty had achieved during his first full season as head coach. While there may have been initial disappointment that a genuine play-off charge had turned limp since the turn of the year, there was an almost universal understanding that, given the trying circumstances behind the scenes, McNulty had actually done a tremendous job in galvanising a group of players who visibly gave their all for the badge. It seemed the only ask going forward was for a more 'entertaining' brand of football that equated to more victories. Essentially, the ask of any football supporter the world over.

I met McNulty for the final time four days after the season had concluded, which, he said, had afforded him time to get some initial 'end-of-season' business out of the way. I found him in a philosophical mood and already planning for the next campaign.

'I feel strange now it's all done, to be honest with you,' he said. 'I'm already looking at next season but haven't had a chance to reflect on what has just gone until now, speaking to you.

'It's been the biggest rollercoaster of emotions I've ever had - and that includes the seasons where we stayed in League One by the skin of our teeth. My range of emotions have never been higher or lower than this season. I've felt elation and anger, happiness and despair – all right off the chart.

'The season was a real marathon, but, at the same time, it felt like it was over in five minutes because it was so intense and there were always so many fires to put out. Everything was always so urgent that it completely dominated my life.

'Analysis is when I'm in my most comfortable state. Only a couple of hours ago I finished clipping up video footage of our last game against Southend and then sent the clips to the players individually, despite the fact the season has finished and some of those players will be leaving us. This is the inclusive culture I have sought to create, and this is what makes me feel achievement – sharing the players' own with them.

'I know most people had empathy for the club's situation this season, but we're all humans at the end of the day, and I really felt that empathy disappear on matchdays at times. The vast majority in the stadium supported us through 90-

plus minutes, and that really helped us, but people became crazed about results. We're all vampires baying for blood at the end of the day and that blood in football terms is positive results. I get that. I get that it's all part of football. You could feel the balance return in the middle of the week and then we'd have another game and the cycle would start all over again. I had to remain focused and not get drawn into that noise.

'I often listen to the voices in football that are logical and reasonable but are farthest away from my situation. This is how I bring balance to my emotions and outlook. People from much higher up the football pyramid, friends and former colleagues, could see what we were achieving on the pitch and that gave me a feeling of pride and reassurance.

'I told you at the start of the season that I didn't want to adopt a survival mode on the pitch. I wanted to build something here from scratch, something that has been missing from this club for a few years now – an identity. That is what I struck out to achieve and I believe, in my first year, we have laid the foundations.

'I get that most of the noise around the club is from people who genuinely just want to see the team win and I'm on board with that. Of course, there will always be those who just want to see the world burn, no matter what, and they have their echo chamber on social media. I don't like it either when a very small minority boo our goalkeeper in the stadium for a choice they don't agree with, or likewise a young centre-back. That behaviour is never going to be helpful. I feel the same emotions as the supporters and am equally invested, but I have a duty to protect my players and, when those same choices by those same players lead to something wonderful, you can see, and hopefully understand, why they attempt what they do.

'With all that said, the winter presented our toughest circumstances. We were in the play-off positions, but it felt like a hollow victory as the squad began to wither away game by game. I asked for help in terms of strengthening the squad, as you know, but help couldn't be found. There was just no money at that point, which I respect. Through that, the players still persevered, playing the style I asked of them, that they had bought in to, even though I could see at times we struggled doing so.

'It would have been so easy to give in. It would have been so easy to go more attritional or drastically change the style game to game. It would have been easy to put the best 11 players on the pitch over the system itself. If I had done any of that, I'd have lost the players. They would have seen right through me and my beliefs, the very beliefs I had instilled in them from day one and then every day of every week at training since. We weren't fighting for the league table, believe it or not, we were fighting to create a footballing identity, for the club, as a group – an identity we were willing to go up or down with. They all bought in to that. That is how you start to build a successful team from a relegated one and it can take more than one season to bed in.

'My primary focus has always been having 11 guys out on that pitch who all know exactly what they are doing. This proved our biggest protection against some mid-season hammerings, when we were depleted. We always wanted to win playing this way, of course we did, but, sometimes, I just had to ensure we didn't get battered during this period, because that's where we found ourselves.

'The other benefit of every player knowing the system is that I can bring guys like 16-year-old Corey Edwards into the team, and it protects them, too. Against Southend, Corey constantly transitioned between three different positions throughout the game, and he knew all the moments in which to do it, while also handling the ball well and with bravery. His understanding of how to work cohesively with the team in this system protected the fact that he was 16 and was up against guys that could just bully him or blow him away, which is what would have happened if he was exposed by a system where not everyone was on the same page. This is part of the overall strategy.

'Despite the rocky periods, the players have all enjoyed it. Even though some went without pay at one point, they say this has been the most enjoyable season of their career to date. Even players who had to leave us, such as Louie Moulden, feel part of the story. They were back in the changing room for the final game of the season for the team talks – just to be part of the vibe.

'Now, I can say this because I *was* a footballer and have spent 20 years in various dressing rooms: footballers are snobbish and judgey when it comes to playing styles and managers. Football is a village. They all move in the same circles, and they all talk. They all like being known for playing in effective and attractive teams. Of course, they all want to win, but, if you allow them the opportunity to create something that they feel is unique, it becomes more special to them than the wins, I think. That is part of my role as head coach. Yes, I must deliver wins ultimately, but I must also create an environment where the players feel comfortable and enjoy themselves. The latter will, more often than not, lead to the former.

'And creating that environment meant I had to hide my feelings at times. I said earlier that I felt anger this season like I had never felt before. I truly did. It was usually to do with the situation at the club, behind the scenes. I had to swallow this anger, though, for the greater good.

'I will give you one example. We almost didn't have a bus for the Ebbsfleet away game. The players were all waiting to be picked up at the service station and the bus didn't arrive because there was a disagreement over money owed. We had to tell the players the bus had broken down on the motorway and that it was going to be fixed, which bought us a little bit of time. They then all went back to looking at their phones sat in Costa Coffee and I became part of a mad scramble to get alternative transport sorted where they couldn't see or hear.

'The club managed to scramble a bus through another company, but then we're late arriving in Ebbsfleet, which affects preparation. I could have easily brought this into the public domain in my anger, but what would it have achieved at the time? The negativity would have affected the players' morale. People would think I was making excuses for losing the game. It would have invited criticism of the board. It would have been damaging, is the bottom line.

'I only say this now just to give you one example of the many times I had to clench my jaw and get on with it during the season.

'So, considering all that, I think a lot of people were thankful that there was such a calm feeling at the end of the season. OK, we didn't make the play-offs, but we also weren't fretting about further decline via relegation, or worse.

'It's easy to lose sight of the good moments. For example, I absolutely loved our goal of the season competition. I thought it was the best one I could remember for ages, and I think it was quite reflective of what we tried to do this year, whether we failed or succeeded. I think we were a difficult team for other teams to play against because of the different challenges we asked of the opposition. I feel we made problems for ourselves more often than opponents did for us, and that is the main learning I am taking into next season.'

McNulty said he had already sat down with the club's new owners, the Ogden family, and had discussed plans for the next season.

'The vibe I got from them was an extremely positive one,' he said. 'I feel extremely excited by their involvement. They came across as having real intellect despite the fact they confessed football has never been their thing. It doesn't need to be, though. They are incredibly good at what they do and seek advice where they need it. That's what I gave them when they asked about the team.

'I told them there are two ways to get success in the National League, throw money at the squad or adopt a process of continuity. I told them I didn't need a Wrexham-style budget. I said that the club needed infrastructure investment so that it has everything it needs to play whatever style of football it wants in the years long after I have gone. We were a club that used to blood youngsters and have them play in the first team with bravery. We have been getting further away from that year after year, so, it was on that basis our discussion was built.

'They said their own business had been built incrementally and that will be their approach to the football club. That chimed with what I outlined. Neither of us like the boom-and-bust approach of chucking money at a problem.

'I'm still waiting for final confirmation of my budget for next season. What I do have now, though, that I didn't last year, is time. I've had a whole season of watching players and I know, in my mind, who I would like to approach to play for us. Some will still be experimental at this level, for sure, but I have a good idea of who I can move on already, whereas last year I missed out on the first round of players.

'Naturally, I will also need to adjust the squad based on the players who may wish to leave us. I was pleased with the recruitment we ultimately did this season and a lot of those players have caught the eye of clubs in the EFL with their performances. Myself and the staff are happy for them and they deserve that recognition.

'There has also been some internal learning and acceptance here at the club. This internal learning has been vital, because, as in any business, it is important that you fully understand the marketplace in which you are operating. You totally need to know what the other guys are doing and exactly where you sit amongst that.'

National League 2023/24 final table

	P	*W*	*D*	*L*	*F*	*A*	*Pts*
Chesterfield (C)	46	31	5	10	106	65	98
Barnet	46	26	8	12	91	60	86
Bromley (P)	46	22	15	9	73	49	81
Altrincham	46	22	11	13	84	59	77
Solihull Moors	46	21	13	12	71	62	76
Gateshead**	46	22	9	15	88	64	75
FC Halifax Town	46	19	14	13	58	50	71
Aldershot Town	46	20	9	17	74	83	69
Southend United*	46	21	12	13	70	45	65
Oldham Athletic	46	15	18	13	63	60	63
Rochdale	**46**	**16**	**14**	**16**	**69**	**64**	**62**
Hartlepool	46	17	9	20	70	82	60
Eastleigh	46	16	11	19	73	87	59
Maidenhead United	46	15	13	18	60	67	58
Dagenham & Redbridge	46	14	14	18	69	63	56
Wealdstone	46	15	11	20	60	72	56
Woking	46	15	10	21	49	55	55
AFC Fylde	46	15	10	21	74	82	55
Ebbsfleet United	46	14	12	20	59	74	54
York City	46	12	17	17	55	69	53
Boreham Wood (R)	46	12	16	18	59	73	52
Kidderminster Harriers (R)	46	11	13	22	40	59	46
Dorking Wanderers (R)	46	12	9	25	54	85	45
Oxford City (R)	46	8	9	29	54	94	33

* Southend deducted ten points for failing to pay an existing tax bill.

** Gateshead refused permission to participate in the play-off eliminators due to failing to meet the entry criteria for membership of the EFL.

Epilogue

THE 2023/24 SEASON had been a relentless grind for Rochdale AFC chairman Simon Gauge. The club's debut in non-league football after more than a century in the Football League had weighed heavily, both emotionally and financially. Gauge had shouldered this burden, pouring his own resources into keeping the club afloat while tirelessly seeking investors to secure its long-term future.

As the May sun peeked through the windows of the boardroom at Spotland Stadium, Gauge exuded a weariness that belied his relief. The turbulent campaign was finally over and, with it, the agonising search for new owners had reached its conclusion. The Ogden family, seeking to firmly establish the club as a pillar of the Rochdale community, had answered the call, pledging their personal wealth and benevolence to the club's revival.

With cautious optimism, Gauge recounted the trials and tribulations of the past year, one that had tested his resolve like no other. Yet he seemed energised by the glimmer of hope on the horizon, which promised brighter days ahead under the steadying influence of the Ogdens' stewardship.

'Personally, I think it was a satisfactory but frustrating season,' Gauge told me. 'There was every chance we could really have struggled in this league and there are plenty of examples of that from previously relegated EFL teams. This was always going to be a year where we needed to stabilise and secure investment, so we could plan for the long term and not just exist on a short-term survival basis.

'The season was frustrating because it was only a really poor February, and fine margins through the rest of the season, that prevented us achieving a play-off place.

'The money I, and others, invested in the club during the season was done so knowing we would probably never get it back. We did this so that the club could survive long enough to secure outside investment. Without that money, the club would not have completed the season.

'Therefore, stability is the key word when looking at what the Ogdens will now bring to the club. We can now sit in a board meeting and conversations will not be around how we are going to survive the next month.

'That financial environment was exhausting and every decision was based around short-term survival. The difference now is we know we will be here in five years' time, so can plan and make decisions for the medium and long term. Foundations can now be laid for success, knowing we will be here to reap the rewards of those foundations. The Ogdens are open to investing in infrastructure, on the proviso it will provide the club with income driving it towards its sustainability targets, or add significant community value.

'Everything to do with the club will benefit. Immediately, off the pitch, we will have the cash flow to employ a director of commercial operations, which will help drive revenues, and, on the pitch, we can look at medium-term plans to achieve success.

'The club will naturally evolve from this point and achieve more success year on year. Off the pitch, there will be infrastructure investment that will drive significant social value and put us at the heart of the community to a greater extent than we ever have been before.

'The major change that people will see from the club will be our community initiatives. We will be equally proud of success achieved here as any success achieved on the pitch.'

No sooner had I spoken to Gauge than changes were immediately implemented at the club via a restructuring of its board of directors. Cameron Ogden, scion of the Ogden family, joined as co-chairman. Jamie Willoughby and Adam Saul, both employees of the Ogden family business, were also appointed as directors. The FA had given its approval for these individuals to serve as officers of the club. Jan Wormald stepped down from the board.

The Ogden family - Cameron, Edward and Tiffany, children of Sir Peter and Lady Ogden - then made a significant commitment. Should any profits ever be made from their ownership of the shares, those profits would be held solely for the benefit of the Rochdale AFC Community Trust.

In line with their stated intentions, the Ogdens also planned to introduce a golden share to be held by the Dale Trust.

'I am delighted to join the board as co-chairman of this great club,' Cameron Ogden stated. 'Our family's connection to Rochdale runs deep, and we envision the club becoming an integral part of the local community. We don't underestimate the challenges ahead, but we'll work tirelessly toward our ambitions.'

A new era was dawning at Rochdale AFC under this new bold leadership and ambitious vision. Challenges lay ahead, but also great aspirations - to be financially viable, ascend to higher leagues and become an invaluable asset to the local community - and we, the supporters, were ready for it.

Thanks and appreciation

AS WELL AS offering my eternal thanks to all the wonderful people who agreed to be interviewed, the writing of this book wouldn't have been possible without the additional support of:

- The Dale Trust, the new chair of which, George Brigham, championed this book's cause
- Roger Graham, a meticulous eye
- Matt Smith, a tactical football brain and amazing sounding board
- Mark Wilbraham, a statistical genius
- Daniel Youngs, a super snapper
- Tom Bodell, Vanarama
- Samuel Carter, Aldershot Town
- Aimee Cocksedge, Bromley
- Cheryl Cooper, Solihull Moors
- Paul Fruin, Wealdstone
- Suzanne Geldard, sports journalist and assistant sports editor
- Lewis Hawkins, Barnet
- Ed Miller, Ebbsfleet United
- Matt Paddock, Kidderminster Harriers
- Shannon Sullivan, Tangerine Holdings
- Steve Thompson, Dagenham & Redbridge